Palgrave Philosoph

CW01023851

Series Editor
Vittorio Bufacchi
Department of Philosophy
University College Cork
Cork, Ireland

The Palgrave Philosophy Today will help all philosophers, established and aspiring, to understand, appreciate and engage with the intricacies which characterize all the many faces of philosophy. They are ideal teaching tools as textbooks for more advanced students. These books may not be meant primarily for those who have yet to read their first book of philosophy, but all students with a basic knowledge of philosophy will benefit greatly from reading these exciting and original works, which will enable anyone to engage with all the defining issues in contemporary philosophy. There are three main aspects that make the Palgrave Philosophy Today series distinctive and attractive. First, each book is relatively concise. Second, the books are commissioned from some of the best-known, established and upcoming international scholars in each area of philosophy. Third, while the primary purpose is to offer an informed assessment of opinion on a key area of philosophical study, each title presents a distinct interpretation from someone who is closely involved with current work in the field.

More information about this series at
http://www.palgrave.com/gp/series/14672

Anthony Robert Booth

Analytic Islamic Philosophy

palgrave
macmillan

Anthony Robert Booth
School of History, Art History & Philosophy
University of Sussex
Brighton, UK

Palgrave Philosophy Today
ISBN 978-1-137-54156-7   ISBN 978-1-137-54157-4   (eBook)
https://doi.org/10.1057/978-1-137-54157-4

Library of Congress Control Number: 2017959461

This Palgrave Macmillan imprint is published by Springer Nature
The registered company is Macmillan Publishers Ltd.
The registered company address is: The Campus, 4 Crinan Street, London, N1 9XW, United Kingdom

To Margaret

Preface and Acknowledgements

One of the great scandals in philosophy from around the beginning of the 20th century has been the perpetuation of the idea that there is a substantial distinction to be made between so-called analytic and continental philosophy—one that goes beyond issues regarding style and sociology. And, even though *none* of the respective participants in the dispute admits to being able to give the distinction any articulation that does not slip between their fingers, the distinction remains today very real (in the stylistic and sociological sense), wielded by both sides for diverse, abject, *anti*-philosophical ends (inter alia): the perceived winning of arguments via the appeal to authority; ensuring that one's arguments will not be subject to wide-ranging critical scrutiny; the maintenance of one's image and identity as a member of a particular philosophical *club* at the expense of others' membership; the perceived entitlement to ignore (and dismiss without reading) vast tranches of literature as some "non-U" other. In short, I think that the belief in the viability of the distinction is ideological in nature (in the pejorative, Marxist sense that I discuss in Chaps. 7 and 8, and which, in a sense, is the guiding theme of this book). One then ought to ask in the present context: why include the word "analytic" in the title of this book? Am I not further securing the credibility of this ideology (used to maintain the positions of power of *individual* philosophers belonging to each camp) by so doing? Am I not thus indicating my desire to engage with Islamic philosophy (depending on one's perceived sense of tribal belonging) in terms of the "right" or "wrong" way?

My answer has to do with, first, how I think the pejorative ideology is best eschewed and what I think a more favourable alternative would be. And, second, it has to do with some of my own methodological commitments on how

I think that History of Philosophy (a discipline that for me is not simply Intellectual History) should be conducted.

With respect to the first point above, it seems to me that it has become unfortunately *de rigueur* for a certain camp to use the word "analytic" as a means to insult a body of scholarly work in the History of Philosophy. For instance, one can find in certain discourses the idea that so and so is really an "analytic Nietzschean" or (perhaps most paradoxically, yet most *de rigeur* of all) an "analytic Heideggerian"—and as such a traitor to "real" history of philosophy, a Trojan horse ultimately dreamt up by the resourceful "analytics". This present book, however, has no disguise. It is explicitly written by someone who has primarily worked on issues and in a style that, sociologically speaking, are considered to belong to the analytic tradition. There can thus be no clever uncovering, unweaving, deconstruction (and attendant summary dismissal) that the book is *really* something connected to the analytic tradition. And, further, I really want to bring it home to the analytic community (such that it is) how congruent the Islamic philosophical tradition is to theirs, and that it did not deserve the fate imparted on it by the summary dismissal of the "father" of the analytic movement:

> Arabic philosophy is not important as original thought. Men like Avicenna and Averroes are essentially commentators. Speaking generally, the views of the more scientific philosophers come from Aristotle and the Neoplatonists in logic and metaphysics, from Galen in medicine, from Greek and Indian sources in mathematics and astronomy, and among mystics religious philosophy has also an admixture of old Persian beliefs. Writers in Arabic showed some originality in mathematics and in chemistry—in the latter case, as an incidental result of alchemical researches. Mohammedan civilization in its great days was admirable in the arts and in many technical ways, but it showed no capacity for independent speculation in theoretical matters. Its importance, which must not be underrated, is as a transmitter. Between ancient and modern European civilization, the dark ages intervened. The Mohammedans and the Byzantines, while lacking the intellectual energy required for innovation, preserved the apparatus of civilization—education, books, and learned leisure. Both stimulated the West when it emerged from barbarism—the Mohammedans chiefly in the thirteenth century, the Byzantines chiefly in the fifteenth. In each case the stimulus produced new thought better than any produced by the transmitters—in the one case scholasticism, in the other the Renaissance (which however had other causes also). (Bertrand Russell – *A History of Western Philosophy*, p. 396)

The claim that "Mohammedan civilization … showed no capacity for independent speculation in theoretical matters" is rather striking—particularly given the supressed premises that Analytic philosophy is essentially something that requires a capacity for that kind of speculation, and that Analytic philosophy (in its various historical guises) is the proper ("U") philosophy. For anyone who has read any philosophy in Arabic, it is hard not to resist the temptation to conclude that Lord Russell himself must not have read any of it. And yet, given Russell's stature, it's hard to imagine that his words fell on deaf ears, especially given the historical fact that the study of Islamic philosophy in Western Universities continues to be predominantly considered *at best* optional in terms of a good philosophical education. My aim in this book is precisely to show that a distinctive feature of Islamic philosophy was in fact in its making theoretical *innovations,* and that the innovations it made bear the marks of considerable insight, relevant to the problems facing the world today.

My approach, then, is to treat the historical protagonists of Islamic philosophy as living, breathing figures in conversation with contemporary philosophy. My approach does *not* belong to what people sometimes call "comparative philosophy". The aim is here to do philosophy with the Islamic philosophers—not merely to compare theirs to others. With Oliver Leaman (2009) I share the ambition of bringing Islamic philosophy (as he put it) "out of the Islamic Studies ghetto"—but let me emphasise that the significance of the historical and philological work done in the former should never be underestimated. And I agree with Muhammad Ali Khalidi's (2006) claim that treating these figures as items of *mere* historical interest (items of curious exotica) is a kind of "Orientalism" (a pejorative ideological discourse in the guise of a scientific study of the Islamic World, designed to shore up imperialism and oppression).

In order to facilitate the sort of dialogue I have in mind, I have given maximum hermeneutical priority to the principle of charity—to making the works of historical figures come out as the philosophically best possible versions. I think that the methodological ends of pursuing historical accuracy and the application of the principle of charity in doing History of Philosophy are hard to balance; just as the ends of empirical adequacy and explanatory power are hard for scientists to balance (see Kuhn 1972; Laudan 1984). Ultimately, which end we favour is likely to boil down to value choice: my choice is the principle of charity.[1]

First and foremost I would like to thank my friend and colleague at Sussex Mahon O'Brien. He gave me valuable written feedback on Chap. 2 and our many philosophical discussions have "copper-fastened" (to use one of his favourite expressions) in me the belief that there is no useful or meaningful distinction between analytic and continental philosophy to be had—that the distinction is nothing other than an appalling sham. I would also like to thank the following for either written comments on various draft chapters, or useful discussion: Katerina Deligiorgi, Gordon Finlayson, Alastair Grey, Christos Hadjioannou, Dimitri Kladiskakis, Michael Morris, Elliot Rose, Umut Sahverdi, Neeltje Spoor, as well as the students who have taken my modules *Islamic Philosophy* and *Philosophy, Politics and the Middle East*. Chapters 4 and 8 draw heavily on my book *Islamic Philosophy & the Ethics of Belief*—thanks to Palgrave for the permission to do so. And thanks to Brendan George and April James (and an anonymous referee) at Palgrave for making it such a pleasure to publish one's work with them.

Finally, I would like to thank my history teacher (turned friend) at Bootham School: Margaret Ainscough. I have no doubt that she would find the lack of detail and nuance in my historical excursions excruciating, and my avowed methodological priorities deeply dissatisfying—but keeping her in mind has helped me keep these from being even more embarrassing to the professional historian than they are. In any case, her model of conscientious scholarship, inexorably involving a "feeling intellect", continues to be an inspiration for me. The book is dedicated to her.

Notes

1. I disagree then with Maria Rosa Antognazza's recent claim (Antognazza 2015) that the two are easily balanced since I think that they can be in competition, and there is no overarching end that can settle which to favour in any given context.

References

Antognazza, M.R. 2015. The Benefit to Philosophy of the Study of Its History. *British Journal for the History of Philosophy* 23: 161–184.

Kuhn, S. 1972. Objectivity, Value Judgement, and Theory Choice. In *The Essential Tension*. Chicago University Press.

Khalidi, M.A. 2006. Orientalisms in the Interpretation of Islamic Philosophy. *Radical Philosophy* 135: 25–33.

Leaman, O. 2009. *Islamic Philosophy: An Introduction*. Polity Press.

Laudan, L. 1984. *Science and Values: The Aims of Science and Their Role in Scientific Debate*. University of California Press.

A Note on Translation, Transliteration, Dates, and References

Throughout this manuscript I have transliterated Arabic words into English, with the use of diacritical marks, and have put the words in italics. However, I have used Anglicised versions of certain well-known Arabic words and names. For instance, I use Koran instead of Qur'ān or Hadith instead of Hādīth, and the names al-Kindi al-Farabi, al-Ghazali instead of al-Kindī, al-Farābī, al-Ghazālī. I used the Latinate names Averroes for Ibn Rushd and Avicenna for Ibn Sīnā. I use diacritical marks for the transliteration of less well-known (than the above) Islamic philosophers, but do not use them for the word Falasifa and its cognates, since I use it so often. When quoting and referencing works in medieval Islamic philosophy, I use the full name of the work in English translation, and in italics, followed by page numbers; for those referred to in the original Arabic, I use the Arabic name of the work, also in italics, and with a footnote on the translation. All works, in translation or in the original, are referenced at the end of the book, before my list of secondary sources. All dates used refer to the Common Era calendar.

Contents

1

Islam and Reason

Introduction

To get things off the ground, I will begin this book by introducing some of the fundamentals of the Islamic faith, both historically and in terms of doctrine. In particular, I want to discuss aspects of the religion that lend it to what I will call an "Evidentialist" interpretation (or as some scholars have put it, a "Rationalist" interpretation). In this context I will discuss the first ever state-sponsored (and Evidentialist) theology of Islam—Muʿtazilite theology—and compare it with its later (anti-Evidentialist) rival Ashʿārite theology, as well as to some of the more traditional, literalist understandings of the faith that one finds in Hanbalite theology and jurisprudence. As we will see, both the Muʿtazilite and Ashʿārite theological schools were extremely philosophically sophisticated (they are both known as part of *Kalām* (rational) theology)—to the point where the boundary between philosophy and theology become rather blurred. And it was during the period of Muʿtazilite dominance that we see the great Islamic philosophers (the Falasifa) first come into ascendance, often appropriating (but also going beyond) philosophical moves made in *Kalām*, and indeed the dialectic they follow often mirroring the fundamental differences between Muʿtazilite and Ashʿārite views. The central and most fundamental issue was a rather simple one: what is the role of independent reason in Islam?

© The Author(s) 2017
A.R. Booth, *Analytic Islamic Philosophy*, Palgrave Philosophy Today,
https://doi.org/10.1057/978-1-137-54157-4_1

Islam: The Beginning

Islam begins with a series of events that befell the Prophet Muhammad. These events occurred when Muhammad was 40 years old, in the year 610. The Prophet was born in Mecca in the year 570 into an Arab clan. The Arabs at this time were a pagan collection of disparate nomadic, Bedouin tribes living in the Arabian Peninsula. The tribes were disunited and often at war with one another, but they shared a number of values, especially tribal loyalty and independence. They lived in the shadow of two more unified and dominant empires in the region: the Eastern Roman Empire and the Persian Empire.

Importantly, in respect of the rise of the Islamic philosophers (who were known in Arabic as the Falasifa) two centuries later, the Eastern Roman Empire underwent significant change towards the middle of the mid-seventh century and Greek (as opposed) to Latin was instituted as the official language. Historians refer to the Eastern Roman Empire from this point on the "Byzantine Empire", after the Greek name for Constantinople (modern-day Istanbul) before Constantine had made it his capital.

In 610, in a cave in Mount Hira (in modern-day Saudi Arabia) where he had taken to meditating, Muhammad was said to be visited by the Archangel Gabriel (in Arabic *Jibrāʿīl*). The Archangel commanded Muhammad to *Recite!* And though Muhammad was reluctant at first, and though (so it is sometimes said) also illiterate, he wrote down the words Allah sent via the Angel. Some say that these were then written on codex (a kind of parchment),[1] and some say that these may have been merely recited and remembered. These words, together with several other revelations that occurred throughout Muhammad's life, constitute the Koran—the Islamic bible.

Muhammad's central message was that Allah commanded him to "Purify my house" (Koran 2:125). That is, to "purify" Mecca from the pagan, polytheistic (*shirk*) idols and to set the path for *Tawhīd* (from the Arabic for "One"— *Wahed*): monotheism, divine unity, oneness, and the idea that there was one God under which all tribes should unite.

Tawhīd and Reason

I think it is this emphasis on divine unity—*Tawhīd*—that, at least partly, explains how for very many people (and a certain kind of Islamic theology) Islam is thought to be a religion that promotes the use of reason. This has several underlying causes.

First, the overwhelming emphasis on divine unity was not new. It is a concept Jews, Christians, and the Zoroastrians also endorsed. Indeed, Muhammad did not think his message really contradicted those religions and in the Koran we see that Jesus, for instance, was considered a genuine prophet. Moreover, the Koran *requires* us to believe in the message of Jesus, qua messenger of God. However, Muhammad seemed to have thought that Christianity had somehow warped the truth of divine unity (the *Tawhīd*) in countenancing the notion of the Holy Trinity. In the Koran, Jesus never himself endorses the Holy Trinity, and one reason why God may have chosen to speak again through a new messiah was to ensure that his true and pure message, which had been somehow adulterated, was properly received, once and for all (Muhammad is said to be the "seal of the prophets"). Muhammad's prophesy is thus said not just to be an interpretation of the word of God, but the word of God itself. This emphasis on divide unity and rejection of the Christian Holy Trinity gives Islam some resemblance with the Jewish faith. Indeed, the two religions appeared so similar to Muhammad that he is sometimes thought to have assumed that the Jews would automatically convert to Islam. But Muhammad did not assume that they would convert simply because he was offering the same religion to them, just differently packaged. He must have thought that there was something about Islam that made it an improvement over Judaism. It is interesting to surmise what exactly that improvement was supposed to be; and the answer shows us something important about how Islam was perceived.

Perhaps the explanation is simply this: the Koran is the unadulterated word of God. When we read the Koran we are reading the word of God, and not an interpretation of what God says. So, in this respect, compared with the Torah (for instance), which was composed by many writers over several centuries, it could be considered superior, and certainly more homogenous or monolithic. But why should Muhammad have expected the Jews just to accept his word that he was reciting the word of God? Perhaps he felt that they would be able to immediately and directly see the intrinsic divineness of the words of the Koran. That Muhammad might have thought that is plausible; but I think it can only be part of the story, given the spiritual sensibility required to do so. It seems to me that part of why Muhammad must have thought the message of the Koran so persuasive was just that, that it was *persuasive*. That is, that if we engage our God-given faculty of *reason*, we will come to see the superiority of the Koran over what had come before and that, as such, the Koran constitutes *progress*.

Importantly, this seems to imply one can be a Muslim without labelling oneself as such. For instance, Jesus is said to be a Muslim and to have "walked the straight path". This is, on the face of it, a rather radical idea. In fact, I cannot overestimate how radical this appears. Martin Luther, much later in the sixteenth century, was considered a radical by virtue of his edict that the "just shall live by faith"; that is, so long as you had faith (i.e., correct Christian beliefs) you can enter Heaven (the test of whether or not you have lived the just life). But the Muslim religion seems to imply here a much more radical thesis—one does not have even have to read the Koran to qualify as a good Muslim (Jesus could not have read the Koran, for instance) and one does not even need to identify one's beliefs as Islamic in order to qualify as a Muslim. That said, the *šahāda*—the profession (witnessing) of faith for a Muslim, and one of the "five pillars" of Islam—involves profession not just that "there is no God but God" (*lā ʾilāha ʾillā llāh*) but also that "Muhammad is the messenger of God" (*muḥammadun rasūlu llāh*). So it does seem that belief in Muhammad's being the seal of the prophets is required in order for one to qualify as a Muslim. However, one might ask: on what grounds must a good Muslim believe this? As we will discuss in later chapters, according to many of the Falasifa, we should believe that he is the messenger because the message withstands rational scrutiny. The ultimate proof for determining whether a prophet is genuine is the *truth*.

A second reason why we might think that Islam is a rational religion is that the word *Islam* means "submission" or "surrender". A Muslim is someone who surrenders his whole being to the divine will (i.e. practises Islam, "walks the straight path"). There are two important observations to note about this.

Islam is often taken to be a religion that is all about obedience. And it is easy to see how the words "submission" or "surrender" can suggest that. But I would like to risk presenting another, I think better, way of interpreting this here (and one that is a rough approximation of how the Falasifa (the Islamic Philosophers) and Islamic mystics (*Sufis*) have taken it, as we will discuss in much more detail in later chapters). The key aspect of being a Muslim is not about people's existing physical or spiritual selves *obeying* what God says, but rather that Muslims give up the illusion that they are fully discrete and independent selves, unities, at all. To the extent that we matter, are spiritual beings more than mere animals, above the contingent everyday world of decay, we must be in harmony with—or in some sense are connected but are not identical with – the One, Allah. But since Allah is essentially One, to the extent that we, as Muslims, are in harmony with Him, we cannot see ourselves as distinct selves. So, to the extent that we matter, we are not individuals. I think this interpretation chimes in well with part of what so displeased Muhammad about the way the pagan Arab tribes were behaving at his time, characterised by infighting and by massive inequalities of wealth. To emphasise divine unity and submission, then, is to emphasise the senselessness of our base need to characterise ourselves as individuals, driven by selfish desires. The point is not about blind obedience, but rather to surrender the "idol" (false God) of the self.[2]

I think this can also be seen by considering the five pillars of Islam: the Creed, Prayer, Alms-Giving, Fasting, Pilgrimage. One does not walk the straight path by simply obeying the instruction that these things ought to be done. One needs to do them in the spirit that in doing them one is abandoning one's corrupt, lower sense of self. For instance, during pilgrimage, Muslims are enjoined at one stage to wear the kinds of clothes worn by the Prophet and his entourage. The symbolism of shedding one's ordinary vestiges at this stage can be taken to be about our shaking off our worldly, mortal selves to prepare our coming into communion with the One.

A third reason why we might take Islam to promote the use of reason is that the Koran and Hadith (accounts of the sayings and activities of the Prophet, which also constitute holy scripture for Muslims) contain explicit edicts to do so. Here are but a few examples:

> ... among his servants, only those who have knowledge are in awe of God. Koran 35:28
>
> Say, 'My Lord, increase me in knowledge!' Koran 20:114
>
> Say, 'to God belongs the convincing argument.' Koran 6:149[3]
>
> If anyone travels on a road in search of knowledge, Allah will cause him to travel on one of the roads of Paradise. The angels will lower their wings in their great pleasure with one who seeks knowledge, the inhabitants of the heavens and the Earth and the fish in the deep waters will ask forgiveness for the learned man. The superiority of the learned man over the devout is like that of the moon, on the night when it is full, over the rest of the stars. The learned are the heirs of the Prophets, and the Prophets leave neither dinar nor dirham, leaving only knowledge, and he who takes it takes an abundant portion.
>
> The Prophet Muhammad (Recalled by Abu Dhara) Abu Dawud, Book 19.

This emphasis on knowledge in Koranic scripture has led the renowned scholar of Islam Franz Rosenthal (2007), to claim that "Islam *means* Knowledge".[4] And this idea is further vindicated by the fact that the Koranic terms for the time preceding the Koranic revelation is *al-jāhilīyah*—a term that is usually translated as "ignorance". This suggests that the central contribution of the Koranic revelation is knowledge. What is meant to mark out Islam over other religions is that its propositions are meant to be believed not out of blind faith or obedience, but because in engaging one's faculty of reason one comes to see them to be true.

A famous Hadith from Caliph Umar is often used to validate this idea:[5]

The Prophet once came across a stranger who asks him: What does *Islam* mean?

The Prophet answers: "Islam means that you should testify that there is no God but God and that Muhammad is the Messenger of God, that you should observe the prayer, pay the zakat, fast during Ramadan, and make the pilgrimage to the Kaba if you have the means to go."

The stranger agrees, but asks: what is meant by *belief* (*Imān*)?

The Prophet replies that it means that you should believe in God, his angels, his Books and his Prophets. [The stranger turns out to be Archangel Gabriel]

A common way, and I think a very natural way, of interpreting this passage is that it is saying that *acting* merely in accordance with the prescriptions one finds in the Koran (such as *testifying* that there is no God but God, or *performing* the pilgrimage to the Kaba) is not sufficient (though necessary) for "walking the straight path", for being a good Muslim. These deeds need to be performed with certain accompanying beliefs—these are propositions *we ought to believe*. And we might think that these beliefs are correct just in case they are true, or (to put it another way) in accord with our evidence. That is, the Koran enjoins us not merely to *act as if we believe* but to come to have the relevant beliefs via rational reflection.

This interpretation, however, makes an assumption about what Islam says about the metaphysics of belief (about what beliefs *are*).[6] It assumes that beliefs are things whose essence it is to *represent* the world. From this metaphysical assumption it derives a normative or epistemological thesis about what correct belief is, namely that correct belief is belief that accurately represents the world (that is, true belief is correct belief). But a different way of interpreting the Hadith (given the similarity of the two answers) is to understand it as telling us that Islamic belief is a matter of performing the relevant required actions. In this view, we might take the passage to suggest that the Islamic view of belief (at least as far as religious belief is concerned) is a thoroughly *dispositionalist* one, where "S believes that p" just means that S has a set of behavioural dispositions associated with a belief that p. For instance, believing that there is a cake in the fridge just means (for someone who enjoys cake, like me) that I will be disposed to open the fridge and eat the cake when hungry.[7] So to believe that there is no God but God is, under this view, *nothing but* the *act* of proclaiming that there is no God but God in relevant circumstances. As such, beliefs are not correct only in so far as they represent the world, but rather they are correct in so far as the actions that constitute them are *correct actions* as determined by the will of God. We will return to this issue in many of the chapters that follow.

Sunna and Hadith

By the time Muhammad died in 632, the Muslim population had grown to inhabit large parts of present-day Saudi Arabia, including Mecca and Medina. (The taking of the latter in 662 marks the start of the Muslim lunar calendar.) Muhammad had not only been the spiritual leader of the Muslims, but also their political leader. So his death, naturally, raised all sorts of questions for the Muslim community. These can be divided into two sets:

First, who was going to succeed him qua spiritual/political leader? This was especially pressing, given that Muhammad himself had not inherited his political and spiritual legitimacy. Was the right successor to be related to him? Or was the right successor to be the closest amongst his followers? Or was the right successor to be the most gifted leader and spiritual guide?

Second, what would happen if a situation arose that required guidance that the Koran had not explicitly addressed?

The answer to the second was largely to focus on the practices of the Prophet (the Sunna) which were collected through a series of Hadith. Of course, having the resource of knowing how the Prophet has behaved considerably increases the likelihood of being able to answer, for any question x, what is the correct (Islamic) answer to x. But, of course, the Prophet was finite (he died!), and the number of possible situations that can arise infinite. So it is impossible for the Hadith and Koran to inform us of what should be done explicitly in every situation. So the need arises to *extrapolate* from the known Hadith and the Koran to answer the question of what Muhammad would have done about a situation, or what follows from the Koran that is not explicitly addressed. But doing this involves the use of *reason* (what is called in Islamic jurisprudence *Ijtihād*). And it is endorsing the use of reason to settle such debates that is the cornerstone of the first Islamic rational theologians: the Muʿtazilites. We will discuss them shortly.

The Caliphate

Let us now discuss what the answer to the question concerning political/spiritual succession and legitimacy turned out to be. The leader of the Muslims, both spiritually and politically, is called the *Caliph*. The word "Caliph" is related to the Arabic for "representative" or "vice-regent" of God. Muhammad, obviously, was the first Caliph. At the time of his death there were effectively three groups among his followers. The **first** group was composed of his most inner circle, and family, who had been with him since he first embarked upon cleansing Mecca from polytheism. The **second** group comprised the group of Muslims from Medina who had made Muhammad's taking of the city possible—as you will recall, the taking of Medina (called the *Hijrah*) marks the start of the Muslim lunar calendar. The **third** group was made up of prominent people from Mecca who had recently converted to Islam and who had, until recently, been enemies of Muhammad. Somewhat surprisingly, perhaps, it was people in this latter group who eventually rose to power.

The first Caliph to immediately succeed the Prophet, however, was 'Abu Bakr. He was a member of the first group of Muhammad's followers, and father to one of Muhammad's favourite wives, *Ā'isha*. The decision to appoint 'Abu Bakr as Caliph, taken by the Medina elders (in a kind of proto-democratic way, referred to as *shura*), was to prove a controversial one (to say the least). A strong faction among the Prophet's followers had expected to see his cousin and son-in-law Ali succeeding him. This rift marks the beginning of the distinction between Sunni and Shiite Muslims (the term "Shiites" is connected to the phrase "the party of Ali" (*Shiʿatu ʿali*)). The Shiites believed that the Caliphate should have been hereditary and that Ali should have been made Caliph to begin with. Ali was later to be installed as (the fourth) Caliph, but his caliphate was marred by civil war and he was opposed by the armies of the Umayyad clan, from Damascus in Syria. (The Muslim empire had, from the time of 'Abu Bakr, expanded to encompass parts of Syria (taken from the Byzantine empire) as well as Arabia). Ali was assassinated in 661 as was his son and heir Hasan in 680, whereupon the Umayyad clan took control of the Arab empire and set up the Umayyad dynasty which was to rule for over 150 years from Damascus. Under the Umayyads the Arab empire grew vastly until it stretched from the Atlantic coasts of Spain and Portugal in the west to the borders of China in the east.

The Muʿtazilites

The Umayyads were vanquished by the Abbasids in 750. The Abbasid Caliphate ruled the Islamic empire from 750 to 1258, when it was broken up by the Mongol invasions (the Mongol sack of Baghdad took place in 1258).[8] The Islamic empire was vast during this time, encompassing most of the Middle East, Persia, and North Africa (Islamic Spain was mostly an independent caliphate during the Abbasid tenure). This was an empire that had grown at an astonishing speed from 622 to 750 but there was now diminishing scope for further significant territorial gain for the Abbasids, and their attention seemed to be turned inwards, towards glorifying their dynasty from within. They made Baghdad their capital (it had been Damascus under the Umayyads) which they sought (and succeeded) to turn into the world's foremost centre of learning and culture—they built there the famous *Bayt al-Hikmāh* (the House of Wisdom), a vast library, and a centre for the translation and study of the Greek scientific and philosophical works the Islamic world had come into contact with (often originally in Syriac[9]) as they made territorial gains in the Levant and, in particular, on taking Alexandria, with what was left of its wonder of the world library. And the Abbasids during this time—especially the early Abbasid Caliphs Hārūn al-Rashīd (786–809), al-Māʿmun (813–833), and al-Muʿtaṣim (833–842)—sponsored and gave extensive patronage to individual scholars, translators, and philosophers, many of whom they invited to their courts.[10] Thus they gave rise to a period often referred to as the Islamic Golden Age, or sometimes the Islamic Renaissance.

Muʿtazilite theology became the state-sponsored, official interpretation of Islam and was quite vigorously enforced.[11] Muʿtazilite theology was an especially *rationalistic* theology, in the sense that it promoted the role of reason in religious faith.[12] I think they can be classified as endorsing Evidentialism. Evidentialism is a thesis that addresses the question: what ought one to believe? And the Evidentialist answer is that what one ought to believe is determined by one's evidence. If one's beliefs are in accord with one's evidence, then one's beliefs are *justified*—they are the beliefs that one ought to have.

Evidentialism: A subject S's belief that p[13] is justified iff S has sufficient evidence that p.

The "iff" above denotes what is known as a bi-conditional—it tells us that the condition *having sufficient evidence* is thereby a *necessary and sufficient* condition. So, according to the Evidentialist, saying that a belief is supported by sufficient evidence *is* to say that the belief is justified (is a belief that one ought to have). According to the Evidentialist then, to say that one ought to believe a religious proposition—such as the proposition that there is a God—is the same thing as saying that we have sufficient evidence for that proposition. For the Evidentialist, therefore, there can be no tension between faith (that is, religious belief) and reason.

Evidentialism has become a popular view in the West. It seems to be the default view of contemporary atheists such as Richard Dawkins and Sam

Harris (Harris 2004). However, it is important to note that without the—controversial—premise that there is no sufficient evidence for any religious proposition, Evidentialism *does not* entail atheism. For one may be a theist precisely because one believes there to be sufficient evidence in favour of theism (Richard Swinburne (1981) is a notable contemporary proponent of this view). The first and archetypal Evidentialist in the West is often considered to be W.K. Clifford, a late nineteenth-century British mathematician and philosopher who famously wrote in his work *The Ethics of Belief*:[14]

It is wrong, always, everywhere, and for anyone, to believe anything upon insufficient evidence. (Clifford 1877)

The view seems to follow the view of the famous British empiricist John Locke (and other British empiricists[15]), however:

Faith is nothing but a firm assent of the mind: which if it be regulated, as is our duty, cannot be afforded to anything, but upon good reason; and so cannot be opposite to it. He that believes, without having any reason for believing, may be in love with his own fancies; but neither does he seek truth as he ought, nor pays the obedience due to his maker, who would have him use those discerning faculties as he has given him, to keep him out of mistake and errour. (Locke, *Essay Concerning Human Understanding*, iv, xvii, 24)[16]

In the contemporary debate, Evidentialism as a normative doctrine has followed an account of doxastic metaphysics: belief is *essentially* (or constitutively) something that is subject to a truth norm: belief that p is correct just in case p (Shah and Velleman 2005).

The Muʿtazilite core theological principles consisted of five essential tenets, the first two of which seem to have been given priority:

(i) God is unity, One (*Tawḥīd*).
(ii) God dispatches Justice (*ʿadl*).
(iii) There is a "promise and the threat" of Paradise and Hell.
(iv) One should adopt an "intermediary position".
(v) One must "command the right and forbid the wrong".

Principles (iv) and (v) require a further explication. Principle (v), simply, is about the need (indeed the obligation for Muslims) to impose justice via any means (consistent with justice) necessary, including the use of force. Principle (iv) is rather more complex. The Arabic name '*Muʿtazila*' translates as withdrawers or those who withdrew. This refers to an (arguably folkloric) account of how it was that the Mu'tazilites came to be known as people who had a particular response to a theological question. The question was something like the following: can someone who has sinned be appropriately considered a true believer? This, of course, is importantly related to the issue of how to interpret the difference (or if there is a difference) between *imān* and *Islam* as it appears in Caliph Umar's Hadith. The issue concerns whether one's actions must accord with one's belief that p if one is said to believe that p. As I hinted at earlier, answering the guiding question above in a negative might well come with a commitment to what modern, Western epistemologists call *disposition-alism* about belief, or even a broader more pragmatic account of the content of our mental states.[17] This sort of view would then support the idea that faith and *religious* knowledge (here thought of as adherence to religious practice) are identical, such that what determines correct (at least, religious) belief out-runs evidence – it is a matter of *faith*. Being a true believer is a matter of acting in accord with Koranic obligation, and such actions we can choose to com-mit, or choose not to commit. As such, belief can be considered voluntary (a function of our actions, or our dispositions to action), adequately the object of blame and praise, and, further, has non-evidential correctness conditions—namely compliance with strictures about how to *behave*. The Mu'tazilites, however, did not take this line, and thought that there was no determinate answer to the question whether someone who has sinned can be considered a true believer. They literally withdrew from debates on this question, and pro-posed an intermediate answer – that is, they *withheld judgement* with respect to the question.

The position had some very serious political implications at the time. First, it meant that the Mu'tazilites did not have to take sides on certain pressing contemporary arguments, such as whether Uthmān was really a heretic,[18] or whether to accept that 'Ali was properly a *Rashidūn* Caliph. As such, until 850, when the more orthodox Sunni Abbasid al'Mutawakkil became Caliph, the Abbasid Empire had been one where a Sunni/Shiite quarrel had been rela-tively marginal. Second, it allowed the early Abbasid establishment to freely be seen to sponsor and give patronage to scholars whose views might be con-sidered to have been too close to blasphemy, or even plain apostasy for com-fort. During this time one could not be legally tried for apostasy if one explicitly claimed allegiance to Islam, even where one's *actions* seemed to sug-gest otherwise, or even if one had other beliefs that seemed to contradict it.

It is the Mu'tazilite's view on God's Justice, Principle (ii) that really marks them out as Evidentialists. For the Mu'tazilites here seem to be endorsing the ideal of personal freedom and moral responsibility, and, especially, the ideal (derived from the work of nineteenth-century German philosopher Immanuel

Kant) that "'ought' implies 'can'", that we are only morally responsible over things within our voluntary control. A just God punishes those who have *chosen* to sin, and rewards those who have *chosen* to do good and abide by God's law. If Zayd is *forced* to sin, and could not have done otherwise but sin, then it is an unjust God that punishes him.[19] Now, via parity of reasoning, the same principle seems to apply to our beliefs as well as our actions. The issue relates directly, I think, to how we are to think of the difference between infidels (*kufrs*), and apostates (*riddahs*), and on whether and how to punish them. Infidels do not believe the religious principles of the Koran, but do they do something morally objectionable in cases where they could not but have failed to have that belief—that is, when there was no way that they could have had access to the Koranic revelation, or to testimony of the Koranic revelation? The Mu'tazilites—and here is where the nineteenth-century perception of them qua "free thinkers" parts company with reality—took a hard line on this, and thought that in many cases the infidels were indeed doing something morally wrong in failing to follow Koranic belief. What must underlie this—compatible with ought implies can—is the thought that through their use of *reason*, that is, by considering the *evidence* around them, they would have come to have beliefs that at least resemble (if are not completely identical to) Koranic belief in all but name. And they could have come to acquire these beliefs even when they had no way of accessing (directly or indirectly) the Koran. People who fail to have Koranic belief are simply failing to exercise their capacity of reason, and since whether or not we use our capacity of reason *is* within our control, we can be—at least indirectly—held to blame for having beliefs that we would not have believed had we exercised reason.[20] It is important to note that there is a thematic connection here, with respect to beliefs that at least *resemble* proper Koranic beliefs, between infidels and apostates. Consider whether those who introduce "innovation" (*bidʿah*) into religion—what Islam considers heresy—are also apostates. The typical Mu'tazilite response to this issue, at least politically speaking, was to here take a more lenient stance, and claim the matter was in many instances indeterminate, subject to suspension of judgement. Certainly the early Mu'tazilites seemed to take this line, as we briefly discussed, with respect to Shiite Islam. The key determinant of apostasy here being about whether a putative apostate has done all that he can with respect to arriving at correct belief: if he seems to have done, by having beliefs that at least resemble the correct Koranic ones, then—though he may still be guilty of lesser crimes, one cannot charge him with apostasy (the matter is too indeterminate for us humans to judge, to be resolved only at day of judgment), and he thus escapes the death penalty. Again, the keystones here are that ought implies can, and that the teachings of prophecy do not tell us anything that cannot be learnt—at least in approximation—via the use of reason alone. And part of the relevant indeterminacy here also concerns the issue regarding whether one can sin and be a true believer. The view that we cannot—at least in certain cases—for certain judge whether someone believes as she does in good faith, that is, has done all that is within her control in order to arrive at what she thinks is correct belief, seems to cohere better with a view of belief according to which the latter is a private, occurent mental state.[21] This all adds up, I think, to a reasonable case for taking (at least the pre-850) Mu'tazilites to be committed to the view I earlier called *Evidentialism*.

The Mu'tazilite case for Evidentialism, premised as it is on the idea of God's justice, as I have tried to suggest, looks to be vulnerable to certain philosophical troubles. Among them are at least the following. First, it does not appear that the Mu'tazilites left much scope for indeterminacy when it came to their own core doctrines—there was hardly much leniency given with respect to what they considered incorrect answers to their inquisition. However, notice that the guiding question of their inquisition was not "Do you accept the principle of God's Unity?", but, rather, the more indirect and intellectual one regarding whether the Koran was created or not. Understanding how this latter question relates to the issue regarding the oneness of God requires some thought, the application of the instrument of reason. Arguably, this could be said to demonstrate the Mu'tazilites primary concern with the latter as the proper determinant of faith, rather than blind commitment to rote learning, even if the consequences of their inquisition were obviously going to militate against that end. Second, one might wonder what the fate—in terms of heavenly rewards and punishments—the Mu'tazilites could think were appropriate for those who die before being given the opportunity to enact any free choice (doxastic or otherwise). Third, what special role could the Mu'tazilites think that prophecy could have, once they seem to have ruled that one could in principle reason one's way into correct belief? Perhaps they could hold that it role is to *guide* reason (in a resonant manner perhaps to how Socrates guides the slave boy of Plato's *Meno* to correct opinion[22]), but this will look deflationary, to say the least, to those for whom revelation has an essentially indispensible role.[23] Of note here is Ibn Tufayl (a twelfth-century al-Andalus philosopher) who allegorizes the idea that we can achieve wisdom through the use of reason alone in his philosophical novel *Ḥayy ibn Yaqẓān*. In an interesting discussion of the latter, Oliver Leaman (2009) compares the story with Daniel Defoe's *Robinson Crusoe*—where Robinson Crusoe is seen as a civilizing influence on the "savage" Man-Friday, the opposite is the case for the Man-Friday correlate in

Ḥayy ibn Yaqẓān, whose unadulterated conception of the faith (acquired independently in his desert island) is the true civilizing force of the novel. Intriguingly, during the time of the Mongols' tenure in the Islamic world, the philosopher Ibn al-Nafis wrote a counter-novel (sometimes known as *Virtuous Son of the Rational*) where the protagonist, while having been able to arrive (alone through the use of reason) at some religious truths (such as that there must be a God), *learns* indispensible religious truths through the testimony of others.

The Hanbalites and Ashʿārites

Ahmad Ibn Ḥanbal (780–855) was the founder of the eponymously named *Hanbalite* theological movement. It constituted—and continues to constitute in its various new guises—a challenge to a more rationalist or Evidentialist account of Islamic religious belief. The Hanbalites were and continue to be traditionalists, and literalists: they thought that what was in revelation was to be taken as *literal* and never metaphorical truth. Revelation factively represents the world, but aspects of it that would be hidden were it not for God's having sent us a prophet. Where prophetic knowledge seemed to contradict ordinary human knowledge, or itself, then *bi-lā –kayf* applies: the contradiction is only seeming to our human minds, which cannot comprehend how there is really none, and such that we should trust that there is none. This has consequences for Islamic jurisprudence, or *fiqh*, on the question of how to turn revelation into operational law (*Sharia*)—that is, there is no place for independent reasoning (*ijtihād*).

Ashʿarite theology can be thought to take a middle-ground position between the rationalism of Muʿtazilism and the anti-rationalism of Hanbalite theology. It begins with its founder, al-Ashʿarī, defecting from Muʿtazilism and embracing Hanbalite theology, and its reverence for revelation over reason. As I have mentioned, the folkloric story is that he did so on considering the story of the "three brothers"—in short, one brother lives a moral life in accord with the Koran and ends up in Heaven, another fails to live such a life and ends up in Hell, and a third dies as a child and ends up in a sort of purgatory, an afterlife short of Paradise. Since the child has not had the chance to either show him or herself to be worthy of an afterlife in Heaven, the story is meant to be a *reductio ad absurdum* of the Muʿtazilite emphasis on God's Justice and human freedom of the will. Unlike Muʿtazilism, Ashʿarite theology espouses what might be called a kind of *voluntarism* about the source of moral normativity. That is, the former, to put it in terms of the Euthyphro dilemma, takes God to love the good because they are good, such that there is an independent source of normativity that exists outside of God's will. As such, Mu'tazilite theology is often thought of as a kind of moral realism (the idea that there exist moral facts independently of any mind or will). The Ash'arites reject this and take the other horn of the Euthyphro dilemma, and think that the good are good because God loves them. That is, God's *will* is the ultimate source of moral normativity, hence the label voluntarism (from the idea that moral obligation comes from what is *willed* by God). Of course, taking each horn of the dilemma comes with having to deal with certain problems (otherwise we could hardly call the problem in question even a seeming dilemma). The Mu'tazilites have to accept having ceded that there is an authority in moral matters that God merely responds to and does not have power over, as well as the issue regarding how to think of the moral status of children, animals, and those others whose action fall somewhat short of being under full voluntary control, but who nevertheless have moral status. The Ash'arites face the long-standing issue of whether they can account for God's justice, an objection which is a particular form of a more general realist strategy sometimes known as the "open question argument" (Moore 1903) (since the Ash'arites *define* the good in terms of what God wills). Briefly: take any attempt to define what Good is (say that Good = what makes the greatest number of people in any situation happy), according to Moore, for any instantiation of that definition we can ask: but is it really Good? So, we might determine that my making a cake is going to make more people happy than any other action of mine at t, but it still makes sense to ask: is that action really *Good*? Moore took this to show that Good was not something that could be *defined*. But one could take it to show that there is no way of defining 'Good as something out there in world—such that there would be moral "facts" for us to find, and not a product of some *will* (God's will for example).

The Ash'arites follow the Hanbalites in thinking, as Montgomery Watt puts it, that "faith (*imān*) consists of word and act, that is, profession of belief and fulfilment of the prescribed duties" (Watt 1985, p. 67). Put differently, they hold a sort of behaviourist, or dispositional, account of the contents of belief. This bears directly on the question regarding the criteria for ascertaining apostasy, and meant the abandonment of the Mu'tazilite decree that professing belief in the *Shahāda* was sufficient for being cleared of apostasy. This once again expediates a Sunni confrontation with Shiite Islam, since even if proponents of the latter profess belief, their putatively divergent practices may be taken to militate against the proposition that they actually believe. This is in accord with Hanbali doctrine, as is their rejection of metaphorical readings of the Koran towards a more literalist understanding of the latter (where putative contradictions are passed off as beyond human comprehension—*bi-lā kayf*). However, in their voluntarism, they differ from the Hanbalites. The latter see that the works of prophecy are statements of fact, propositions representing the deep nature of reality, and are as such to be taken an infallible testimony as regards these facts, that is, as constituting *evidence* that the relevant propositions are true. One cannot reason one's way to having the appropriate beliefs because this evidence is uniquely available through this special testimony. This is in accord with Evidentialism, as defined earlier. The Ashʿarite line in the ethics of belief constitutes what I am going to call anti-Evidentialism, on the other hand. This is because, parallel to their line on the Euthyphro dilemma, they think that what we ought to believe is determined by what God wills. That is, they take a voluntarist line about doxastic normativity, such that one believes religious propositions because God decrees it, and *not* because there is independent evidence that shows the propositions to be true. Thus, the view is much stronger (and entails) non-Evidentialism (simply the denial of Evidentialism), since it claims that *all* beliefs are to believed for non-epistemic reasons, not only that it is permissible to sometimes believe for non-epistemic reasons. To summarise:

Anti-Evidentialism: S's belief that p is justified iff S has non-epistemic reason to believe that p.

The relevant non-epistemic reason for Ashʿarites is clearly God's will, such that a S's belief that p is justified just in case God wills that S believes that p. This is compatible, incidentally, with the idea that God commands that one believe on the basis of good evidence, since God's will is nonetheless doing all the normative work.

A second difference between Ashʿarite and Hanbalite theology is that proponents of the former thought it legitimate to engage in rational methods/philosophy in support of revelation, or as Watt puts it "the support of revelation by reason" (Watt 1987, p. 65). This is in fact a consequence of their anti-Evidentialism and belief that in the uniqueness of the role of prophecy. The combination of belief in the uniqueness of prophecy and Evidentialism—as per Hanbalite doctrine—seems to entail a sort of exceptionalism about the *evidence* (through testimony) one receives in reading the Koran, where that evidence is unavailable by any other means. And this entails that there is no other way of properly engaging with religious matters than by consulting revealed texts. Rejecting Evidentialism (of the stricter variety—i.e. not moderate Evidentialism) frees one from having to accept this conclusion. This is not necessarily, as the Ashʿarites show, to place reason above revelation, since the use of the former is merely an instrument to demonstrate the necessity of the latter – indeed in the last of three dreams that are said to have immediately preceded al-Ashʿarī's conversion, Muhammad is said to have appeared to him and told him (angrily) not to reject rational methods altogether, despite having in the previous dreams recommended him to have more strictly followed the paths set out in the Hadith and Koran.

A third difference is the Ashʿarite commitment to a proto-compatibilist account of free will. The Ashʿarite subscribed to an Occationalist metaphysics, according to which God intervenes at every point in the causal order of things—that is, underlying every event, God is the *proximate* (immediate) cause. If God is the proximate cause of every event, and actions are events, if follows that all human actions are predetermined by God. And so the issue regarding God's justice returns: if I had no control over whether or not I acted according to God's law, is it really just of God to punish me for violating God law? The Ashʿarite compatibilist answer is something like this (fabulously resonant with some of the work by the contemporary American philosopher Harry Frankfurt (1971) and perhaps a precursor to Thomas Hobbes's classical compatibilism): part of what it is to be human, and not an animal, is that we have higher-order desires and beliefs. That is, we can reflect on our own desires and sometimes come to endorse them, and sometimes come not to endorse them. My desire for gorging myself on dates all the time, for example, might not be a desire that I endorse, given that I think that I ought not to be so gluttonous. To act as one wants then is to act in such a way that one's higher and lower order desires are in sync. When my base desires take over and I do gorge myself on dates, I no longer act as I want, but rather am just an animal and a mere product of the chain of cause and effect. The same can be said about our higher-order and lower order belief—when I have a belief that I think I ought not to have, I am no longer the agent of my own beliefs.[24] My action or belief s is free then just in case I have not been prevented from acting or believing as I wanted. Since God's being the proximal cause of my action or belief x does not *prevent* me from acting or believing as I wanted, it is no obstacle to my acting freely. And, as such, no obstacle to my being held responsible for either my actions of my beliefs.

Concluding Remarks

We have now explored the broad contours of the Islamic faith and its three major theological impulses centred around the normativity and metaphysics of belief. In other words, whether belief is really a kind of public action, a private mental representational occurrence, and relatedly whether belief is correct only where it corresponds with our evidence, the world, the literal word of revelation, the will of God. As we will see, all these positions have inherent and interesting *philosophical* problems and I think we can see the fixing of these problems to be a unifying theme of Islamic philosophy—Falsafa: a project of doing "Philosophy in the land of Prophecy". Falsafa emerges in the Islamic world during the Abbasid Caliphate when Islamic civilization was first coming into contact with Greek philosophy. The project of Falsafa was in large part and in the first instance an attempt to come to terms with this exciting and for them new discovery. In order to understand Falsafa then, we must first have a working understanding of some of the key themes and ideas in the Greek philosophy they were inheriting. This is the task of the next chapter.

Study Questions

- Is there a tension between Hanbalite doxastic metaphysics and the Hanbalite account of doxastic normativity?
- If one can reason one's way to correct religious belief, what might be the unique epistemic purpose of revelation?

What to Read Next?

- Ibn Tufayl – *Ḥayy ibn Yaqẓān* in Lenn Goodman (trans.) *Ibn Tufayl's Hayy Ibn Yaqzan: A Philosophical Tale* (2009) (Chicago: Chicago University Press).
- Watt, M. 1985: *Islamic Philosophy and Theology* (Edinburgh: Edinburgh University Press).

Notes

1. Fakhry (2004) calls it an "eternal codex (the Preserved Tablet, referred to in Koran 85, 22)", p. xviii.
2. This partly also explains the Muslim emphasis on the importance of the *umma* (community).
3. For an interesting exploration of Koranic verses and their philosophical relevance, see Leaman (2016).
4. Indeed, he goes as far as claiming that "From the Qu'ranic attitude toward knowledge, it would be possible almost to predict the course that Muslim

theology, mysticism, jurisprudence and the like were to take, as well as the fate that had to befall the liberating influences set in motion by the reception of the Classical heritage in the ninth century. The triumph and defeats of Muslim civilization are foreshadowed in Muhammad's understanding of 'knowledge'" (Rosenthal 2007, p. 32).

5. Retrieved from www.hadith.com
6. Metaphysical questions ask what the nature of things: what *is* an x? This in contrast to epistemological questions that ask about how we know x.
7. For a modern defence of this view, see Schwitzgebel. For a related more general pragmatic account of the contents of our mental states, see Stalnaker (1984).
8. Though the Seljuk Turks were in de facto control of much of the Empire from 1037.
9. Syriac is a dialect of Aramaic, the language spoken by Christ.
10. For an account of why this might have been politically expedient, see Gutas (1998).
11. For instance, the instituted a famous "test" or inquisition whereby subjects were required to answer whether the Koran was itself infinite or created (a wrong answer to the question would bring about harsh punishment for the subject), see Adamson (2015).
12. For a good account of Mu'tazilite doctrine, see Watt (1985, chapter 8).
13. 'p' stands for proposition here. For instance, S believes the proposition that Baghdad is the capital of Iraq, or S believes the proposition that Jupiter is a planet.
14. It is said that Einstein developed theories in geometry that Clifford had first suggested (Kallfelz 2009).
15. For Hume this approach famously led to atheism; see Hume (1779).
16. For discussion on Locke on the ethics of belief, see Wolterstorf (1996).
17. Of the sort espoused by Wittgenstein and Elizabeth Anscombe, and more contemporary Neo-Wittgensteinians such as Bob Stalnaker.
18. The Kharijites, among others, accused the Caliph Uthmān of having sinned due to his not having meted out to other sinners the punishments that are prescribed in the Holy Koran.
19. As many scholars have noted (Adamson 2015; Frank 1983), a good way to think of the position here is as taking the first horn of the Euthyphro dilemma: does God love the good because it is good, or is the good, good, because God loves it? As we will shortly discuss, an opposing theological group in Islam—the Ash'ārite theologians—take instead the second horn, as well as espouse a compatibilism with respect to moral responsibility and a kind of determinism.
20. This is because there are two ways in which blame supervenes (depends) on obligation: we are blameworthy simply for breaking an obligation, and we are also blameworthy when a state of affairs occurs that would not have occurred had we not broken an obligation (Alston 1989; Zimmerman 1996).

21. Though, in particular when one allows *dispositions* to action to play a role in determining the contents of belief, it may well be sometimes difficult to judge what a subject believes just by investigating their actions, even if belief is just a function of how one acts, or is disposed to act.
22. We will discuss this in the following chapter.
23. Abū Bakr al-Rāzī (854–925) was a philosopher and medic who seemed to bite the bullet and to accept that prophecy has such a minimal role. He was very unpopular for this and his contemporary critic—Abū Hātim al-Rāzī—calls him a heretic in his work *The Proofs of Prophecy.*
24. Although see Shoemaker (2009) for an argument against this possibility.

References

Secondary Sources

Adamson, P. 2015. *Philosophy in the Islamic World: A Very Short Introduction.* Oxford University Press.

Alston, W. 1989. The Deontological Conception of Epistemic Justification. In *Epistemic Justification: Essays in the Theory of Knowledge.* Cornell University Press.

Clifford, W.K. 1877[1999]. The Ethics of Belief. In *The Ethics of Beleif and Other Essays*, ed. T. Madigan. Prometheus.

Fakhry, M. 2004. *A History of Islamic Philosophy.* Columbia University Press.

Frank, R. 1983. Moral Obligations in Classical Muslim Theology. *Journal of Religious Ethics* 11: 205–223.

Frankfurt, H. 1971. Freedom of the Will and the Concept of a Person. *The Journal of Philosophy* 68 (1): 5–20.

Gutas, D. 1998. *Greek Thought, Arabic Culture: The Graeco-Arabic Translation Movement in Baghdad and Early Society.* Routledge.

Harris, S. 2004. *The End of Faith: Religion, Terror, and the Future of Reason.* Norton.

Hume, D. 1779. Dialogues Concerning Natural Religion Original e-copy. http://www.davidhume.org/texts/dnr.html

Kallfelz, W. 2009. *Clifford Allgebra.* VDM Verslag.

Leaman, O. 2009. *Islamic Philosophy: An Introduction.* Polity.

———. 2016. *The Qur'an: A Philosophical Guide.* Bloomsbury.

Moore, G.E. 1903. *Principia Ethica.* Cambridge University Press.

Rosenthal, F. 2007. *Knowledge Triumphant: The Concept of Knowledge in Medieval Islam.* Brill.

Shah, N., and J.D. Velleman. 2005. Doxastic Deliberation. *Philosophical Review* 114: 497–534.

Shoemaker, S. 2009. Self-Imitation and Higher-Order Belief. *Erkenntnis* 71: 35–51.

Stalnaker, R. 1984. *Inquiry.* MIT Press.

Swinburne, R. 1981. *Faith and Reason.* Oxford University Press.
Watt, M. 1985. *Islamic Philosophy and Theology.* Edinburgh University Press.
Watt, M. 1987. *Islamic Philosophy and Theology.* Edinburgh University Press.
Wolterstorf, N. 1996. *John Locke and the Ethics of Belief.* Cambridge University Press.
Zimmerman, M. 1996. *The Concept of Moral Obligation.* Cambridge University Press.

2

The Greek Legacy

Introduction

In Chap. 1, we discussed some of the philosophical and historical underpinnings of Islam. In particular, we considered:

- Why Islam might be considered an essentially rationalistic religion.
- The Mu'tazilite theological movement and their commitment to Evidentialism, especially their emphasis on the oneness (*Tawhīd*) and justice of God, and how they paved the way for the Islamic Falasifa. Evidentialism.
- The competing Ash'ārite theological movement, its focus on divine attributes, such as the omnipotence of God, its underlying anti-Evidentialism and its introduction of compatibilism in respect of the issue of free will and determinism.
- Different accounts of the metaphysics of belief, and Hanbalite literalism.

Falasifa (Islamic philosophy) emerged as a spin off from the massive translation movement of Greek texts into Arabic commissioned during the Abbasid Caliphate. With translation came interpretation and commentary, and hence a concomitant philosophical movement. To understand the Falasifa, therefore, we need to have some sense of the Greek philosophical tradition they were engaging with. The aim of this chapter is to introduce the philosophy of Plato and Aristotle to readers unfamiliar with their work. However, I also want to try to introduce parts of Plato and Aristotle that are typically ignored in mainstream university courses on Ancient Greek philosophy, but which are

© The Author(s) 2017
A.R. Booth, *Analytic Islamic Philosophy*, Palgrave Philosophy Today,
https://doi.org/10.1057/978-1-137-54157-4_2

vital to the development of Islamic philosophy. In particular, I want to introduce the notion of an active (or agent) intellect as found in Aristotle's *De Anima*. This notion of an active intellect takes on a large role in the thought of the Falasifa and forms the keystone for the belief that through engaging in abstract thought we can connect with the One, Allah. Before that, I will try to make a link between certain themes in the works of Plato and the works of the Neo-Platonist philosopher and mystic Plotinus. We will look at Plotinus because he was very influential with both the early Falasifa (engaging in what is sometimes known as the Peripatetic tradition) and the later, more mystical, *Ishrāqi* tradition in Islamic philosophy, and has a special role to play due to the fact that, as the Falasifa worked on the mistaken assumption that much of Plotinus' work had been penned by Aristotle (in the pseudo-work *The Theology of Aristotle*).

Plato's *Heavens First Epistemology*

When people bring to their mind's eye a picture of Plato and Aristotle, they very often think of one of Raphael's Vatican frescos: *The School of Athens*. The fresco has Plato pointing up towards the heavens—the message being that knowledge proper can be attained only by directing our attention towards something beyond our mortal world, towards something more stable and permanent. Next to Plato is Aristotle, who seems to be holding Plato back—almost telling him to "take it easy"—in a pose that seems to convey an attitude of groundedness, of being the sensible one, of being oriented towards the earth. The embedded message here is the opposite of Plato's—true knowledge is to be gained by investigating this, our world, and not the ephemeral heavens. There is more "action" as it were around the two figures, with quite a lot of other famous scholars depicted (the Falaysuf Averroes is made to look like a minor figure to the left of the painting, interestingly). Plato and Aristotle are in the middle, which suggests that their disagreement is the central one in all philosophy, indeed in all civilised thought. Indeed, I would argue that a good case can still be made that it continues to be a disagreement of central importance.

So why might Raphael's Plato have thought that knowledge can only be obtained by directing one's attention towards the heavens, and why might Aristotle have thought the opposite? It is almost certainly the case that the *actual* positions of these thinkers were not the antipodes this caricature suggests. Nevertheless, the caricature can help us take a first stab at understanding their respective philosophies.

Let us begin this attempt by making a distinction between *universals* and *particulars*. As a very rough approximation, we can take universals to be concepts with at least a degree of generality, such as the concept *chair*, or *horse*, or *human*. Particulars, on the other hand, are the things that instantiate those universals, *particular chairs* (the very chair you are sitting on, for instance), *particular horses* (the horses at the Epsom derby, for instance), or particular *humans* (the people watching the Epsom derby). Particulars can even be *all* the horses that there are, or all the chairs that there are, or all the humans that there are. The set of all chairs, however, is not the universal *chair* perhaps since even if all the chairs in the world were broken, we might still think that the universal *chair* is something that one can sit on; even if every buffalo in the world broke a leg, we would still think that the universal *buffalo* has four legs, for instance.

We might then ask: do we know particulars only *through* our knowledge of universals (such that we cannot know particulars without knowing their concomitant universals)? Or, conversely, do we know universals only *through* our knowledge of particulars? Let us call the idea that we can know particulars solely, or principally, through our knowledge of universals: **Heavens First Epistemology**. And let's call the idea that we can know universals solely, or principally, via our knowledge of particulars: **Experience First Epistemology**.

Plato, in Raphael's fresco, looks like a proponent of Heavens First Epistemology. Plato, however, used a specific term for universals—*Forms* (*Eidos* in Greek). Part of what I want to suggest is that these Forms correspond in a way to what Aristotle calls *essences*—even if Forms and essences are, in other ways, quite different. For example, the Form of a *horse* might have four legs (in so far as it is the *ideal* horse), but perhaps it is not the case that the *essence* of a horse is that it has four legs (we will discuss this further later in this chapter).

Raphael's Plato would seem to be advocating a Heavens First Epistemology. What might have been Plato's reasons for this thesis? I think he gives us at least two arguments that I will now explore; one found in his dialogue the *Meno* and one in his dialogue the *Pheado*.[1]

The Argument from the *Meno*

Let us start with the argument in the *Meno*. The *Meno* begins with a question concerning whether virtue can be taught. As is usual in Plato's dialogues, at some point Socrates makes somewhat of a nuisance of himself and in this dialogue claims that (a) in order to know the answer to the question as to whether virtue can be taught, we must know what virtue is; and (b) no one around him (and especially no Sophist) knows what virtue is.[2] So the first part of the dialogue ends, as is usual in Plato's dialogues, in what the Greeks called *Aporia*—confusion, or perplexity (literally meaning not knowing where to go). But then the dialogue takes a fascinating and important turn. A more general question is raised in regard to whether learning in general is possible, and what is sometimes called Meno's Paradox is discussed. The paradox is sometimes also called the Eristic Paradox, and was a paradox that had been in circulation among the Sophists for a while.[3] Plato himself calls the paradox "eristic", in a pejorative way: unlike dialectical arguments which aim at educating, eristic arguments are exclusively aimed at defeating one's opponent for no other benefit. The paradox is supposed to show that learning is impossible and so enquiry futile. What is at stake is whether the Socratic (and Koranic) ideal that we are under an obligation or duty to enquire is true—if learning is impossible and enquiry pointless, we cannot be under an obligation to enquire. The paradox is as follows.

If we embark on enquiry, how can our enquiry come to an end unless we already *know* what it is that we are enquiring into? Otherwise, how would we recognise that we had discovered what we had sought to discover? But if we already *know* what it is that we are enquiring into, what is properly motivating our enquiry?

As Plato puts it (via Meno):

> … how will you look for something when you don't in the least know what it is? How on earth are you going to set up something you don't know as the object of your search? To put it another way, even if you come right up against it, how will you know that what you have found is the thing you didn't know? *Meno* 80d (p. 128 Guthrie translation)

It seems that Plato's solution to the problem is something like the following. Our souls are immortal and once inhabited a transcendent world containing only Forms. Our immortal souls get heavy and come to inhabit the mortal, empirical word (this bit about the souls getting heavy is actually in *the Pheado*). When our bodies die, our souls return to the heavens (populated by Forms), until they get heavy again and return to earth … and so on. Our souls then really know all there is to know, but as they got heavy and returned to the subluminal world (our mortal world), they forget this knowledge. But they are capable of remembering it when adequately prompted. What we think is learning, then, is for Plato, simply remembering—*Anamnesis* in Greek.

Now, to a modern audience this solution looks rather speculative, to say the least. But Plato tries to offer us what might be considered empirical support for his hypothesis. For instance, in the *Meno*, he tells us about how a slave boy can come to have true beliefs of difficult abstract truths in geometry without any previous geometrical education. At first, when just asked to guess the answers to the geometrical problem, the slave boy gets them wrong. But once Socrates asks the slave boy some more searching questions, it turns out the slave boy does have the answers to the difficult geometrical questions. But he is a slave boy—with no education in geometry—how could he possibly have the answers? It must be the case that he is simply remembering what he had learnt when he was an immortal soul. Plato's argument then works as an inference to the best explanation. His recollection theory best explains, so he claims, the phenomenon—namely the fact that the slave boy has true beliefs about complex geometrical matters. So Plato's theory here can be compared with how scientific theories are tried and tested. The question then is whether his hypothesis is really the best explanation. Let's consider some objections.

Objections to the Argument from the *Meno*

Socrates Asks Loaded Questions

One could object that Socrates asks the slave boy loaded questions, and really gives the right answers away. But it is hard to say exactly what we might mean by "giving the answers away" in such a way that makes his practice problematic. To illustrate, take the standard definition of what is sometimes called an argument that *begs the question*, or is a *circular argument* (sometimes also known as a *petitio principi*): the conclusion is somehow "contained" or presupposed by the premises. Here is an example of an argument that is meant to obviously beg the question:

1. A being who creates everything is omnipotent.
2. God created the moon, the stars, the rivers, the seas, the mountains, the animals and everything all around us.

Therefore,

3. God is omnipotent.

The argument above is said to be circular, since premise (2) is just premise (3), simply expressed in different words. In a sense, (2) *contains* premise (3) [assuming the truth of premise 1]. But now take a classic example of an argument that is meant to be valid:

4. All men are mortal.
5. Socrates is a man.

Therefore,

6. Socrates is mortal.

This argument is not supposed to be a question-begging, circular argument. But there is a sense in which its premises (4, 5) "contain" its conclusion, or we could not have worked out (6) by simply considering the premises. And consider the standard definition of a valid argument: an argument where it is impossible for the premises to be true and the conclusion false. That's another way of saying that in a valid argument the premises must somehow contain the conclusion, such that they *necessitate* it. So from this we can deduce that there are arguments whose premises contain their conclusion in a benign (non-fallacious) way, and some arguments where the containing is somehow problematic or non-fallacious. And it has turned out to be much more difficult than is often acknowledged to spell out exactly what that difference amounts to (for a contemporary discussion on this issue see Sinnott-Armstrong 1999).

Now, returning to the charge at hand with respect to Plato's *Meno*— armed with this information, we can respond: the fact that Socrates' questions in a sense "give away" the answers to the slave boy is not in itself problematic, just as it is not problematic for a teacher to ask a young pupil whether Socrates is mortal (when we know that all men are mortal and Socrates is man) in order to test their deductive capacities. Socrates' method would be problematic only if his questions "contained" the answers in some more explicit way such as actually articulating the answer. Here is an example: trying to prove that you know that Google Chrome is a better browser than Firefox, I ask you: isn't it just obvious that Google Chrome is a better browser than Firefox? Your answering "yes" in this instance hardly proves that you already knew this piece of information. And the questions that Socrates asks the slave boy in the *Meno* are clearly *not* like that. Indeed, the exercise is a fine illustration of what Socratic dialogue is meant to be all about—asking pertinent questions that guide one to the answer while making absolutely sure that one does not simply just articulate that answer. As Plato has Socrates say:

> … I simply ask him questions. Be ready to catch me if I give him any instruction or explanation instead of simply interrogating him on his own opinions. *Meno* 84d (pp. 135—136 in Guthrie translation)[4]

The Slave Boy Episode Is Just a Story

Another objection could be this: why are we meant to take the slave boy story to be a genuine phenomenon in need of explanation? Could not Plato have just made this story up?

In response, part of what makes the passage in the *Meno* so interesting is that if you are not familiar (or at least not phenomenally familiar) with the geometry that Socrates refers to, you yourself can take the place of the slave boy. That is how it was for me, and, I must say, I had the same experience as the slave boy—Socrates was a good teacher for me, it seems! Further, something like the slave boy point can be made with respect to the methodology of philosophy (and it is a point that is often made these days): philosophical analyses are often accepted and rejected on the basis of being either *intuitive* or counter-*intuitive*. For instance, knowledge is considered not to be mere justified true belief, because we *intuit* that certain cases of justified, true beliefs (Gettier cases) are not knowledge.[5] The point here is that it seems that we already really *know* what the answer to questions such as: what is knowledge? Our philosophical analyses are, if you like, just a way of teasing out or of making explicit what we already know.

Granted, the fact that these *intuitions* are somewhat mysterious has led certain more naturalistically minded philosophers to countenance a kind of eliminativism about them—that this, they think that use of intuitions in philosophy ought to be abandoned. A nascent movement known as Experimental Philosophy ('X-Phi' for short), also claims to have dislodged the result that such intuitions are universal and not culturally or gender sensitive, for instance. But such movements are still in the minority, and the majority of contemporary philosophers continue to appeal to intuitions. Perhaps the reliability of these intuitions more generally can take the place of the slave boy's having the answers, as the phenomenon that his theory attempts to explain. And this looks like a seriously perplexing thing to attempt to explain, with no consensus currently being enjoyed as to how it can be explained.[6]

Imperfect Knowledge

An alternative attempt to resolve the Eristic Paradox is the following: maybe when we set about enquiry we do not possess perfect knowledge of the thing we want to enquire into, but we possess a less perfect epistemic state (to be contrasted with a total blank, what Dominic Scott calls a "cognitive blank" (2006, p. 76)). Perhaps we are, say, 60 % sure that something is the case, but we want to know for sure. So we do know the thing that we are enquiring into, in a way—but this does not make enquiry into that thing futile, since we go into it hoping to get 100 % certainty (or something closer to that than 60 %) that the proposition we are investigating is the case. As such, there is just a *much* simpler resolution to the puzzle than appealing to Heaven's First Epistemology.

But in response one might ask how we know when we should be 100 % certain that we know. Surely, we are here confusing second-order knowledge about our own cognitive states with first-order knowledge of objects or propositions. In other words, under this picture, when we enquire, the object of enquiry is whether we know (not whether there is such a thing as a particular object, say a Higgs boson particle). And then the paradox arises as to our second-order knowledge: how could we come to recognise what it is to know for certain, without already knowing what it is to know for certain?

Further, it is possible that Plato himself might have at least partly endorsed this *imperfect knowledge* solution to the Eristic Paradox himself. An important part of the *Meno* concerns drawing a difference between knowledge and mere true belief, and the introduction of the question concerning why knowledge is more *valuable* than mere true belief. In fact the slave boy is held by Plato to have true beliefs and not *knowledge* about certain facts about geometry. So the phenomenon to be explained is why the slave boy has *true beliefs* (not knowledge) about geometry, and we might take this to be another way of saying that the phenomenon to be explained is how the slave boy has 60 % (not 100 %) certainty as regards the truth of the propositions of geometry.[7] After all, according to Plato in the *Meno*, part of what makes knowledge more valuable than true belief is that the former involves proper certainty and so is more "secure" than the latter.

But this perhaps calls into question whether Plato seriously endorsed the recollection "solution" to the Eristic Paradox. First, because we might think that the distinction between full knowledge and justified, true belief, or mere true belief, or between grades of epistemic status more generally does all the solving, and so the recollection solution is superfluous. However, as we've said, the puzzle may remain such that the recollection solution is necessary if the paradox is expressed as a puzzle about recognising what "full" knowledge is. But, second, and in my view very plausibly, it seems that when Plato first mentions the recollection "solution" in the *Meno* he aims to entice, or persuade in a dialectical way, his interlocutor (Meno) into further enquiry as to the status of enquiry. As Dominic Scott puts it:

> [Plato] uses his recollection as an incentive to make Meno eager to enquire, and almost panders to his desire for the exotic in the initial exposé of recollection. This includes references to priests, priestesses and the divinely inspired poets— all of whom immediately arouse Meno's curiosity, as does the prospect of hearing about a new theory. (Scott 2006, p. 81)

It's also a well-known aspect of Plato's most famous work, *The Republic*, that he advocates the use of "noble lies"—mythologies, or allegories—to explain difficult truths in metaphorical terms to people who would not otherwise be able to grasp those truths.[8] Further, there is of course the issue of what significance is the fact that Plato wrote his philosophical treatises in the form of *dialogues*. And this is congruent with the fact that at times in the *Meno* Plato seems to reject the doctrine we called Evidentialism in Chap. 1. Since he at times seems to suggest that we should believe that we have a duty towards enquiry (and so reject the putative lesson of the Eristic Paradox) for non-epistemic (moral or pragmatic) reasons:

> So one shouldn't be persuaded by that eristic argument. It would make us idle and is pleasant for the faint-hearted to hear. But this makes us hard working and eager to enquire. Trusting it to be true, I'm willing to enquire with you into what virtue is. (81d)

Plato seems to be saying here that we ought to believe that we have a duty to enquire because not believing it would make us worse people —it would make us idle. Accordingly, he seems to be claiming that there are at least some propositions we ought to believe on non-epistemic grounds and so perhaps on the basis of metaphors and "noble lies", or perhaps (depending on who "us" denotes) some people who ought always to believe for those non-epistemic reasons. As we will see, in the rest of this book, this claim resonates strongly with the Falasifa who were looking for a way to solve the problem concerning what we called the Epistemic Uniqueness of Prophecy.

Heavens First Epistemology in the *Phaedo*

Let's now take a look at the second argument we mentioned in favour of Plato's Heavens First Epistemology. This argument occurs in the *Pheado*, the dialogue where Plato in fact famously first talks about Forms (they are not explicitly mentioned in the *Meno*) and argues in favour of the immortality of the soul. Plato concludes that the only thing to fear in death is what physical entity our soul will grasp hold of upon getting heavy when returning to the subluminal realm.

In the course of arguing in favour of the immortality of the soul, however, Plato runs another argument, arguably less interesting, in favour of Heavens First Epistemology. The argument goes something like this: if we look at the material, natural world we will find no *standard* by which to properly predicate the properties we predicate on objects. Here he uses the example of a stick: put next to a stick that is of the same length, it has the property of "being of the same length". But if you introduce another longer stick and put that next to it as well, the stick has *both* the properties of "being of the same length" and of "not being of the same length" at the same time. Another example might go as follows: compared with Kojak, Prince William is not bald, but compared with Noel Gallagher he is bald. So, by just looking at the natural world, we would have to come to the conclusion that Prince William is both bald and not bald. But this cannot be: something cannot have the property of being both x and not-x at the same time. To think otherwise violates what is sometimes called the *law of non-contradiction*. So in order to determine whether or not Prince William is *really* bald, we need to appeal to some transcendent standard—we need to appeal to the *Form* of baldness.

It appears, then, that Plato's point hinges on the issue between relativism and non-relativism. Relativism here is the claim that there are no objective or transcendent standards to tell us whether someone *really* is bald, for example—all we can say is that someone is bald *relative* to someone or something else (non-relativism, unsurprisingly, is the denial of relativism). The issue for Plato would then be that if relativism is the case then there are no proper standards for assessing whether a particular claim is true—no way of telling whether Prince William really is bald. Thus any proposition would be capable of being both true and false (hence the violation of the law of non-contradiction). The form of his argument seems to be:

(i) Relativism ought to be avoided.
(ii) The only way to avoid relativism is to postulate Forms.
(iii) We ought to postulate Forms.

The argument is a commitment to Heavens First Epistemology: it claims that if we are to avoid relativism, and so for our enquiries to actually make any sense, we need to fix our gaze towards the eternal world of Forms. Of course, this argument is then predicated on the assumption that relativism ought to be avoided. And we might think that there is something rather question-begging about that, since it is not a claim that those who defend relativism will want to accept as a background assumption. Yet one might want to argue, given some of what we have said above, that relativism ought to be avoided because it violates the law of non-contradiction. But perhaps the opponent, qua relativist, could just insist that the law of non-contradiction is not something that they are willing to accept.

Regardless of the philosophical merits of these two arguments, Plato's Heavens First Epistemology has been remarkably influential, especially with the Neo-Platonists. The Neo-Platonists were to have a huge influence on Islamic philosophy, so let us now turn to exploring the work of perhaps the most famous of the Neo-Platonists: Plotinus. We will then have a look at Aristotle's arguments against Heaven's First Epistemology, and the case for his alternative.

Plotinus

Plotinus lived in the 3rd century AD and thus belongs to the period historians refer to as Late Antiquity.[9] Plotinus is usually thought of as a Neo-Platonist philosopher—the word "Neo-Platonist" meaning New Platonist—though it is a matter of some controversy as to whether Plato was really his strongest influence, as opposed to, say, Philo of Alexandria. However, it is clear that Plotinus was greatly influenced by Platonic thought, even if it was indirectly through the work of other philosophers, and he was clearly in awe of Plato. For instance, he made some concrete plans for building a city that was to be run under the principles of governance set forth in Plato's famous political work *The Republic*—this city was to be called *Platonopolis*(!). Regrettably, Platonopolis was never built.

As we will see, however, there is a sense in which Plotinus was more of a mystic than a philosopher. And as such it is hard to engage philosophically with some of the things he says. But I want to give you a very rough overview of some of the broad Plotinian themes since they were very influential for the Islamic philosophers (they have also been highly influential for Jewish, Christian and mystical thought). As I have mentioned, the Falasifa were working under the misapprehension that much of Plotinus' work was written by Aristotle.

I will now concentrate on what I take to be the two central doctrines in Plotinian thought: the centrality of the One; and the emanationist theory of metaphysics.

The One

It is not hard to see how Islamic scholars working at a time of Mu'tazilite dominance (given their emphasis on *Tawḥīd*) would come to have a special affinity with Plotinus' concept of the One. Nor is it hard to see how this concept would have special affinity with Jewish theologians as well as Christians, a fact perhaps nicely illustrated in modern terms by the pop group U2's[10] very spiritual song *One*.

Plotinus thought that unity or oneness is the mark of existence (unity is a condition of being) so that the better one can individuate something the more concretely, or assuredly, we can say that it exists. In the *Enneads* ("the nines"; a work then comprising of nine books) he contrasts the principle of unity of things such as plants and animals, and the principle of unity of armies and houses. Plants and animals have unity essentially and internally, whereas armies and houses have their unity inessentially, from the outside. Yet without their possessing that unity, they would not be the thing we say they are—they would be just a pile of bricks, or a random collection of people carrying weapons. Their *identity* is thus more precarious, because less self-sufficient. Plotinus infers from this that the more *essential* unity a thing has (so the more indivisible it is) the more deeply, permanently it can be said to exist. Put differently, for Plotinus essential (internal) unity = indivisibility. It thus follows, according to Plotinus, that the thing which is most, and most purely, indivisible must be the thing that exists most permanently, deeply, and self-sufficiently.[11] And that if we are looking for the source of all existence, whose existence depends on nothing else so totally self-sufficient, then we must look to the thing which is most indivisible—that thing which by its very essence is indivisible: the *One*.

Now, for Plotinus, the One is ineffable. Put differently, the fact that the One is essentially indivisible means that the One cannot be described at all. This has inspired what has been called negative theology, the idea that we can only talk about God in terms of what he is not—assuming that God is identical to the One. I think this is a mistake however, as we discussed in Chap. 1, since it seems that saying that God does not have certain properties nonetheless involves predication. And predication seems to violate the essential indivisibility of the One. I do not think that Plotinus really espoused negative theology—so construed—in saying that the One was ineffable, however. He was saying, rather, that we cannot *say* anything about God at all—in fact we cannot even say that. Ultimately, the One is a concept or object that is beyond human cognition. Of course, if we identify the One with God, the problem arises as to how we can reconcile God's fundamental indivisibility with God having divine attributes, such as omnipotence and omniscience.

But though Plotinus thought that the One was a something beyond human cognition (when cognition is thought to involve the subject-predicate logical form Fa, and the One cannot be predicated on since it completely simple) but he seems to have allowed the possibility that we can come into communion with it via other means. We achieve this communion, according to Plotinus, by *becoming* the One. According to his student and editor, Porphyry in the *Life*, Plotinus achieved this communion with the One four times in his lifetime.[12] But we are not told exactly how this happened and the method—if there is a *method*—here must surely be described as *mystical* as opposed to philosophical, in the sense that it does not involve patterns of reasoning.[13] Nevertheless, this idea of how communion with the One is possible does resonate with the interpretation I gave in Chap. 1 as to how to take the fact that the word 'Islam' means submission or surrender. That is, that we should not take it to mean that we must be *obedient* to what is said in the Koran, but rather that in order to be close to God we must surrender our sense of self, our sense of being a unity distinct from God. But then this puts pressure on the idea that Islam is an Evidentialist religion, since knowledge of God could not then be *propositional,* and seems to involve idolatry in perhaps implying that we, humans can also be divine. As we will discuss, these issues were taken up by the various Islamic philosophers, and by the mystical understanding of Islam as found in Sufism.

Emanation

So the One exists, according to Plotinus, more fundamentally than anything else. And it is to it that we must look to if we are looking for an answer as to what the supreme source of existence is, since it is the thing that exists most permanently or robustly.

For Plotinus, then, the One constitutes the first on the four levels of existence in his famous, four-level "emanationist" metaphysics. Let me now attempt a sketch of his emanationist system.

Level One—The One. The One is thought to be the source of all that exists, like the source of light. From the One the other levels of existence come into being, like an overflowing fountain. For this reason, for certain theologies, such as Ash'arite theology in Islam, God cannot be identical to Plotinus' One—since according to that theology God created (and maintains) the world gratuitously by *deciding* to do so.

Level Two—Noûs. From the One overflows the next level of existence: the intellect. This is *pure* intellect and resembles Aristotle's characterisation of God as Noesis Noeseos—"thought thinking itself" (we will discuss this in due course). Thought at this level has no concrete object aside from itself. The Platonic Forms exist here.

Level Three—Souls. Here, the Forms merge into matter and create things such as animals and plants, and humans.

Level Four—Nature. Finally, at the last emanation, emerges the material, physical world. Sometimes referred to as the world of "generation and corruption". However, we should note that Plotinus held this world to be illusionary, less real that the world of Forms. Here perhaps it is helpful to recall Plato's allegory of the cave in *The Republic*, where perceptions in the physical world are compared to watching mere shadows on a screen. To see what reality is in itself, we must remove our shackles and turn towards the light that is behind and projects the shadows—ultimately the Form of the Good: the Form of all Forms. This corresponds to Plotinus' One—the difference is merely that for Plotinus the One is not a Form but is, as we mentioned, ineffable (Plotinus often calls the One, "the Good").

As with Plato's solution to the Eristic Paradox, Plotinus' emanationist metaphysics is going to look rather speculative (to say the least) to a modern audience. But, like with Plato, Plotinus' metaphysics is meant to be a solution to a real (and continuing) problem, and so can even be thought along "scientific" lines as an inference to the best explanation. What needs explaining here is the relationship between the immaterial world of Forms or universals and the material world of particulars: how do particulars come to "instantiate" the universals? In more modern terms we might parse this in these terms: if we accept that abstract thoughts exist and are real independently of the humans actually thinking them then how is it that they can be used to explain the constitution of the material world? There must be some passage from the abstract to the concrete for this to be possible, and this is what Plotinus' theory of emanation is meant to try to capture. Perhaps you think that this just shows how problematic it is to think of Forms as something in some transcendental or immaterial sense. And perhaps you are in good company, since I think this is the central thought motivating Aristotle's (as the caricature would have it at least) non-Platonic alternative.

Aristotle and Experience First Epistemology

Let us return to the picture we started with, and explore the question of why the caricature Aristotle held the negation of Plato's Heaven First thesis, what we dubbed Experience First Epistemology—the idea that the true source of knowledge is the physical, material world.

Recall the universals and particulars issue that we mentioned in opening. The question is, which is the more epistemically fundamental? Can we know particulars without knowing their universals? Or do we come to know universals *via* knowing their particulars? Aristotle has a simple argument against Plato's Heavens First Epistemology, the claim that we cannot know particulars without knowing universals in so far as it relies on the existence of Platonic Forms conceived of as transcendent, and existing, idealisations. This argument is known as the third man argument. We will now look at this argument, and then explore Aristotle's alternative to how we should think about universals, and how that underscores an Experience First Epistemology (though as ever with the caveat concerning caricatures).

Aristotle's Third Man Argument

Aristotle—Plato's most famous student, and later tutor to Alexander the Great—discusses what is called the third man argument in his *Metaphysics*. Strangely enough though, it is an argument that he develops from Plato himself, who discusses the objection to his own theory of Forms in his dialogue the *Parmenides*.

The third man argument is really fairly simple. Recall that we can take Plato to be conceiving of universals in terms of Forms. This means that, whatever it is that all men have in common—that is, the necessary and sufficient conditions for the category "man"—must constitute a separate, ideal Form; that is, an ideal man. But this raises a problem, since the Form of the man (i.e. the ideal man) must be a man itself—assuming this principle: every Form of F-ness is itself F. But then the man itself must belong to the class or set of *particulars* not universals—that is, it is a member of the set of men. So then we need to postulate an ideal man that is the form of all man (including the ideal man we postulated earlier) and so on ad infinitum. There is a lot one could say about this argument, especially about the assumed principle above. However, given how much we still have to discuss about Aristotle, let us move straight into thinking about his alternative way of thinking about universals, in terms of *essences*.

Essences

For Aristotle, universals are better thought of, not in terms of transcendent forms, but in terms of *essences*—the necessary and sufficient conditions for a thing being the thing that it is. And to know what the necessary and sufficient conditions of a thing are we must look to what their *functions* are.

To know what the essence of a house is, we must look to what its function is—to give shelter from the elements (roughly speaking). We cannot describe the essence of a house, for instance, merely in terms of its physical properties—whether it is made of brick or stone, or mud or straw. A house that does not give shelter is not really a house. A house without a roof is not really a house, though it does in certain respects *resemble* a house.

To know what the essence of humans is, we must also, then, look to what the function of being a human is. For Aristotle, this is to strive towards a certain *telos* (goal), what he calls *eudamonia* in the Nichomachean *Ethics*—which according to him is the contemplative life. Our essential nature then is to be *res cogitans* (to use the famous Latin phrase)—thinking beings.

Function and Matter

Now, Aristotle makes a distinction (mainly in his *Categories*) between the function or form (not to be understood in Plato's way, but more like a guiding principle or organisation) of a thing and its matter. Imagine here the carbon that you are made up of, and the guiding principle in which it is organised that make you a human being. Or think of the carbon that makes up a buffalo, and the guiding principle that makes it a buffalo and not a human like me (though the buffalo and I are made of the same matter).

However, according to Aristotle, neither I (nor the buffalo) can exist qua mere principle of organisation. I only exist as a combination of *matter* existing and its being organised in a particular way. Matter can never be created or destroyed, but it can take on different forms. This combination of matter and form gives me my *substance*. For Aristotle <What is it that is?> and <What is

substance?> are the same question. And the principle that substance is a combination of matter and form is called Aristotle's *hylomorphism*.[14] Universals are then not to be thought of as *Platonic* Forms, that is as free-standing, idealisations existing in the ephemeral heavens, but as the essences of substances whose matter displays a given organisational form. So that if Aristotle's hylomorphism is true, it must be the case that we can only know of a thing's (qua substance) essence through experience since a substance's form is carried via its matter (so we can only know universals through experience).

Understanding, Knowledge, and the Four Causes

Further, for Aristotle, to truly know something, it is not enough to know its essence; we must know the following four things about it (that Aristotle calls 'causes'):

- Its *material* cause: what the thing is made of (this might not be essential to the thing's being what it is).
- Its *formal* cause: the entity's principle of organisation/its organisational form.
- Its *efficient* cause: what or who the agent was that brought the entity into existence as the thing that it is (again this might not be essential to the thing's being what it is).
- Its *final* cause: the *purpose* or *goal* the agent had in bringing the entity qua substance into existence.

In order to know things we must *understand* why those things are what they are. Of course, we do not only know *things* or objects, but we also know discrete propositions. Aristotle has a correlate account of what the best kind of propositional knowledge is—what he calls demonstrative proof (in his *Posterior Analytics*—a work of epistemology/meta-logic).[15] Aristotle is well known as the inventor of logic. In his logic, good (i.e. sound) arguments take the form of what he calls *syllogisms*. These syllogisms have two premises (with a term in common) that yield a conclusion; for example:

(1) Socrates is a man.
(2) All men are mortal.
(3) Socrates is moral.

As in modern informal logic, for Aristotle, the premises must somehow *necessitate* the conclusion. However, in contrast to modern informal logic, Aristotle defines knowledge that is the culmination of demonstration as a belief that is the conclusion of a sound and *explanatory* syllogism where the middle term (2) of the syllogism is either a "first principle" or directly derived from a "first principle". The argument is supposed to be explanatory in the following way: it not only has to show that a conclusion must be true, but *why* it is true. In the above syllogism, we learn not only that Socrates is mortal, but with no explanation: we learn that he is mortal *because* he is a man. As such we come to *understand* why the conclusion is true. The middle term is a "first principle" if it is a necessary truth—that is, it denotes an essential property as opposed to an "accident" (a contingent property), that cannot be derived from any other proposition—for instance, that the law of non-contradiction is true, or the proposition that every object is self-identical. Aristotle thought that necessary truths are propositions that are *eternally* true, so that we can only have proper *episteme* (knowledge admitting of demonstrative proof) of eternal truths too. This makes the account extremely demanding, and as we will see creates controversy for the Falasifa as to how God—whose knowledge is held to to be perfect—could have knowledge of particulars. As we will see, this leads Avicenna in particular to offer a novel and improved understanding of what it is for things to be necessary and for things to be merely possible (what are sometimes known as the "modalities" of existence).

However, partly because his epistemology is so demanding, Aristotle seems to have allowed that there may be sub-demonstrative knowledge, and to have followed Plato on the belief that the use of dialectics and rhetoric was essential when done in the right way and in the right hands.[16] As we will also see in what follows, this was something that the Falasifa took very seriously, and, as I hope to show in Chap. 4, underscores al-Farabi's political philosophy. Before we get to all that, however, I want to address an important question, related to our discussion of the *Meno*, and that arises out of Aristotle's criterion for demonstration that the middle term be a first principle, or derived from a first principle: how do we come to know these—seemingly a priori—propositions?

Aristotle's *De Anima* and the Active Intellect

As we have seen, according to the standard account of the *Meno*, Plato claims that we learn a priori truths in another reality made up only of Forms (not this world of generation and corruption), and that we merely recollect what we learnt there when we come to "learn" universal truths in this world. Unlike his teacher, however, Aristotle claims at the end of his *Posterior Analytics* that we learn these truths—through the special faculty of *noûs* (intellect)—through experience in *this* world (this is part of his Experience First Epistemology, of course). Aristotle thus owes us an account of how *noûs* can do this, and this is not forthcoming in the *Posterior Analytics*. He does seem to do this, however, in his more psychological work in *De Anima*—of course, this stands to reason given the naturalist turn that the question of how we know a priori propositions ("intelligibles") takes at the end of the *Posterior Analytics*.

In the notorious, and very short, section 3.5 of *De Anima* we find a first allusion to the concept of an *active* intellect (*noûs poiêtikos*, as Themistius called it). Because Aristotle wanted to explain the workings of *noûs* naturalistically, in the sense that it has an experiential base, he ends up maintaining a strong parallelism between the workings of ordinary perception, and the workings of *noûs*—now considered to be a sort of intellectual perception. The idea that we have a unique faculty that allows us to cognize a priori propositions, and that it is to be modelled on perception, as if it were a sort of mind's *eye,* is a common one in contemporary epistemology, especially among Foundationalists,[17] though here the faculty is often called the faculty of intellectual *intuition.*[18] And current proponents of this view, such as George Bealer (1996), offer arguments which may render Aristotle's parallelism more palatable, since all that Aristotle has given us as grounds to accept it is the mere assertion that we know a priori truths in the same way we know accidents, or contingent propositions—that is, through sense perception. For example, Bealer's argument is—briefly[19]—that if intuitions were beliefs or judgements, then it intellectually seeming to S that p would not survive S's learning that not-p. But this is not the case, as per when one attends to naïve set theory, and the theory seems right, even though one knows that it is not (being familiar with Bertrand Russell's famous objections to it). Perceptual seemings also share this feature: two Muller-Lyer lines still perceptually appear to be of differing lengths, for instance, even if we know that they are not. On that basis then, intuitions seem to be more like perceptual seemings than beliefs or judgements.

Whatever the merits of Aristotle's parallelism here, it is the case that, if it is true, and given Aristotle's naturalism, then knowing how ordinary perception works should give us insight into how we come to know Aristotelian first principles. Aristotle gives us an account of the workings of perception in *De Anima*. In rough approximation, it goes as follows. Suppose I am about to go into a field where there is a buffalo grazing. Before I go into the field my perceptual apparatus is in a state of *potentiality* whereby it is possible for it to be *actualised* into a state where I am seeing a buffalo before me. What prompts the change from being in a state of merely potentially seeing a buffalo to actually seeing a buffalo is, for Aristotle, and naturally enough, a change in my physical circumstances. But what is slightly curious is what, for Aristotle, constitutes the property of actually seeing. Again very roughly, it seems to be for the perceptual apparatus to have taken the (phenomenal, not essential) *form* of the object seen, so that when I see the buffalo, my perceptual apparatus takes the buffalo form. That is not to say that my perceptual apparatus has *become a buffalo*, since the substance of the seeing is a compound of the form of the buffalo and the material that constitutes my perceptual apparatus. In this sense, the theory is what modern scholars in philosophy of mind would call a "representationalist" or "intentionalist" theory of perception (in its modern form derived from Franz Brentano (1874) who was deeply influenced by Aristotle's *De Anima*)—a perceptual state for Aristotle has what could be deemed intentional content, in its having a particular *form*. But it also has elements in common with modern "adverbial" theories of perception (see Chisholm 1957) which hold that when one perceives something, then there exists an object of which one perceives—but this object is not a physical object, nor a "sense datum"; rather, the object exists in the perceptual experience itself, to be thought of in an adverbial way. So when I come across a brown buffalo and perceive brownness, my perceptual apparatus does not *become brown*, but, rather, I perceive *brownly*—in Aristotelian terms, my perception has changed merely its *form*.

Now, with the account of perception on the table we can now look at Aristotle's account of intellection—the mechanism that allows us to grasp essences and first principles. The intellect, says Aristotle, has the potential to grasp all forms. Since the intellect is a *potentiality* it is passive, like our capacity for perception. *But,* when I see the buffalo, for instance, the buffalo's form is transmitted to me via its matter—its matter, as we said, is the active agent on my passive sense organ. It actualises my mere potential seeing the buffalo. *But,* and here is the rub, when I grasp the essence of the buffalo, purely intellectually as it were, there is no matter to act as an active agent before me. So how is it possible for me to intellectually grasp the essence of the buffalo? If *noûs* is to be thought of as a kind of perceptual faculty, then when we change from merely potentially apprehending some intelligible and actually apprehending it, something having the corresponding form must have it in *actuality*. But the experience of seeing, for instance, just *one* buffalo can only ever impress on me the *phenomenal* form of a buffalo—its "phantasm"—not its essence, and certainly not any more fundamental first principle such as the law of non-contradiction. So what it is then that can cause my intellectual faculty to change from a state of potentiality to actuality? Here Aristotle invokes the force of an "active" or "agent" intellect, an all-encompassing intelligence that is permanently in actuality—that is permanently thinking all the universal thoughts there are to think. Experience still plays a role in our coming to apprehend first principles, since the agent intellect cannot switch our minds "on" such that we also come to be thinking all there is to think. Rather, once we have in our imagination the right number of phantasms, we will have set up our intellects such that they are ready to be actualised by the active intellect and so that we end up actively grasping a first principle. For instance, having had the right experience, I become able to imagine a house, and a house without a roof, or without windows, a mansion house, a mud hut, and then all of a sudden such come to "see" that the essence of a house is that it gives shelter. Thus there are various degrees of potentiality in between, say, a child's mind, a mind that is ready to cognise intelligibles, and one that actually comes to apprehend any given first principle.

Now, of this agent intellect, Aristotle says that it is always in actuality, incorporeal, and infinite. So it looks at first blush as if Aristotle is here talking about the God in his *Metaphysics Lambda*—*noesis noeseos*: thought thinking itself.

But the matter is complicated because we tend to think that when we engage in abstract thinking, it is *us* who are the directors of how we think— that we are the agents. So the alternative interpretation of Aristotle here is that our souls constitute (at least in part) the active intellect. But this is controversial given how Aristotle has characterised the active intellect as something that is necessarily incorporeal and infinite—so without death. Thus under this interpretation it seems that Aristotle has reneged on the idea that the soul is *not* immortal. So on this reading Aristotle is with Plato on the claim that the soul *is* immortal. One can then imagine how this reading taken together with the misapprehension that Aristotle was the author of Plotinus' works could lead the Islamic philosophers to believe that a project harmonising the works of Plato and Aristotle was not so ill conceived.

There is of course quite a controversy as to what Aristotle really thought the agent intellect is—is it something that exists in all of us? Is it God? Other people, perhaps our teachers? John Philoponus seems to have held something akin to the interpretation of Aristotle whereby it is other people, and this is the view that some (e.g. Endress 1980) think al-Kindi shared.[20]

The Peripatetics were the followers of Aristotle; some were his contemporaries and some wrote years later. They are the counterparts to Plato's Neo-Platonists, though the Neo-Platonists actually came after the Peripatetics. A word of warning: Leaman and other scholars sometimes seem to refer to the Falasifa as Peripatetics. The Falasifa were acquainted with the Peripatetics' works (often just in paraphrases, however). One of the central Peripatetics was Theophrastus who succeeded Aristotle as head of the Lyceum (the school of philosophy founded by Aristotle, the equivalent of Plato's Academy). He introduced the term "*noûs poiêtikos*" to denote the active intellect and thought it denotes the God of *Metaphysics Lambda*, qua *noesis noeseos*. Another important Peripatetic was Alexander de Aphrodisias who introduced a new category in the active/passive intellect distinction (in his works *De Anima* and *De Intellectu*). We have passive minds that we acquire at birth; the active mind which acts on us from without; and a mind that the active mind turns the passive mind into the thinking mind. Through the thinking mind we come to participate in immortality. But it means that there is no such thing as *personal* survival after death. His view heavily influences Averroes, whom we will look at in Chap. 6. More influential with Chap. 5's Avicenna was Themistius. He lived just before the Roman closure of the Greek schools in 529 and countenances a tripartite view of the intellect similar to that of Alexander de Aphrodisias, but held that the mind was individual and that as such there could be *personal* survival after death through communion with the active intellect.

I'll save critical engagement with these ideas until the Chap. 3, where we will discuss al-Kindi's take on them, as in doing so really kicks-off Falsafa.

Concluding Remarks

We have now explored in broad brushstrokes the philosophies of Plato and Aristotle and also how their ideas were developed by some of their respective followers. Following the usual charicature, I called Plato's overall philosophical stance a commitment to Heavens First Epistemology, and Aristotle's a commitment to Experience First Epistemology. I hope we can now see that there are issues for both of these (meant to be mutually exclusive) approaches. To summarise: Heavens First Epistemology faces the issue of how transcendent forms come to have an influence on the material world; Experience First Epistemology faces the issue of how we can properly generalise from experience in an imperfect world of "generation and corruption" to grasp of universal and eternal first principles. One might reasonably conclude from this that therefore the right approach must somehow take on both Platonic and Aristotelian elements. This was very much the line taken by the Falasifa, and in trying to do that they come up with ingenious and fascinating systems of thought, with insights, I hope to show, that are relevant for some of the real problems facing our world today. As such, while they do participate in the commentary tradition they inherited from the Neo-Platonists and Peripatetics, they cannot be dismissed as Bertrand Russell did so glibly in his famous *History of Western Philosophy* as insignificant commentators with nothing original to say.

Study Questions

- Is Plato's recollection theory the only way to explain how Plato's slave boy could have had true beliefs about geometry without ever having studied geometry?
- Given Aristotle's hylomorphism and the idea that matter can never be created of destroyed, how might Aristotle explain change?
- Is intellection really a kind of perception? If not, what else might it involve?

What to Read Next?

- Plato: *The Meno* (2005, Penguin Classics Edition, *Protagoras & Meno*, translated by W.K.C. Guthrie).
- Aristotle: *De Anima* (1987, Penguin Classic Edition, *De Anima* (*On the Soul*), translated by H. Lawson-Tancred).
- Scott, D. 2006: *Plato's Meno* (Cambridge: Cambridge University Press).
- Shields, C. 2013: *Aristotle* (2nd Edition) (London: Routledge).

Notes

1. Significantly, Plato wrote his philosophical works in the form of *dialogues*.
2. The Sophists were rhetoricians working at the time of Plato.
3. For example, some scholars suggest that the paradox echoes the style of the well-known fourth/fifth century BC Sophist (see Hoerber 1960).
4. As a slight aside, I hope you have noticed the resonance this part of *the Meno* has with the issue we discussed in the previous chapter in regard to the role of spiritual guides in rationalistic, Evidentialist religions like Islam in certain interpretations. The slave boy here is potentially taking the place of the Man-Friday correlate in Ibn Tufayl's *Ḥayy ibn Yaqẓān* that we discussed.
5. If you look at a stopped clock (that has stopped at 12.00) at 12.00, you may have a justified true belief that it is 12.00 but not knowledge that it is 12.00. These kinds of scenario are known as Gettier cases, after Edmund Gettier's classic 1963 paper. It is worth noting, however, that for Plato knowledge was *not* justified, true belief (Antognazza 2015).

6. Booth and Rowbottom (2014).
7. Irwin (1977) argues that the distinction between knowledge and true belief is Plato's actual solution to the Eristic Paradox.
8. This will be discussed in Chap. 8.
9. The period that marks the transition from the Classical period to the Middle Ages.
10. In fact, in a version of the video for U2's *One* that played on MTV at the time the song was released, we are shown a series of shots of buffalo and plants. I think this is a certain reference to Plotinus on the internal principles of unity of plants and animals.
11. Another way of thinking about things here in more modern terms is that, according to most scientists, simplicity is a virtue of scientific explanation—the simpler the theory, the more explanatory it is. This is what motivates some physicists, for example, to look for a "Theory of Everything". One might think that the One for Plotinus just takes this to its logical conclusion: the most simple theory (postulating only one explanatory entity) is the most explanatory theory there can be since the one postulated entity is supposed to explain everything (see Emilsson 2017, p. 71).
12. "To Plotinus 'the goal, ever near, was shown'; for his end and goal was to be united to, to approach god who is over all things. Four times while I was with him he attained that goal, in an unspeakable actuality" (23, 14–17).
13. However, see Emilsson (2017) for scepticism about the idea that for Plotinus this sort of communion with the One was central to Plotinian thought, since, he asks: "how could the human soul transcend the level of soul and become one with the Intellect, not to mention the One, and still remain a soul?" (p. 337). And, further, "there is no hint anywhere in the *Enneads* that anything other than philosophical thinking can prepare the way for this sort of awakening" (p. 339).
14. Though there has been a lot of controversy about exactly how exactly to understand this.
15. The *Posterior Analytics*, with the *Prior Analytics*, were Aristotle's classic logic texts.
16. Works such as the *Rhetoric* were considered part of Aristotle's *Organon*—the collection of his logical works.
17. Roughly, the idea that all knowledge is inferentially based upon indubitable propositions (foundations), such as (classically) the proposition that you exist (Descartes being the classic Foundationalist).
18. Of course, not all contemporary epistemologists espouse this view. Williamson (2011) is a monumental case in point, since according to the latter, intuitions are nothing but judgements or beliefs (or propensities to make judgements or beliefs) about counterfactuals. Thus we have an alternative *doxastic* model of intuitions. For a critique of the idea that Aristotelian "grasp of essences" is

parallel to a modern non-doxastic (perceptual) model of intuitions, see Lowe (2014).

19. We will return to this argument in Chap. 5.
20. An Aristotelian philosopher living in Alexandria (c. 490—570).

References

Secondary Sources

Antognazza, M.R. 2015. The Benefit to Philosophy of the Study of Its History. *British Journal for the History of Philosophy* 23 (1): 161–184.

Bealer, G. 1996. A Priori Knowledge and the Scope of Philosophy. *Philosophical Studies* 81: 121–142.

Booth, A.R., and D.P. Rowbottom. 2014. *Intuitions.* Oxford University Press.

Brentano, F. 1874 [1995]. *Psychology from an Empirical Standpoint.* Routledge.

Chisholm, R. 1957. *Perceiving: A Philosophical Study.* Cornell University Press.

Emilsson, E.K. 2017. *Plotinus.* Routledge.

Endress, G. 1980. Review of *L'Intellect selon Kindī* by J. Jolivet (1971). *Zeitschrift der Deutschen Morgenlandischen Gesellschaft* 130: 422–435.

Hoerber, R.G. 1960. Plato's *Meno. Phronesis* 5: 78–102.

Irwin, T. 1977. *Plato's Moral Theory.* Oxford University Press.

Lowe, J. 2014. Grasp of Essences vs. Intuitions: An Uneven Contest. In *Intuitions,* ed. Booth and Rowbottom. Oxford University Press.

Scott, D. 2006. *Plato's Meno.* Cambridge University Press.

Sinnott-Armstrong, W. 1999. Begging the Question. *Australasian Journal of Philosophy* 77 (2): 174–191.

Williamson, T. 2011. *The Philosophy of Philosophy.* Wiley Blackwell.

3

Al-Kindi and the Rise of Falsafa

Introduction

Let's take a moment to recapitulate.

In Chap. 1, "Islam and Reason", we introduced the Islamic faith and some of its underlying philosophy and historical context. We also introduced the Muʿtazilite theologians and their opposite number, the Ashʿārite theological school. As we mentioned, under the Abbasid Caliphate the Muslim empire began to expand north into territories in the Levant area (today's Syria, Lebanon and Jordan, for instance), territories that had previously been under the control of the Greek-speaking Byzantine Empire. Here the study of the ancient Greek philosophers had survived despite the Roman Empire's closure of the Greek schools in 529. As the Arab empire expanded into this area, then, it came into contact with the Greek philosophers, in particular on taking Alexandria, with what was left of its library that had been a wonder of the world. How would the Abbasid caliphs that were leading this expansion react to the contact? Like the Romans, they could have refused to accept the legitimacy of Greek thought and have the circulation and reading of it banned. They did not take this course of action, however. Instead, they chose to amalgamate its teachings into Muslim culture—that is, show that it was consistent with the Koran while at the same time attempting to demonstrate the intellectual superiority of Islam over the Greek philosophical tradition. The two aims are not inconsistent, since showing the consistency of the Greek philosophical tradition, as well respected and well developed as it was (perhaps the cornerstone for the entire Greek civilisation) with Islam, would demonstrate just how intellectually resilient and fertile Islam was. And, further, it would

© The Author(s) 2017
A.R. Booth, *Analytic Islamic Philosophy*, Palgrave Philosophy Today,
https://doi.org/10.1057/978-1-137-54157-4_3

perhaps show just how visionary the Prophet's teachings had been, such that those philosophies could have been canonised so elegantly and beautifully (the Koran is written in verse, remember) into a religion. This might further have vindicated the belief in the holiness of the Koran—that it was the unadulterated word of God. The implicit question was: what else could explain how an isolated man meditating in a cave could independently come to apprehend what was considered the pinnacle of civilisation's intellectual achievements?

But besides these theoretical benefits, why did the Abbasid caliphs choose to take this course of action?

Here are three possible explanations.

(1) Islam as rationalistic

As we have discussed, it is arguable that there is something inherently *rationalistic* about the Islamic religion, and this was something captured in the teachings of the Muʿtazilite school. The Muʿtazilites constituted the dominant theological school of the Abbasid Caliphate. Their philosophical sophistication must have contributed to a certain confidence in the intellectual merits of Islam.

Further, the ninth century was when the business of collecting Hadith was *de rigueur*. This came alongside the project of trying to determine what were, and what were not, genuine reports of the Prophet's practices. This involved a great deal of scholarship, of course, which was seen as central to the development of the Islamic faith. As such, the Muslim self-image at this time must have viewed scholarship and Islam as a package deal, as it were. Thus it could well have been seen as appropriate for Muslims to take on Greek thought because of its intellectual merits, and not to dogmatically cast it aside.

(2) Islam as a nascent movement

It is also the case that, relatively speaking, Islam was in the ninth century a relatively young religion. It saw itself as providing, in a sense, the state of the art and the final word on religious matters: Muhammad is said to be the "seal of the Prophets". As such, it must have been seen as important that Islam could demonstratively prove its intellectual superiority in order to achieve the goal of Islamic homogeny. In short, at this point in history Islam had a great deal of ambition and as such a lot to prove.

(3) Cultural legitimacy

Being seen to confront the Greek philosophical tradition and come out triumphant must also have played into the Abbasid political ambitions of the time. The Abbasids' political enemies were the Persians and of course the Byzantines. It is likely that they were keen to establish the Arab culture as a new, learned culture, superior in every sense to those of their enemies.

The Islamic empire had grown at an astonishing speed from 622 to 750, first under the Prophet Muhammad, then the *Rashidūn* ("rightly guided") caliphs,[1] and then under the Umayyad dynasty. As we disussed in Chap. 1 there was little scope for further significant territorial gain for the Abbasids (who had vanquished the Umayyads), and their attention seemed to be turned inwards, towards glorifying their dynasty from within. They made Baghdad their capital (it had been Damascus under the Umayyads), and they sought to (and succeeded in) turning this into the world's foremost centre of learning and culture: they built there the famous *Bayt al-Hikmāh* (the House of Wisdom), a vast library and a centre for the translation and study of the Greek scientific and philosophical works. And the Abbasids during this time—especially the early Abbasid caliphs Hārūn al-Rashīd (786–809), al-Māʿmun (813–833) and al-Muʿtaṣim (833–842)—sponsored and gave extensive patronage to individual scholars, translators, and philosophers, many of whom they invited to their courts.[2] Thus they gave rise to a period often referred to as the "Islamic Golden Age", or sometimes the "Islamic Renaissance".

Whatever their motivations, it is an historical fact that the Abbasids sponsored the massive translation movement of Greek texts into Arabic. But if at least some of their motivations were those we have just discussed, merely translating these texts into Arabic cannot have been enough to meet their ends. The Greek texts also needed interpretation, and most importantly to be understood in a light that viewed Islam favourably. It is in this context that al-Kindi, the first Islamic Falaysuf, or as he is sometimes called "the Philosopher of the Arabs", came to prominence.

Al-Kindi: A Short Biography

We do not know exactly when al-Kindi was born or when he died. The best estimates, however, are that he has born in Basra (in modern Iraq) in around 800 and died in around 870. We do know, however, that he was called "the Philosopher of the Arabs" because he was born the son of the Emir of Kufa. He was thus of noble birth, his family having been important in the Kinda tribe, whose existence preceded the advent of Islam. Indeed, al-Kindi is said to have been a direct descendant of one of the kings of Kinda, who was also a companion of the Prophet. It is likely that this fact alone gave al-Kindi's works a great deal of internal authority.

Al-Kindi worked in, and under the protection of, the courts of both the caliphs al-Māʿmun (in his earlier days) and al-Muʿtaṣim (later). Al-Māʿmun, if you recall, was the caliph whom legend recounts had a dream in which it was revealed to him that the translation project must take place. It was under al-Muʿtaṣim that al-Kindi wrote most of his famous works. For instance, his magnum opus *On First Philosophy* was dedicated to al-Muʿtaṣim's son Ahmad, to whom al-Kindi was tutor. Al-Muʿtaṣim was perhaps not the most likely caliph to have been the sponsor of philosophy, given his reputation for dexterity in the battlefield. But nonetheless he seemed to follow the Abbasid's tradition for affinity with the intelligentsia and certainly it seemed like al-Kindi was allowed to pursue his very grand intellectual ambitions unfettered.

At the end of al-Kindi's life, Caliph al'Mutawakkil was in power. This was not the best of times for al-Kindi. The so-called " Banu Musa brothers"—both well-known mathematicians—sought to discredit al-Kindi's work. Why they did this is unclear; professional jealousy perhaps, or maybe a sense that his work was, as they said, contrary to Islam; or, as is most likely, they were keen to establish their intellectual discipline as the most fundamental and the discipline to be worthy of the most patronage by the caliph. Whatever the reason, they persuaded their caliph to have al-Kindi's library seized and their rival badly beaten up. Later, however, the mathematical brothers suffered ignominy when they made some crucial mistakes with respect to the building of a canal for the caliph. They escaped his wrath, but the caliph ordered al-Kindi's library to be returned to him.

From this episode we can see just how competitive the intellectual environment was at this time. In this context it is also important to point out that the word Falsafa is a word derived from the Greek *philosophia* and as such it was a new word, and always then (to this day I suspect) considered something foreign, not purely Arabic—a questionable import. This meant that al-Kindi was not merely trying to understand Greek philosophy and how it bears upon Islam, nor merely just doing philosophy—but was rather in the business of almost *selling*, certainly advocating, the whole idea of philosophy. Being an academic philosopher in the so-called age of "austerity", I can certainly sympathise.

But this had at least two consequences. First, al-Kindi was at real pains to make Greek philosophy appear to be a unified whole. We have already mentioned how some of Aristotle's work was only available in paraphrases that were perhaps slightly misleading, and that the work of important Neo-Platonists—Plotinus and Proclus—had been taken in error to be authored by

Aristotle. So we can understand how it would have seemed, per¹
than it does now, that there was a genuine case to be made foı
the work of Plato and Aristotle. However, it also seems to be the cₐ
where there were clear points of divergence between them (as well as betweᴄ
other Greek philosophers) al-Kindi was not all that forthcoming in pointing
them out.

Secondly, it meant al-Kindi was also at pains to show how Greek philosophy is never inconsistent with the teachings of the Koran; or, at least, that an
Islamic philosophy inspired by the Greek philosophers was never in competition with the Muslim faith. Indeed, al-Kindi argued that *not* taking the work
of the Greeks seriously was un-Islamic—*kufr*. Here he makes use of a point in
Aristotle. Philosophy is inescapable, because to claim that it is meaningless,
redundant or in some way defective is to make a philosophical claim that
needs to be established by rational argument—philosophy. So it would be
incoherent to claim, using philosophy, that philosophy is pointless, since at
the very least philosophy would have shown that philosophy was pointless,
and therefore not *completely* pointless.

This underscores what I think is al-Kindi's dominant philosophical standpoint and contribution (shared in part with Muʿtazilite theology): Islamic
Evidentialism.

Al-Kindi's Evidentialism

Evidentialism is a thesis in the field of what in contemporary terms is called
the ethics of belief. The central question posed by this is as follows: what ought
we to believe? Another way of posing the same question is: what justifies
belief? The Evidentialist answer is that only our evidence justifies belief; we
ought to believe in accordance with the evidence. Slightly more formulaically,
we can express it like this:

Evidentialism: A subject S is justified in believing any proposition that p
just in case S has sufficient evidence for believing that p.

According to Evidentialism, because only evidence can justify belief there
can be no non-evidential, non-epistemic (justificatory) reasons for belief. In
Western philosophy, the most famous Evidentialist is probably the nineteenth-
century British philosopher and mathematician W.K. Clifford, who wrote,
emphatically: "It is wrong, always, everywhere, and for anyone, to believe
anything upon insufficient evidence" (Clifford 1877). In contemporary
Philosophy of Religion, this view is defended by the Oxford philosopher and

theologian Richard Swinburne (cf. 1981): since religious beliefs are *beliefs*, then they too are justified by evidence and nothing else. Swinburne goes on to argue that our evidence justified belief in religious propositions, such as the proposition <God exists>. In the context of Islamic philosophy (and also in more contemporary discussions about Islamic politics), this stance is sometimes called Rationalism—the thought being, as we discussed in Chap. 1, that we have good *reason* to believe in God. In some interpretations of the Hadith collected by Caliph Umar, to be a proper Muslim it is not enough to blindly believe the propositions contained in the *šahāda*, but one must believe those propositions for the right reasons; and in some interpretations those reasons are epistemic (evidential) reasons. I prefer to call this last view Evidentialism and not Rationalism, since Rationalism can make it look as if some Islamic philosophers and theologians took a stance with respect to the correlate European debate between Rationalists such as Leibniz and Descartes and Empiricists such as Berkeley and Hume.

Evidentialism in a religious context has obvious implications as regards the relationship between faith and reason—this being often used as a shorthand for denoting whether religion is compatible with science. Evidentialism's answer is that *if* religious belief is justified, then *ipso facto* religious belief must be compatible with science. This is because according to Evidentialism any belief is justified just in case it is compatible with available evidence, such that if religious belief is justified it is compatible with the available evidence, as will be any scientific belief that is justified. The underlying assumption here is that two beliefs that are both compatible with the evidence cannot be contradictory.

The Muʿtazilites, as previously discussed, were Evidentialists. Their Evidentialism is derived from a Doxastic Metaphysics, according to which belief is an *occurrent, private* state constitutively aimed at *representing* the world. The correctness of such beliefs must be conditional upon accurate representation—that is, truth. The beliefs we ought to have, in other words, are those beliefs that are true: we ought not to have beliefs that are false. Two beliefs that are justified, then, cannot be incompatible, since both will be justified by virtue of their relationship with the truth.

In his work *On First Philosophy* al-Kindi further elaborates this line of thought. The idea here is that two true propositions cannot contradict each other, so two true beliefs cannot contradict each other. If truth (evidence) is the measure of correct (justified) belief, then two justified beliefs cannot contradict each other. Al-Kindi, ever the salesman for Falsafa, uses this as a marketing technique. Assuming that Muslim beliefs are justified, and therefore correct vis-à-vis the measure of truth, they cannot be in opposition to other evidentially justified beliefs. To think otherwise would amount to being an infidel, since it would involve believing that Muslim beliefs are not true, and are therefore unjustified. Al-Kindi does not so much give us an argument for Evidentialism, but, rather, using Evidentialism as a background assumption (recall that al-Kindi is working at a time when Muʿtazilite theology was *dominant*), argues for the compatibility of Falsafa with Islam. Nowhere does he illustrate this better than in this famous passage:

> We ought not be ashamed of appreciating the truth and of acquiring it wherever it comes from, /even if it comes from races distant and nations different from ours. For the seeker of truth nothing takes precedence over the truth, and there is no disparagement of the truth, nor belittling either of him who speaks it or of him who conveys it. (The status of) no one is diminished by the truth; rather does the truth ennoble all. (Al-Kindi *On First Philosophy*, p. 58)[3]

Notice the locutions "nations different to ours" and "races distant", which seem to be a reference to the Greek civilisation. The implicit thought is that we (Muslims) should not be afraid of studying Greek philosophy. We know that Muslim belief is true, and so anything that we find in Greek philosophy, in so far as it is true, can only be in accord with Muslim belief. Not only that, it is incumbent on the student of the Koran—who studies truth—to study Greek philosophy. Muslims are enjoined to study it. In other words:

> … it is right that one who resists the acquisition of knowledge of the real nature of things and calls it unbelief be divested of (the offices of) religion. (*On First Philosophy*, p. 59)

The underlying thought here is that if truth is the measure of justified belief, then it must follow that beliefs have their value only in virtue of whether or not they are true. Put figuratively, what matters is the destination, not the means by which one arrives there. For example, suppose that all you care about is reaching the central railway station by 12.00. If this is the case then it shouldn't matter to you *how* you arrive there, so long as you get there by 12.00. You can cycle, walk, get a taxi, persuade your friend to give you a lift: any of these will be as good as any of the others, provided they are effective in achieving your end. The same is true for arriving at true belief: it does not matter how you achieve it. You can do so by studying the Koran, or you may have done so via Falsafa, or if you are clever enough you may get there under your own steam by critically engaging with the world; but what matters is just that you get to the truth, so any of these means is as good as the others.

There seem to be two primary advantages to Evidentialism for al-Kindi. First, it makes it possible to discern true prophets from counterfeits: true prophets speak truly, and so there will be verisimilitude (congruence between the world and a statement about the world) between the prophet's message and the world. Second, it accords with the Mu'tazilite idea that the Muslim God is a Just God, giving people the faculty of reason in order to work out for themselves what at least approximates to the correct beliefs, and so gives us the possibility of salvation even when we have not been lucky enough to read the Koran.

Questions for al-Kindi's Evidentialism

Al-Kindi's idea that the truth is the truth, no matter who utters it, certainly looks like a noble idea, and is one that resonates so well with us today that we might consider it platitudinous. But it was certainly not an idea that was uncontroversial at the time, given the alternative Hanbalite Doxastic Metaphysics. In particular, it makes no further progress as regards the issue of the epistemic uniqueness of prophecy that we discussed in reference to Mu'tazilite Evidentialism; indeed Al-Kindi seems only to exacerbate this given the emphasis on truth as the sole value that matters. He addresses the issue by claiming that prophetic knowledge differs from the knowledge of ordinary humans in that the former and not the latter is attained instantly, "without study, effort, or human methods" (this from *On the Quantity of Aristotle's Books* translated by Adamson in Adamson (2007a, b, p. 43)). This hardly solves the problem, however, since it renders the function of prophecy to be a matter of sheer expediency—that is, the attainment of knowledge *faster* and with *less effort* than otherwise. This means that humans might well have gained the knowledge that is said to be in the Koran independently of its having been revealed to us, but it would have taken longer and would have been a more painful process.

Further, perhaps we can question the validity of moving from the premise that the truth does not alter with respect to who utters it to the conclusion that it does not matter how one arrives at the truth—and that if there is a valid way of getting at the truth of Islam, it is *kufr* to reject that way. Here, perhaps al-Kindi did *not* learn one of the important lessons of the *Meno*—the professed difference between mere true belief and knowledge. According to Plato in the *Meno*, the latter is more valuable than the former, and is the stuff that we are really after. But the question concerning whether we *know* can be taken to depend on how it was that we gained our belief. Lucky guesses are true, but not knowledge. So the opponent of al-Kindi could say that what matters is not that we merely have true Muslim beliefs, but rather that we *know* the truth of Islam. One could then say that one can only *know* the truth of Islam via divine revelation, even if it is possible for us to come to believe it via other means. These other means, however, would be analogous to mere lucky guesses. The point is that from the fact that the truth is the truth no matter who utters it, it does not follow that whichever route we take to the truth is as important as the next.

However, we might, on al-Kindi's behalf, question the idea that knowledge is more valuable than true belief. Perhaps al-Kindi would have taken it as obvious that the aim of inquiry is to arrive at true beliefs, and that anything that is supposed to mark the difference between mere true belief and knowledge will be such that a belief's having it will make it more likely to be true than not. For example, we might think that the reason we want our beliefs to be *justified* as well as true, in, say, a tripartite analysis of knowledge,[4] is because justified beliefs are more likely to be *true* than not. As Laurence Bonjour puts it:

> if finding epistemically justified beliefs did not substantially increase the likelihood of finding true ones, then epistemic justification would be irrelevant to our main cognitive goal and of dubious worth. (Bonjour 1986, pp. 7–8)

But, if our epistemic aim is truth, then really what exactly is more valuable about a belief that is knowledge as opposed to a belief that is merely true? To illustrate, if all we want out of a cup of coffee is that it's a tasty cup, does it matter to us if a tasty cup of coffee was—by luck—produced by a faulty machine? Isn't the tasty cup of coffee produced by the faulty machine as valuable to us as the tasty cup of coffee produced by a non-faulty and reliable machine?[5] If so, then perhaps it's also just as valuable to get to a true belief, no matter how we get there.

We might also question al-Kindi's position as regards his claim that prophecy does not reveal truths which are in principle beyond human reason; but that it reveals to us the truth in a way that is simpler and clearer than any way in which us mortals could ever hope to express it. Surely, if we take this position we commit ourselves to there being some truth that we *are* after all cognitively closed to; some truth that is forever beyond our reach—namely, the truth regarding how to express whatever truths prophecy reveals to us in the most simple and clear way possible.

But perhaps here al-Kindi's position could easily be remedied by making the following simple alteration (or interpretative move): it is not really true that it is *in principle* impossible for us mortals to find the way to express truths in the same way as divine revelation. But it would take lifetimes of work (if not millennia) to do so, such that it is *practically* (not metaphysically) impossible for us to do so, given our other ends and activities, and our finite lives. Still, this does not help us with regard to the *epistemic* uniqueness of prophecy, if we think that prophecy—as a matter of principle—teaches us something that evades independent human reasoning.

As we will see, solving this issue motivates the other of the great Falasifa to modulate al-Kindi's Evidentialism while attempting to maintain the compatibility of Falsafa with Islam, and in doing so come to invent some important theories that impinge on the politics of today. And whatever its faults, I think that the influence of al-Kindi's position on the relationship between philosophy and the established religion of the day cannot be underestimated, since he seems to have been to a large degree successful in his aims qua salesman. Al-Kindi effectively made possible the achievements of some of the biggest intellectual giants that humanity has ever produced, in Avicenna and al-Farabi in particular. And at a less meta-philosophical level, al-Kindi provides us with some fascinating philosophical thoughts and arguments that highly influenced the Falasifa who came after him. He took control of large parts of the translation movement, and was instrumental in deciding which text got translated (he did not himself do any of the translating). For instance, he led the circle of translators that took on the works of Aristotle, Alexander de Aphrodisias and the Neo-Platonists Proclus and Plotinus. We certainly see their influence in what I take to be the three central topics to which al-Kindi made a philosophical contribution. These three topics are:

The Immortality of the Soul and the role of the Active Intellect in Knowledge.
The Oneness of God.
The Eternity of the Universe.

We will now look at each of these topics in turn.

The Immortality of the Soul and the Role of the Active Intellect in Knowledge

In Chap. 2, we discussed Plato and Aristotle's ideas concerning the immortality of the soul. As we mentioned, the *De Anima* was only available to the Arabs in Greek paraphrase, and this paraphrase possibly over-emphasised the role of controversial section 3.5 in *De Anima*, where it may be argued that

Aristotle is countenancing the immortality of the soul. We can imagine how this played into the hands of al-Kindi, who was keen to (a) present Greek thought as a unified whole and (b) show how it is in harmony with Islam, which of course (as do the Christian and Jewish faiths) postulates the immortality of the soul. According to the Koran, on the Day of Judgement our souls will be reunited with our bodies.

In his works *That There Are Incorporeal Substances*, *Short Statement on the Soul* and *Discourse on the Soul* al-Kindi addresses the issue. In *That There Are Incorporeal Substances* he puts together an intriguing argument in favour of the claim that the soul is incorporeal and immortal, using some of the intellectual machinery he finds in Aristotle's *Categories*. It goes as follows.

First, al-Kindi makes a distinction between what he calls "univocal" and "equivocal" characterisation, or definition. For a description A to characterise a thing B univocally, it must both give B its name and definition. Equivocal characterisations are then simply non-univocal characterisations. The word "buffalo" characterises James the buffalo in the world univocally, because buffalo and James the buffalo share the same definition (gruff-looking horse-type animals) and the word "buffalo" is a name that buffalo and James the buffalo share. The word "buffalo" only characterises a *picture* of James the buffalo equivocally, because the definition of a *picture* of James the buffalo does *not* share the same definition with "buffalo".

Al-Kindi then says that the *essence* of something (an idea he gets of course from Aristotle) is captured in univocal characterisation and not captured in equivocal characterisation. That is, if A characterised B univocally (gives both name and definition), A is then the essence of B. Equivocal predication, by contrast, involves accidents or accidental (non-essential) properties.

Al-Kindi then argues that (a) the human body (divorced from the soul) is not essentially alive, (b) that the soul is essentially alive, and (c) that the soul is an incorporeal, immaterial substance.

The argument for (a) should go through fairly easily:

(i) The human body can perish (premise; no one denies this).
(ii) No body that can perish can have being alive as an essential property.
(iii) Thus, the human body is not essentially alive.

Al-Kindi then can then continue:

(iv) But being alive is an essential property of being a person.
(v) Thus, we are not persons essentially in virtue of our human bodies.

If (v) is true, then it must be something else than our having human bodies that makes us essentially alive qua humans. If it is not the body, it must be the soul which must be essentially alive, in other words immortal. Therefore (b) is the case. QED.

Now comes the argument for (c): that the soul is an incorporeal, immaterial substance.

(vi) Living beings (including persons) are substances [premise taken to be uncontroversial].

(vii) Living beings are alive essentially in virtue of their souls (from (i) to (v); in other words, no living being exists without a soul.

(viii) Therefore, souls are substances.

In support of (vii), recall that al-Kindi defines essential predication in terms of univocal characterisation—in terms of giving both name and definition. This means that the nature or "form" of both "living thing" and "soul" will be identical.

Finally then, once he has established that souls are substances, and that we are essentially alive in virtue of having souls, the argument for why they are immaterial should be straightforward:

(ix) We are not essentially alive in virtue of having material bodies (premise v).

(x) We are essentially alive (premise iv). We are essentially alive in virtue of having *immaterial* souls. (from ix, x)

(xi) Souls are substances (premise viii).

(xii) Human substances are immaterial souls (from xi, xii).

(xiii) Therefore, souls are immaterial substances.

Al-Kindi's argument is ingenious, though we might worry that it trades on conflating the following two claims:

(a) *F* is an essential property of *a* just in case it is impossible for *a* to cease to bear *F*.

(b) *F* is an essential property of *a*'s being an *x* just in case if *a* fails to bear *F* it is not an *x*.

We might then complain that (b) is true while (a) is not. For example, it is true that if it is an essential property of a house that it provides shelter then something that does not provide shelter is not a house. However, it is false that if it is an essential property of a house that it provides shelter then it is impossible for a given house to stop providing shelter. Think of a house that has been ravaged by a storm such that it no longer provides shelter to its inhabitants: it may no longer be a house, but the fact that it is no longer a house did not protect it from such storms! Similarly, we might worry about al-Kindi's premise (ii) above that no body that can perish can have being alive as an essential property: (ii) would be true if (a) was true, but unfortunately it is not. So one might think that from the fact that humans are essentially alive it does not follow that it is impossible for them to perish. When a person dies their body is no longer strictly a person, but that does not obviate the possibility that persons can stop being persons.

Further, we might worry that as Aristotle defined it, substance is a composite of form and matter.[6] So if souls are substances then they too must be a composite of form and matter. If this matter is not physical matter, then we seem forced to postulate an odd type of *immaterial* matter or "ether"— perhaps what Aristotle called the "Fifth Element" in his *On the Heavens*. This material looks mysterious at best, and conceptually impossible at worst.

The Active ("First") Intellect

As we have just discussed, al-Kindi held a kind of substance dualism as regards the material body and the immaterial soul. As we will now see, this metaphysical dualism comes with a concomitant epistemological dualism as regards how we come to know material objects and how we come to know immaterial, abstract objects.

Here, of course, it will help to remind ourselves of our discussion on Aristotle's *De Anima* in Chap. 2. Recall that Aristotle wants to maintain a structural similarity between perception (through which we know material objects, such as buffalo) and intellection (through which we know first principles and essences). Al-Kindi follows Aristotle here, and also maintains that:

> there are two kinds of human perceptions, one of which is nearer to us and further from nature. This is the perception of the senses which belongs to us from the beginning of our development... The other is nearer to nature and further from us, being the perception of the intellect. It is right that there should be two kinds of perception, sensory perception and intellectual perception, since things are universal and particular. (*On First Philosophy* pp. 61–62)

As you will recall, Aristotle seems to say that the matter of the buffalo acts as a kind of causal agent between the form of the buffalo and myself. My sense faculty is always in potentiality and can become all forms: the buffalo's matter (indirectly perhaps by creating changes in air pressure) causes my sense faculty to take its phenomenal form, its phantasm. However, we were careful to note, if you recall, that the form now interacts with the matter which constitutes my sense apparatus, not the matter constituting the buffalo. So my perception of the buffalo is merely a representation of the buffalo; it does not actually become a buffalo.

Note the distinction here between what the Greeks called phantasia and species or genus. We can see the phantasm of a buffalo (its phenomenal form), for instance, when we perceive a buffalo—that it's a hairy beast, brownish and so on. But we cannot see the genus or species it's a member of when we perceive the buffalo. So we can after all, just by ourselves, *imagine* (bring to our mind's eye) the *phantasm* of the buffalo—an image of a buffalo—having already seen a buffalo. But, crucially, we cannot come to (intellectually) grasp the concept mammal merely by imagining it, since we cannot see it in the perceived buffalo. Here is where the active intellect comes in: to act as a causal agent between the genus mammal and our passive intellect, which then comes to intellectually grasp the notion.

What exactly this active intellect is supposed to be is an incredibly vexed question. For those who wish to see a possibility of harmonising Plato with Aristotle as regards the idea that the soul is immortal, the active intellect will usefully seem to be inextricably connected with the immortal soul. For one thing, they will ask, if I can be the agent of my imagination when I bring to my mind's eye the phenomenal form of a buffalo, why can't I—my rational soul—also be the agent of my intellections? Further, no concept is more abstract than that of God. And we take ourselves to be responsible as regards whether or not we grasp that notion: we might think that unbelievers will be punished at judgement day, for instance. So it must be down to *us, our agency*, that makes us grasp the notion, not some external force bearing down on us. Recall here the Mu'tazilite emphasis on the justice of God, and the idea that a just God would not punish us for not doing things that were out of our control. So if our individual immortal souls somehow individually constitute this active intellect, and the active intellect is something that cannot be destroyed, then it must follow that there is something in our souls that cannot be destroyed, which survives the perishing of our bodies.

But for others, such as the Peripatetic philosopher Theophrastus, it is clear that the active intellect in *De Anima* is supposed to be God himself, the purely active intellect *Noesis Noeseos* (the Greek for "thought thinking itself") of Aristotle's *Metaphysics* Book *Lambda*.

Many scholars think that al-Kindi's major influence here was the commentary of John Philoponous, a Christian theologian and philosopher (and commentator on Aristotle) who worked in Alexandria in the sixth century. His take is a really interesting one, I think. Briefly, it is that the active intellect is not God, or some transcendent agency, but rather *other humans*. Here he makes use of Plato's theory of recollections as found in the *Meno*. Our souls—or passive intellects—tacitly already know all there is to know, but merely need to be prompted by a tutor such as Socrates (whose mind is already active in this instance) into remembering what it is they know. The active intellect, then, is just a term that denotes members of the human species intellectually interacting with one another.

The trouble with this account, I think, is perhaps that it makes learning dependent on our interacting with other humans. This might seem prima facie attractive, but it does mean that the paradox of learning—the Eristic Paradox we raised in the previous chapter—has not been solved. The human species is not infinite, and at one point the human mind must have learnt abstract thought without interacting with other human minds.

In any case, I do not think al-Kindi's account of the active intellect is Philoponous', even if he was influenced by it. His account is rendered in his *On the Intellect* as well as *On First Philosophy*. I think it is rather somewhere between the two antipodes I identified earlier—between taking God or part of ourselves to be the active intellect. Here something like Plotinus' Emanationist scheme presents itself. At the first level we have a transcendent God, One, that is thought thinking itself and is always in actuality: the "first intellect" as al-Kindi labels it. From the first intellect, another level of intellect emanates or is "caused by" (loosely speaking) the first intellect. This is the intellect that is acquired by the soul—but it is in a state of quasi-potentiality. At this point the intellect can actualise itself at will (this seems to be what Aristotle says in *De Anima* iii.4). Before the human intellect was in this state of quasi-potentiality, it was in a state of complete potentiality—the first intellect—which causes it to move from complete potentiality to quasi-potentiality (in a state that al-Kindi calls the acquired intellect). Then once the first intellect has completed this activation we can, at will, start thinking, and when we do we get a human mind that is actually thinking (what al-Kindi calls the actual intellect). What al-Kindi is doing here is identifying different degrees of potentiality when it comes to our intellect's union with the first intellect. To illustrate, there is a sense in which new-born babies have the potential to engage in abstract thought, even though they cannot do so at will. Teenagers, on the other hand, have the capacity to engage in abstract thought at will, and so when they are sitting idly, they have a different kind of potential to think (since, in al-Kindi's language, they have an acquired intellect). At some point between being a new-born and being a teenager something happened such that we can think at will. This is the first intellect actualising our minds so that we acquire this elevated potential, such that we have acquired intellects.

> It is like writing in the writer. For writing prepares the writer and makes it possible for him to write; he has acquired it, and it is firmly established in his soul. Then he actualises it and uses it, whenever he wishes (*On the Intellect*).

Here al-Kindi ingeniously steers a middle course between the Scylla of claiming that the active intellect is God or something other than us (as individuals or a collective), and the Charybdis of claiming that the active intellect is something in our individual (or collective) souls. We are involved in intellection, yet there is also a force involved in getting us to the stage that is beyond our control.

One issue that seemed to concern al-Kindi, however, was the question whether we, in grasping abstract entities, become those abstract, otherworldly entities themselves. In other words, in abstract thinking do we transcend ourselves and *become* something superluminary? That is, do we become God? Recall that Aristotle, on perception, seemed to hold that there was *some* sense that on perceiving orange we become orange. On grasping the immortal forms of things, do we then become those immortal forms? Al-Kindi points out, however (as we did), that our sense organ in perception only takes the *form* of orange on perceiving an orange, the form then interacts with our sense organs to become something different (a representation) of the orange: they do not become an orange themselves, nor do they become orange. Similarly, our souls only take on the form of the transcendent forms on grasping them; they do not become identical to them qua substance. In other words, we come close to God in engaging in abstract thought, but we do not become God in so doing.

Al-Kindi draws a few ethical conclusions from all this, as well as his acceptance in his *Discourse on the Soul* of Plato's tripartite division of the soul that we find in *The Republic*. As we will discuss further in Chap. 8, Plato thought that the soul is divided into three parts: an appetitive part, a spirited part and a rational part. Al-Kindi claims in *Discourse on the Soul* that the rational part of the soul is where its true essence lies, and not to take heed of it would be to pay too much attention to the "world of generation and corruption"—the Aristotelian phrase for this material world. Nurturing the intellectual part of the soul will not only make us happier, since we are then more in tune with our true natures, but also has the following consolation he describes in his *On the Method of How to Dispel Sadness*. The point he makes here is that, following Plato, the true reality lies beyond ours and is immutable and permanent with the world of generation and corruption only a poor copy, a shadow of reality. This means that we should not really be concerned by the things we care about perishing; the true source of the things we care about (what they are a mere shadow of) will never cease to exist. So we need not ever be sad about losing them.

I am now going to address the other two topics which figure most prominently in al-Kindi's thought: the subject of eternity and of the Oneness of God. I'll deal with them in much less detail than I have done with respect to al-Kindi's thoughts on the soul and epistemology. That is because I think that the major moves he makes here are those the Mu'tazilite theologians made, and the main issues with them are those we have already discussed.

The Oneness of God and the Eternity of the World

Al-Kindi, like the Mu'tazilites, held the Oneness of God to be of paramount importance to Islamic dogma. More explicitly than perhaps the Mu'tazilites, he made use of Plotinus' work on the One, and he cites the principles of unity we discussed in Chap. 2 as regards animals and plants—that is, that the more unity a thing has, the more permanently, deeply, it can be said to exist. Thus the thing which has the most unity is going to exist the most and be the source of all existence. It is not difficult to see how al-Kindi would have thought that this played straight into his hands with respect to showing how philosophy and Islam are in perfect harmony. All al-Kindi had to do was interpret Plotinus' One to be God, and it would look as if Plotinus' philosophy was in accord with Islam. And so here the fact that a part of Greek philosophy could be seen to vindicate Islam, and therefore be used as a propaganda tool for furthering the Islamic cause, could in turn became a propaganda tool for the study of Falsafa. This was especially the case given the Koran's explicit repudiation—and for conceptual, philosophical reasons to boot—of the Christian Trinity: that God cannot be both fundamentally indivisible and yet admit of this trifurcation:

> Lo! Whoso ascribeth partners unto Allah, for him Allah hath forbidden Paradise. His abode is the Fire. For evil-doers there will be no helpers. They surely disbelieve who say: Lo! Allah is the third of three; when there is no God save the One God. (Koran 5:72)

The philosophical problem here is, as we have discussed, that of the viability of a negative theology that seems to form part and parcel of the Plotinian view of the One, and the emphasis on the complete indivisibility of God. That is, we cannot say sensibly anything about the One, even that it is indivisible, or that it is the source of all things, or even that it is ineffable, without compromising its indivisibility. Whatever there is to know about the One, then, we must pass over in silence. And this seems to obviate the possibility of doing theoretical, philosophical work on the One; if we think that the former is not something that can be done in silence, so to speak.

For al-Kindi the fact that God is fundamentally indivisible meant that God bears no properties, and, as such, has no properties that are subject to change ("generation and corruption"): He is incorruptible. Thus, emphasising God's unity was, for al-Kindi, paramount to recognising God's eternity, since he exists and cannot change (time, according to Aristotle in the *Physics*. [7] And this meant that for al-Kindi the Hanbalite (literalist) interpretations of passages of Koranic claims such as that God sits on a throne were akin to denying God's eternal existence. Further, in contrast with later Islamic theology as found more explicitly in the Ashʿārite school, under an Emanationist Metaphysics, God does not wilfully, gratuitously, create the world (the universe and everything in it), but rather the world emerges from God owing to his irresistible unity—and so his overwhelming force of existence. And correlatively, and even more inconveniently, there is the Aristotelian idea that the world is pre-existent—that it is never created, never had a beginning and has existed infinitely. This is an instance of Aristotle's idea, derived in part from Parmenides, that nothing can come from nothing—in the famous Latinate expression *ex nihilo nihil fit*. For Aristotle, things exist either potentially or actually. For something to turn from potentially existing to actually existing, something actually existing must actualise something potential. On pain of infinite regress, then, we must think that something must always exist in actuality, since otherwise there would be nothing. As we will see, Avicenna later turns this idea into an argument for the existence of God qua something that must necessarily exist. However, the issue here is, granting that God exists necessarily, if God exists he exists in space and time, or somewhere perhaps not *physical* space and time (the heavens), so could not possibly have created that space and time (in the heavens), else he would not exist. In the Koran, however, we are told that God created the world and time.

An interpretative possibility is that the passage ought to be taken metaphorically and not literally. But this was not the way al-Kindi responded, and in *On First Philosophy* he tackles the issue head on. Here al-Kindi does seem to draw again from the work of John Philoponous, commentator on Aristotle, and thus takes his line to be the line of Greek thought *tout court*. He omits telling us that Philoponous was arguing *against* Aristotle on this point. The argument, in paraphrase, goes as follows:

(i) If the past is infinite, then an infinite amount of time would have elapsed before we get to the present.
(ii) But it is in principle impossible for an infinite amount of time to have elapsed. [If that amount of time had elapsed, then it would not be infinite.]
(iii) Therefore, the past cannot be infinite.

In al-Kindi's words:

> Before every temporal segment there is (another) segment, until we reach a temporal segment before which there is no segment, i.e., a segmented duration before which there is no segmented duration. It cannot be otherwise—if it were possible, and after every segment of time there was a segment, infinitely, then we would never reach a given time – for the duration from past infinity/to this given time would be equal to the duration from this given time regressing in times to infinity; and if (the duration) from this known time to temporal infinity would be known, and then the infinite is finite, and this is an impossible contradiction. (*On First Philosophy,* p. 74)

Of course, this does not rule out the future being infinite; and this is of course in accord with theological dogma—that God creates time and space *ex nihilo* and then it is up to him to decide whether it carries on existing indefinitely.

There is something quite compelling, I think, about al-Kindi's argument. However, as Peter Adamson points out, the argument trades on ignoring Aristotle's distinction between the *potential* and *actual* infinite (cf. Adamson 2007a, b, pp. 92–98). Aristotle agreed that the *actual* infinite was impossible: if we could hold in our minds the entirety of π then it would not involve infinite recursion, for example. But that is not to say that π does not exist, involving infinite recursion. Rather, the recursion is *potentially* infinite. But whatever the merits of the argument, in terms especially of *al-Kindi*, what is most important here is how ingenious al-Kindi is—in tandem with his thoughts about Evidentialism, the immortality of the soul and the fundamental indivisibility of God—in making it look as if Greek philosophy and Islam are in concert.

Concluding Remarks

We can conclude, then, that al-Kindi was a successful salesperson for Falsafa in the Muslim world. Even if his arguments are not all entirely successful, they are all ingenious. His Evidentialism is a thesis that later became an axiom of the Enlightenment—though it was not explicitly attributed to him—and the connections al-Kindi makes between Aristotle's psychological work in *De Anima*, his epistemological work in *Posterior Analytics* and Plato's epistemology in the *Meno* are insightful and robust. Further, his weaving of these ideas into the Neo-Platonic fabric of an Emanationist metaphysics make for a fascinating set of co-ordinates for an intellectual movement, and they set the course for the intellectual contours Falsafa was going to move in for centuries afterwards. Al-Kindi's project of harmonising Greek philosophy with Islamic dogma also meant that from the outset Falsafa was in part a religious enterprise, not wholly distinct from rational *Kalām* theology. As Sayyed Hossein Nasr puts it, Falsafa is best described as a kind of theosophy, and its practitioners' central problem that of doing "philosophy in a land of prophesy" (Nasr 2006). Al-Kindi's doctrine of Evidentialism appeared to be fertile territory in terms of solving that problem. However, as we will see, the Falasifa who followed al-Kindi came to see it as incomplete, and in doing so led their programme into both extremely fertile but perilous intellectual territory.

Study Questions

- Does al-Kindi's Evidentialism really provide us with a way to reconcile faith and reason?
- Does al-Kindi's account of the active intellect really account for the idea that we are the agents of our own thoughts?
- In what ways, if any, does al-Kindi's notion of Falsafa resemble our modern notion of philosophy?

What to Read Next?

- Peter Adamson (2007) *Al-Kindi* (Oxford: Oxford University Press).
- Al-Kindi: *On First Philosophy – fī al-Falsafa al-Ūlā*. Translated by Ivry, A.L. (1974): *Al-Kindi's Metaphysics* (New York: SUNY Press).

Notes

1. The "rightly guided" Caliphs are those four or three who immediately followed Muhammad, and were either close companions of his, or his genetic descendants. Here, of course, is where the split between Sunni and Shiite Islam occurs—the former acknowledging the Prophet's nephew 'Ali as a legitimate Caliph, and maintaining that the Caliphate should have been hereditary in the first instance ('Ali the only hereditary candidate was not immediately installed as Caliph), while the Sunnis deny this.
2. For an account of why this might have been politically expedient, see Gutas (1998).
3. Incidentally, we do not know the chronology of al-Kindi's works. All we have of his works are collected in one single manuscript discovered by Helmut Ritter and which is now held in Istanbul. We know that he wrote other works from a contemporary book-merchant's book list, but again we do not know the chronology of them.
4. According to which knowledge is justified, True Belief. See of course Gettier (1963) for an attack and articulation of that view, which he attributes to Plato; though see Antognazza (2015) for an argument for why that was *not* Plato's view.
5. I take the coffee example from Linda Zagzebski (2003).
6. Though recall the controversy as to what exactly Aristotle meant by "substance".
7. Time, according to Aristotle in the *Physics*, enumerates *motion* and so change.

References

Secondary Sources

Adamson, P. 2007a. *Al-Kindī*. Oxford University Press.
———. 2007b. Knowledge of Universals and Particulars in the Baghdad School. *Documenti e Studi Sulla Tradizione Filosofica Medievale* 18: 141–161.
Antognazza, M.R. 2015. The Benefit to Philosophy of the Study of Its History. *British Journal for the History of Philosophy* 23 (1): 161–184.
Bonjour, L. 1986. *Empirical Knowledge*. Rowman and Littlefield.
Clifford, W.K. 1877[1999]. The Ethics of Belief. In *The Ethics of Belief and Other Essays*, ed. T. Madigan. Prometheus.
Gettier, E. 1963. Is Knowledge Justified True Belief. *Analysis* 23 (6): 121–123.
Gutas, D. 1998. *Greek Thought, Arabic Culture: The Graeco-Arabic Translation Movement in Baghdad and Early Society*. Routledge.
Nasr, S.H. 2006. *Islamic Philosophy from Its Origin to the Present: Philosophy in the Land of Prophecy*. SUNY.
Swinburne, R. 1981. *Faith and Reason*. Oxford University Press.
Zagzebski, L. 2003. The Search for the Source of Epistemic Good. *Metaphilosophy* 34: 12–28.

4

Al-Farabi and Islamic Moderate Evidentialism

Introduction

In Chap. 3, we introduced the first of the great Islamic philosophers, al-Kindi. In particular, we discussed how through his doctrine of Evidentialism, he sought to prove the harmony between Falsafa and Islam. We also had a look at al-Kindi's epistemology and how it comes together with certain views about human psychology and the metaphysics of the soul. In this chapter, I want to introduce the second of the great Islamic philosophers, Abu Nasr al-Farabi. I will do so by taking up themes that were raised in the previous two chapters: meta-philosophy, epistemology, and the relationship between philosophy and prophecy. As we will see, I propose that al-Farabi's overall meta-philosophical position departs from al-Kindi's Evidentialism in subtle but important ways, to formulate a position I will call Islamic moderate Evidentialism. As with the chapter on al-Kindi, I will begin by giving a very brief biographical sketch of al-Farabi's life.

Al-Farabi: A Very Short Biography

We know very little about al-Farabi's life, and there is some controversy in regard to certain details. We know he has born in around 870, almost immediately following the death of al-Kindi. What is not known with certainty is where he was born and what his ethnic origins were. Two places of birth are put forward, in what are now Kazakhstan and Afghanistan. There are also two theories about his ethnic origin: that he was of Turkish origin (this is Fakhry's

© The Author(s) 2017
A.R. Booth, *Analytic Islamic Philosophy*, Palgrave Philosophy Today,
https://doi.org/10.1057/978-1-137-54157-4_4

contention[1]), or that he was of Iranian/Persian origin. The matter is sensitive, since implicitly the question can be taken to turn on whether he was a Sunni or Shiite Muslim—and thus whether his controversial views on religion have something to do with the denomination of which he was a member. The matter is further compounded by the fact that al-Farabi always refers to religion in the most abstract terms and never, for example, quotes scripture to illustrate any of his points. There is something about his views that make this fact unsurprising, and makes it highly improbable that his views are in any way affected by the particularities of the denomination to which he belonged.

We do know that al-Farabi was educated and spent most of his intellectual life in Baghdad, where a particular school of philosophy had developed. This school, known as the Baghdad school, was composed of predominantly Christian Peripatetic philosophers; that is, followers of Aristotle (following the model of Themistius and Alexander de Aphrodisias). They were especially concerned with understanding and disseminating Aristotle's logical works. Of particular importance here, I think, is the fact that Aristotle's *Posterior Analytics* was available to them in translation, and that they were not afraid to tackle it. Previous Christian scholars had stopped at the *Prior Analytics*, taking the *Posterior Analytics* to be potentially heretical.

Al-Farabi seems to have quickly outshone his teachers in Baghdad, and his biographers are unanimous in pouring heavy praise on his intellectual abilities. He is often referred to as the "Second Master"—the first Master thought to be, implicitly, Aristotle. This would reasonably make one think that al-Farabi was a Peripatetic philosopher; indeed a card-carrying Aristotelian, who in logical prowess was second only to Aristotle himself. Yet he is also credited with founding the Islamic tradition of Neo-Platonism. Majid Fakhry's book on al-Farabi, for instance, is subscripted *"Founder of Islamic Neoplatonism"*. The reason for this, of course, is that al-Farabi was explicit—more so than al-Kindi—in his attempt to harmonise the work of what he called the "Two Sages". His work therefore contains elements of both Plato's and Aristotle's work, as we shall see. Therefore I feel it is misleading to label him either a Neo-Platonist or a Peripatetic; rather, he was following in the footsteps of the Neo-Platonising Aristotelians of Later Antiquity.

I think that al-Farabi's central contributions were to (a) philosophical methodology and the primacy of logic within it; (b) relatedly, the relationship between philosophy and prophecy; (c) epistemology and the theory of human psychology and metaphysics to match. We will now discuss al-Farabi's contribution to these things in turn. We will not discuss his contributions to music or to alchemy, which are also said to be important.

Al-Farabi lived during the rule of the Abbasid caliphs. For reasons that I hope will appear obvious during the course of this chapter, he had a harder time than al-Kindi in securing the patronage of the caliphs. Especially during the latter stages of his life, he was forced to move around in search of patronage—in particular within Egypt and Syria. He died in 950 in Damascus, the capital of modern Syria.

Philosophy Versus Prophecy

In Chap. 3, we discussed al-Kindi's take on the issue regarding whether philosophy and the claims of prophecy need to be in opposition with one another. As we discussed, al-Kindi was very emphatically on the side of the idea that they are not at all in opposition and are indeed complimentary—two different ways at getting to the same truth. This is underscored in his commitment to Evidentialism. As we also discussed, this view was part and parcel of his operating as a kind of salesman for philosophy—although in his conception the only real difference between philosophy (Falsafa) and (rational) theology (Kalām) was that philosophy explicitly took on board what the Greeks had said whereas theology did not.

Al-Farabi's approach to this issue is rather different from al-Kindi's. The relationship between the findings of philosophy and the claims of prophecy can be taken to involve the respective statuses within an Islamic context of Falsafa and Kalām theology, and so indirectly an argument about which scholars the caliphs ought to patronise. Perhaps surprisingly, since he is much more of a hermit scholar than the worldly, salespersonesque al-Kindi, he supports the view that philosophy is the epistemically superior method over theology as a means to arriving at truth, religious or otherwise. To summarise the two views:

Al-Kindi: Philosophy and theology are on a par: they are just two different ways at getting to the same (religious) truths.

Al-Farabi: Philosophy is superior (over theology) as a means of reaching (religious) truths.

As I mentioned above, it might strike us as surprising, given the Muʿtazilite accord with Falsafa and their emphasis on the role of human reason, that al-Farabi should turn against them. As commented upon in previous chapters, it was certainly not as if the Muʿtazilites were philosophically unskilled, and the difference between Falsafa (as inaugurated by al-Kindi) and theology was a thin one. I think that two points are in order here:

(i) It has been convenient for me to talk about the Muʿtazilites as a coherent movement, whose proponents shared many beliefs and modus operandi (in just the same way perhaps that it was convenient for al-Kindi to present the Greek philosophers as a coherent unit). But the Muʿtazilites were in historical fact a rather disjointed bunch, holding a whole gamut of different (and sometimes contradictory) beliefs. Many of them were probably much more traditional and literal in their interpretation of the Koran than is presented here. My hypothesis is therefore that when al-Farabi attacks the Muʿtazilites, he has really got these more traditionally minded Muʿtazilites in his sights (and considers the more rationally orientated theologians really to be a kind of Falasifa).

(ii) Al-Farabi, qua member of the Baghdad school, had been taught by several *Christian* logicians.[2] One can again reasonably conjecture that, as such, al-Farabi may well have been keen to make it clear that his philosophy was not constitutive of Christian theology. Philosophy should be seen as a totally independent form of inquiry dealing with timeless logical truths—and thus that it was just a matter of contingency that certain Christians had taken up the study of it. That is, there was nothing *Christian* about the emphasis on logic, the distinguishing mark of the Baghdad school.

What is perhaps even more surprising is that al-Farabi comes to defend the epistemic superiority of Falsafa over Kalām by *rejecting* al-Kindi's Evidentialism, in favour of a modified doctrine that I will call Islamic moderate Evidentialism. To see how he gets there, let us have a look at what he (famously) has to say about the relationship between logic and grammar.

Grammar Versus Logic

The point at issue here has to do with the role of grammar in the explication of the Koran. The traditional (theological) view was something like this: the Koran was revealed to Muhammad in Arabic, so if we want to know what the ultimate structure of thought and language is (and perhaps the world), we had better investigate the grammatical rules of Arabic. It is there that the true underlying structure of thought and language can be seen.

But al-Farabi thinks that this is mistaken: any given natural language's grammar is for him culturally bound, whereas the language of logic is universal and underlies all languages, and indeed all human thought. Perhaps Allah chose to reveal the Koran in Arabic, but that was probably because it was the language of the chosen prophet. What is logic, ultimately? An idealised language whose purpose it is to uncover the deep underlying structure of human thought—and as such also the world, if like the early Wittgenstein you think there is an isomorphism (a structural identity) between the form of language and the form of the world. So al-Farabi here can be taken to have a position very much like the twentieth-century logical positivists (such as Rudolf Carnap, and the early Wittgenstein), who countenanced what is sometimes called Ideal Language Philosophy. Al-Farabi would then be opposed to what is called Ordinary Language Philosophy, espoused by the later Wittgenstein and Oxford twentieth-century philosophers such as Gilbert Ryle and J.L. Austin. These days Ordinary Language Philosophy is out of favour for, I think, very similar reasons to why al-Farabi rejected the emphasis on the grammar of the Arabic language that was made by the theologians. That is, why should we privilege English grammar over the grammar of other languages, and how can we be sure that the way in which our natural language operates is not grossly misleading?

On this point, with respect to al-Farabi's take on language, Oliver Leaman writes:

> The argument was really about power. Who has access to the more profound analysis of language, the grammarian or the logician? If al-Farabi was right, then the grammarians were dethroned from their previous crucial role. (Leaman 2009, p. 6)

Leaman is surely right that al-Farabi's position has this consequence—of "dethroning" the grammarians. And it's probably true that this would mean that the theologians of the day had a vested interest in seeing al-Farabi's work discredited. But I don't think we should attribute this consequence to being al-Farabi's motivation, since surely his reasoning here has pretty good independent standing, and it surely would have been more politic for him to have taken a line like al-Kindi's on this issue.

The central question that gets us to al-Farabi's motivations is why did he think that the theologians could only study our *natural* language, and not logic? That traditionally the theologians have done so is no reason to think that they *ought* to. The answer to this question lies in the limitations of al-Kindian Evidentialism.

Islamic Moderate Evidentialism

The central problem (CP) that is exercising al-Farabi is the following:

CP   How we can verify the veracity of the Prophet, without at once obviating the unique epistemic function of prophecy?

Recall Evidentialism:

Evidentialism: A subject S is justified in believing any proposition that p just in case S has sufficient evidence for believing that p.

Recall that the advantages of Evidentialism (in an Islamic context) seem to be that it allows us to discern genuine from fake Prophets,[3] and that it coheres with the Muʿtazilite emphasis on God's justice: by giving us the faculty of reason, God gives us all the means by which we can come to the correct beliefs and ascend to heaven on the Day of Judgement. And of course the trouble is, what then is the unique epistemic purpose of prophecy?

The issue is one that is familiar to contemporary epistemologists, this time those working on testimony.[4] According to the latter, the problem is a general one concerning *epistemic expertise*: how do we ascertain that a putative expert's claims are true, without ourselves becoming experts? Alvin Goldman (2001) calls this the "novice/expert" problem, and identifies two further similar problems, the "novice/2expert" problem, and the "expert–expert" problem. The former denotes situations in which two putative experts give us, the novices, conflicting testimonies regarding some subject about which they supposedly have expertise. How do we discern which of the two accounts we should trust without ourselves becoming experts? The latter denotes situations in which experts are faced with competing testimonies from two people they consider to be their epistemic peers (i.e. are as expert on the relevant subject matter as they are). What would count as evidence in favour of one expert account over the other? Of immediate concern to us here are the "novice/expert" problem and the "novice/2expert" problem, since we are concerned with how the ordinary layperson (the novice) can rationally come to trust the testimony of the prophet (the expert) and can detect the difference between a real prophet and an impostor. To solve the problem, Goldman makes use of a further distinction between what he calls an expert's "esoteric" and "exoteric" claims. The former are claims that "belong to the relevant sphere of expertise" while the latter are claims that the layperson can understand "either at the time of the assertion, or later" (Goldman 2001, p. 94). According to Goldman, the premises and lemmas of an esoteric argument are "epistemically inaccessible" to the layperson (given the layperson's existing personal knowledge), such that it is impossible for the layperson to assess the soundness of the expert's argument just by considering their esoteric claims. The central issue, then, is about how the layperson can assess the epistemic trustworthiness of the expert by extrapolating from the expert's exoteric claims. This process will give the layperson what Goldman calls "indirect justification", which is grounded by an inference to the best explanation: certain properties of the expert's exoteric claims are such that cannot be explained (or are simply best explained) except by the proposition that the expert is a trustworthy source of testimony on the given domain. One of the relevant properties for Goldman here is what David Matheson (2005) calls "rhetorical superiority"—the genuine expert, unlike a competing impostor, is able to present her exoteric terms such that they bear the following marks:

(i) The presentation of more ostensive rebuttals to ostensive counter-evidence.
(ii) Quicker responses to ostensive counter-evidence.
(iii) Smoother responses to ostensive counter-evidence. (Goldman 2001, p. 95)

But the existence of these marks is certainly not sufficient for ascertaining the trustworthiness of a given expert for Goldman, since, for instance, "skilled debaters and well-coached witnesses can appear better-informed because of their stylistic polish, which is not a true indicator of superior expertise" (Goldman 2001, p. 96). This is why Goldman thinks that the expert also needs to showcase what he calls "dialectical superiority",[5] the ability to present his esoteric knowledge in exoteric terms, relative to the novice's existing opinions. An inference to the best explanation is involved here, too: the quality of the expert's dialectical ability is best explained by the fact that the expert really does know the esoteric claims.

What seems to be missing in Goldman's account, however, is a principled link between dialectical and rhetorical ability and knowledge in respect of certain pieces of esoteric knowledge. Only if there is such a principled link can we run a robust inference to the best explanation here. And it is precisely this link that al-Farabi's account offers us, it seems to me.

To see this, let us have a look at what we can term "Western" moderate Evidentialism.

Moderate
Evidentialism_{western}:   For *some propositions* p but all subjects S, S ought to believe that p iff S has sufficient evidence that p (e.g. when the evidence is indeterminate as to p, then non-evidential considerations can legitimately sway one).

In other words, the Western way of moderating Evidentialism is to restrict the *propositions* that the Evidentialist principle applies to. According to this thesis, there are some propositions that escape Evidentialist treatment; that we can believe without evidence. Candidates for such propositions are of course religious propositions, or propositions where our relevant evidence is inconclusive: where our evidence is inconclusive in regard to whether p or not p, it is permissible to believe that p (e.g. <there is a God>) for non-epistemic (e.g. voluntaristic, moral, pragmatic) reasons. It is arguable that this was the view of St Thomas Aquinas (see his *Summa Theologica*), who claimed that since our evidence that the universe was created or infinite is drastically inconclusive, one ought to believe that it is created because the Holy Bible says it is. As such, for Aquinas, religious faith can never *go against* reason, even if it can at times outrun it.

One problem for this view is that it seems like a case of special pleading to claim that religious beliefs are immune from the Evidentialist principle. And even if our evidence for certain religious propositions is inconclusive, then one might think that the Evidentialist should say that we ought to suspend judgement about them. Regardless, unsurprisingly enough, the Western way of modulating Evidentialism is not al-Farabi's way. Rather, his version is something like the following:

Moderate
Evidentialism_{Islamic}:   For *some subjects* S (the epistemic elite) but all propositions p, S ought to believe that p iff S has sufficient evidence that p.

The modulation here regards the *subjects* that Evidentialism applies to. Here al-Farabi elaborates on a thought that features in Plato's *Republic*—that God does not mete out capacities for rational thought in equal measure throughout his subjects. As such, it is wrong-headed to assume that Evidentialism will apply to everyone without caveat. Put differently, the idea here is that for those with the requisite intellectual ability, they ought to believe in accord with the epistemic reason—and the best kind of epistemic reason for al-Farabi is the Aristotelian *demonstrative proof* that we discussed in Chap. 2. However, for those without the requisite capacity—the non-philosophers or the epistemic non-elite—they are allowed to believe for non-epistemic reasons, and on the basis of something that falls far short of demonstrative proof: they can believe on the basis of rhetorical ploys, symbolism and allegory.

This putatively (and ingeniously) solves the CP above (regarding prophecy): it is *in principle* possible to discern genuine prophets from counterfeits, since an epistemic elite will be able to test their claims against their demonstrative proof. But prophesy still has a unique function: to educate the non-elite—via symbols, rhetoric and allegory—something approaching a truth that they would not be able to discover left to their own devices. I cannot overstate how influential this ingenious move was to prove to be, especially in a political context. We will discuss this in Chap. 8.

But, for now, we might still wonder how the epistemic non-elite know when they are in the presence of genuine prophets? And if they have to take the word of philosophers that a putative prophet is a real prophet, then how do they know which philosophers to trust without themselves becoming philosophers? Here, once again, al-Farabi's answer is ingenious. To see it we need to look further at his epistemology, and his extremely novel account of certainty.

The Conditions of Certainty

In seeing themselves as following a Peripatetic tradition of philosophy, and on commenting on Aristotle's *Organon*, the Falasifa were keenly concerned with logic and on the epistemological foundations of logic. Aristotle's *Posterior Analytics* was well known to them, and al-Kindi had already made a connection (which I mentioned in the previous chapter) between the concept of *noûs* (intellect) that is found in *Posterior Analytics*' last chapter and the concept of *noûs* as found in Aristotle's psychological work in *De Anima*. The guiding question here concerns what is a demonstrative proof—a valid and explanatory syllogistic argument—and, in particular, what explains, or makes possible, direct knowledge of "first principles" grounding sound syllogisms, themselves indemonstrable, indubitable—certain—intellectual truths intuited by *noûs*. Al-Farabi explicitly takes up this question, and attempts to give an account of the conditions of certainty (*yaqīn*) in his works *Kitāb al-burhān* (*Book on Demonstration*) and in particular *Sarā'iṭ al-yaqīn* (*The Conditions of Certainty*).[6] In the latter, we find the following concise definition:

> Absolute certitute is: [1] to believe of something that it is thus or not this; [2] to agree that it corresponds and is not opposed to the existence of the thing externally; [3] to know that it corresponds to it; and [4] that it is not possible that it not correspond to it or that it be opposed to it; and, further [5] that there does not exist anything opposed to it at any time; and [6] and that all of this does not happen accidentally, but essentially. (Al-Farabi *Sarā'iṭ al-yaqīn*)[7]

Deborah Black (2006) paraphrases this as follows:

AFC₁

S has absolute certainty of p iff:

1. S believes that p (the *belief condition*).
2. P is true (the *truth condition*).
3. S knows that p (is true) (the *knowledge condition*).
4. It is impossible that p not be true (the *necessity condition*).
5. There is no time at which p can be false (the *eternity condition*).
6. Conditions 1–5 hold essentially, not accidentally (the *non-accidentality condition*).

I think it is important to note here, however, that al-Farabi's aim is not only to give a definition of certainty, in terms of necessary and sufficient conditions. He also aims to give an account of all the *differentiae* that the genus certainty can admit to—that is, he wants to give an exhaustive account of what different modes certainty can take. As such, some of the conditions he sets out above will either not be necessary for certainty or else will be strictly redundant. The crucial point here for him, which I agree with Black can be considered a considerable breakthrough, is that we can distinguish between what he calls "absolute certainty" (a state that meets all six conditions) and progressively less absolute kinds of certainty, as we consider states that miss progressively fewer of the six conditions.

Now, I think that we should interpret al-Farabi's passage on certainty slightly differently to Black's way, as follows:

AFC₂

S is absolutely certain that p iff:

1* S believes that p.
2* S believes that p for epistemic reason.
3* S (infallibly) believes that S believes that p for epistemic reason [S has taken cognisance of her reasons for belief].
4* S (infallibly) believes that it is impossible for there to be no epistemic reason for her to believe that p.
5* S (infallibly) believes that there can be no time at which there is no epistemic reason for her to believe that p.
6* Conditions 1*–5* hold essentially, not accidentally.

According to AFC₂ *all* except condition 6* are about first-order belief, or how it is that the subject *views* the world, as opposed to how things are in the world. I will now defend each of my modified conditions as exegetical of al-Farabi's position. But first let me note what I take to be the major difference between mine and Black's interpretation of al-Farabian certainty. According to Black, condition 6 is "superfluous", whereas I think that it is of vital importance and its inclusion demonstrates that for al-Farabi "absolute certainty" is only available to prophets. This represents a poignantly fallibilist position where the rest of humanity must make do with something less perfect. This has important implications for his political philosophy, as we will discuss in Chap. 8. Let's go through each condition.

1* and 1 are identical, so need not be discussed further. 2* is more explicitly about S's mental state, and not about the external world as it is in 2, and so I think captures better what al-Farabi means by "to *agree* that it corresponds" [my italics]. 3* is like 3 in the sense that it is supposed to be a higher-order (loosely speaking "K-K") condition,[8] the thought being that S must be *aware* of what it is that is justifying her belief in order for her to be properly certain of it. As Black rightly notices, this is typically considered to be an "internalist" condition on knowledge (in the parlance of contemporary epistemology). However, as Black also rightly notices, the condition's being satisfied must for al-Farabi *guarantee* that the higher-order belief be true. This is why al-Farabi insists on there being, as Black puts it, "direct epistemic contact" between the knowing subject and the object known. That is, the subject must have something akin to a direct intellectual perception of the object in question. Once one has direct acquaintance with the object one can predicate on the object such that one's belief has a proposition as its object. As such, it seems that al-Farabi maintained that only abstract truths can be the object of absolute certainty. I think "infallibly believes" is a better translation here than "knows" since the latter in Arabic is ambiguous (the closest Arabic word for "knowledge", *'ilm*, admits of gradation whereas, usually, the English word "knowledge" does not), and al-Farabi has attempted to disambiguate it accordingly. "Infallibly believes" captures that disambiguation, if we take the former to mean that it is impossible for S to have met the condition and for S's relevant belief to be false. The introduction of this condition, incidentally, kick-starts an interesting tradition in Islamic philosophy, where self-knowledge is taken to have special, infallible status.[9] By "epistemic reason" I mean reason that makes it the case that S ought, all things considered, believe that p. In other words, I do not think that the epistemic reason denoted here is a *pro toto* not *pro tanto* reason.[10] As such, I think 4* expresses something very similar to what Black's 4 does. Things get interesting, however, when we consider why al-Farabi includes condition 4 in the account, since it seems to be entailed by 5, and how he thinks what are denoted by 4 and 5 differ.

Black gives us in effect two reasons for why al-Farabi postulates the two conditions. The first is that where 4 is about a subject's mental state, 5 is about the world. As she puts it: "The necessity condition ... does not point to the *necessary existence* of the object of belief itself ... rather, necessity here is attributed to the *assurance* and *strength* of the belief itself, the feeling of confidence that one cannot be mistaken, that one's belief is both incorrigible and infallible" (Black 2006, p. 24). The second reason is about the "eternity condition" (5): "Only if the extra-mental object of the belief is itself incapable of undergoing change at any time can it provide an additional guarantee that a belief that is true at time t_1 will not become false at some future time, say, t_2" (Black 2006, p. 26). As such, she claims, the introduction of (5) "introduces properly modal concerns into the definition of absolute certitude" (Black 2006, p. 27). This is strange, since in Black's own paraphrase *both* conditions 4 and 5 are formulated such that they are about the world, as opposed uniquely to a subject's mental state. That is, 4 is parsed such that it does not look like a further K-K condition. While I think that it is a K-K condition, unlike Black I think that 5 is too, on pain of making 6 redundant, as I will explain shortly. So I do not think the difference about the objects of 4 and 5 (in terms of 4 being a K-K condition and 5 not) accounts for why both need to be included.

The second explanation Black gives us is that the inclusion of 4 underscores al-Farabi's "willingness to admit an attenuated form of certitude in the case of contingent propositions" (Black 2006, p. 27). The thought here seems to be that there are at least two kinds of necessary truths: those true in every possible world at any time t and those true in every possible world at a given time, say t_1. According to Black's al-Farabi, one has "absolute" certainty only of the former kind of necessary truth. Here al-Farabi seems to follow the Aristotelian stricture that demonstrative proof is only to be had in relation to the eternal, unchanging "intelligibles", but yet departs from it in holding that a lesser kind of certainty, but a certainty nonetheless, can be predicated on our knowledge of necessary, but non-eternal truths. I think that Black is right in thinking that accommodating this difference is the central motivation for including both the 4th and 5th conditions, since al-Farabi explicitly says:

> For sensibles may be true, and it may be impossible for them to be otherwise than we believe them to be. It may, however, be possible for them to cease at an indeterminate time, such as Zayd's being seated; or it may be inevitable for them to cease at some determinate time, such as the eclipse of the moon which one is now seeing. So too with universal existential propositions, like your saying, "Every human is white." (Al-Farabi *The Conditions of Certainty*)[11]

I also agree with Black that this is a significant breakthrough on the part of al-Farabi. It is important in foreshadowing Avicenna's claim that God can know particulars "in a universal way".[12] It might even also foreshadow a discussion in contemporary metaphysics concerning what is known as "real possibility" (Deutsch 1990). The idea here is that what may move you to research the cure for cancer may be that you think there is a possibility *in this world* that a cure can be found, as opposed to the conceptual possibility that it can be found *in some possible world*. Similarly, one might imagine that there are truths that, given the constitution of this world, are *necessary* in *this* world or at a particular time, but not in all possible worlds or at all times. But it is most important, I think, in its concession that perhaps absolute certainty may not be important for all our cognitive enterprises, and this aspect of al-Farabi's thought is lost if we interpret part of the difference between 4 and 5 to be about whether or not they are epistemic or metaphysical conditions. This is because this would obviate the need for condition 6, and 6's inclusion comes with further, parallel, fallibilist insights. Rather, both 4 and 5, as per 4* and 5*, should be taken to be epistemological conditions, albeit about different kinds of epistemic possibility respectively.

As I have already mentioned, Black thinks that al-Farbi's condition 6 is superfluous. As she puts it:

> Farabi's motivations for adding this sixth condition are closely tied up with his concern to differentiate philosophically demonstrative certitude from dialectical and rhetorical conviction. But his account is puzzling in some ways, since the other five conditions taken conjointly (and in some cases in isolation), seem sufficiently strong to rule out any such chance occurrences …suggesting that this 6th condition may in the end be superfluous. (Black 2006, p. 30)

According to Black, meeting al-Farabi's conditions 1–5 already rules out the possibility that 1–5 have been met by luck. Conditions 1*–5* do not rule out the presence of all luck, however. This is because 1*–5* are merely epistemic conditions, about the subject's mental state—they are about what the subject (infallibly) believes about what *her* reasons for belief are. There is a link postulated between the world and what the subject believes, in that she must believe this infallibly, but there is not enough of a link for al-Farabi (such that for him meeting this condition is not enough for absolute certainty). And this is where what Black rightly describes as al-Farabi's "reliabilism" or more generally his "externalism", comes in. Though perhaps, in my view, it is an externalism that is slightly stronger than that found in contemporary epistemology. This is because while contemporary epistemological externalists will concede that knowledge is incompatible with certain varieties of epistemic luck, they allow that it is compatible with certain others. That is, they think that S can know that p even if it is what Duncan Prichard (2005) calls *evidentially lucky* that S believes that a true proposition p—where it is lucky that S is in the possession of evidence that p. Robert Nozick's example here is of a bystander watching a bank-robber's mask accidentally fall off, and thereby accidentally acquiring evidence for the proposition that the masked-man is identical to Jesse James. Evidential luck is contrasted with *veritic luck*—where it is lucky that one believes a true proposition that p *given one's existing evidence* that p; an example being that one believes that Margaret Thatcher has died purely out of wishful thinking on the evening she died. The received view in contemporary epistemology is that veritic—and not evidential—luck is incompatible with knowledge. But this does not, in my interpretation, accord with al-Farabi's view. For him, the strongest kind of justified belief, grounded on absolute certainty, as per 1*–6*, cannot in a sense even be evidentially lucky. However, for al-Farabi the idea is broader than were it to be about considerations about evidence alone, given his K-K conditions: for him the world must somehow guarantee that one is in the epistemic situation one is in (K-K conditions included). This is why I take it that only prophets can satisfy this condition, since God has set the world up in such a way that it is predetermined that such people will be able to satisfy 1*–5*, and, moreover, they know and understand this. This is in accord with al-Farabi's and al-Kindi's—and the Falasifa's in general—view that one can account for the workings of prophecy psychologically, quasi-naturalistically. A person with the correct prophetic psychological makeup will necessarily come to be in an epistemic situation where they have absolute certainty towards those propositions about which there can be absolute certainty—necessary, eternal truths. But this certainty will, as we will now discuss, perforce also come with certain rhetorical and practical abilities.

Black thinks that al-Farabi is a "reliabilist" in the following sense: we cannot come to understand how it is that we can reliably apprehend first principles. We can "intuit" or "rationally grasp" these abstract, necessary propositions through our intellective faculty (the Arabic word used for *noûs*: *'aql)* and come to believe them infallibly, such that we believe such propositions just in case they are true. And we can do so, and in fact always do so, without understanding how and why we do so, because they have the right causal history (involving provenance from the active intellect). Here is where Black sees a tension between the internalist and externalist elements of al-Farabi's thought. He seems to think that in order to be certain that p, one must understand how it is that one is certain that p (internalism). But he also seems to think that in order to be certain that p it is sufficient that certainty that p has the right causal history, and such that one cannot be certain of a false belief that p (externalism). Furthermore, he seems also to think "that we have no conscious awareness of when we acquired knowledge of these intelligibles, and that we can recall no time when we did not know them". But he is careful to assert only that it is "*as if* our souls possessed [knowledge of intelligibles] by nature from the beginning of our existence, and as it were innate in us and we were never lacking in it ... the fact that we are ignorant of the manner of their attainment does not cause our certitude in them to cease, nor does it diminish nor impede us from composing a syllogism from them which causes certitude for us as a necessary entailment from them" (Black 2006, p. 41).[13]

The point of the last "as if" above seems to be to underscore the claim that we *don't know* how we acquired our knowledge of intelligibles. As such, our "knowledge" of them cannot satisfy condition 4 in AFC$_1$ when it is taken—as Black takes it—as a higher-order 'K-K' condition on absolute certainty. In other words, al-Farabi seems to be saying that we do not need to have any attitude at all towards the grounds, or the reasons, for which we believe that p, so long as our belief that p has the right causal history that guarantees it to be true, in order for us to be absolutely certain that p. Since this is a necessary and sufficient condition for absolute certainty, it seems that all the other conditions in 1–6 are made redundant (not only 6, as Black notes), and this is why its inclusion makes a mockery of the idea that there can be gradations of certainty for al-Farabi. Black, though, seems to think that it is the required internalism that does this:

> Because it builds reflexive self-awareness into the very definition of certitude, "knowing that one knows" requires that we be explicitly aware of the grounds which justify our beliefs and able to articulate exhaustively our reasons for claiming to know whatever we know. Such an assumption is clearly present not only in Farabi's knowledge condition itself, but also in his discussion of the powerful weapon that certitude provides to the philosopher who is faced with opposition from the sophist and his ilk. But for these very reasons it undermines Farabi's basic insight that some forms of certitude exist which are secure though not absolute. (Black 2006, p. 47)

I think the underlying mistake here is to think that condition 5 is a metaphysical condition, and not *also* (like 3 and 4) a K-K condition, as per 5*. Both 4* and 5* make the requirement that S infallibly believes that *she* has epistemic reason to believe that p—and that is compatible with the falsity of p, even if the epistemic reasons are all things considered or "conclusive", since

S could be in a sceptical scenario. As such, S has a level of certainty that p, but not such that she has eliminated these special cases. To do so, and to attain *absolute* certainty, she needs to satisfy condition 6/6*. If she satisfies 6/6*, then not only has she eliminated the possibility of what we earlier termed *evidential* luck (luck that she is in the epistemic position that she is), but in so doing she will also eliminate the possibility of her belief being subject to *veritic luck*. As such, she rules out being in a sceptical scenario,[14] and she thus satisfies al-Farabi's desideratum that she is completely immune from the rhetorical strategies of such people as sophists. That is, her belief that p will persist *come what may*. The explanation is linked to the account of prophecy just canvassed. S can only satisfy 6/6* if she has a certain prophetic ability, that God has predetermined that she will know all intelligibles by giving her a special faculty of imagination. The thought here is that all intelligibles are available to us, provided we have set up our imagination correctly. But, and this is the really important part, since the prophet has special rhetorical and practical abilities in that she can see how all truths fit together (in what Black calls al-Farabi's "coherentism"),[15] she also attains a degree of *understanding* that is superior to ordinary humans. This means that satisfaction of 6/6* also carries with it the satisfaction of a further more stringent K-K condition, in line with Aristotle's desideratum for demonstrative proof that it be *explanatory*. Put differently, satisfaction of 6/6* comes with knowledge of how—and why—their souls came to acquire the intelligibles. This further prophetic K-K is for al-Farabi not strictly *new* knowledge, but merely an *understanding* of the prophet's existing knowledge. This is perhaps why, in Black's words, the sixth condition is "offered not as an additional differentia over and above the first five, but rather, as a qualification of the way in which these other conditions obtain" (Black 2006, p. 29). So because the elimination of evidential luck in this manner comes with satisfaction of this more stringent K-K condition, which enables the prophet to properly understand his own grasp of intelligibles, the meeting of 6/6* for al-Farabi also eliminates the possibility of the prophet's belief being *veritically* lucky. That is, there is no sceptical scenario where the prophet is certain that p, but it is not the case that p. And as such, among humans, only the prophet can have absolute certainty.

We are now in a position to see how al-Farabi can make a principled link between esoteric and exoteric knowledge—or between true knowledge and rhetorical ability. The best kind of cognitive state a human can be in for al-Farabi is a state of absolute certainty. Being in such a state demands (as per condition 6*) such a high degree of higher-order knowledge—understanding—that only someone with special cognitive powers can attain it. Put differently, among humans only the prophets, with their God-given, superior faculties of imagination, are able to attain this perfect cognitive state. This means that it is impossible for the prophet *not* to have perfect rhetorical and dialectical abilities with respect to his knowledge: he is in a sense in a state of absolute certainty concerning his belief *in virtue of* possessing these abilities. The prophet is thus *so* persuasive, and *so* dialectically skilled, because she not only knows the truth, but also understands it, that she cannot but persuade one of her testimonial trustworthiness. The prophet's absolute certainty is such that his persuasiveness is guaranteed (that is not to say that his *persuading* is guaranteed). As such, someone who is engaged with a prophet, but still fails to believe her testimony, must perforce have a blameworthy belief: he must be wilfully and deliberately sabotaging his intellect's being in a position where it will see the truth.[16]

The Plato–Aristotle Fusion

Al-Kindi presented Greek philosophy to the Arab world as a unified whole. As we have mentioned several times already, it was politic for him to do so, and he did not seem to be overly forthcoming about pointing out areas where the Greeks might have diverged amongst themselves.

In contrast, al-Farabi is quite explicit about there being at least a prima facie tension between the philosophies of Plato and Aristotle, but he wants to show that the tension is bridgeable. Nowhere is this clearer than in his work *Reconciliation of the opinions of the Two Sages* (the two sages referred to here being Plato and Aristotle, of course). Now, there has been some recent controversy over whether or not al-Farabi actually wrote this work. The main reason to be sceptical seems to be that he ignores the work of al-Kindi and Porphyry (Plotinus' student) in this work (they being two authors who had attempted a similar undertaking). I'm personally not convinced that this is a good enough reason to cast doubt on the work's authorship—especially since al-Kindi is not really up front about where Plato and Aristotle were even prima facie incompatible. But even if I'm wrong on that score, I think that the work is well worth discussing, since it explicitly explains how al-Farabi might have harmonised the two—and is therefore valuable even if not penned by al-Farabi himself.

Whoever the author is starts the work with the following thought: what is more unlikely, that the commentators up to now have made some mistake in the interpretation of Plato and Aristotle, that the difference between them is merely apparent (not real), or that the two greatest sages of all time had in fact been in agreement? It's not unreasonable to work on the assumption that the latter proposition is the more unlikely.

He admits that there were certain differences in the lifestyles of the two philosophers—Aristotle being the more worldly of the two (having been married and amassing quite a fortune through his service to Alexander the Great). He also recounts that there were differences in both of their styles: that Plato was much more prone to use allegory and metaphor, for instance.

Here, the author points out, rightly, that these differences are merely superficial: that Aristotle could at times also write using allegories, and that their lifestyles were irrelevant to the question of what they took the right philosophy to be.

Then he turns to the more substantive issues. The most interesting to my mind is the issue discussed in Chap. 2 regarding the epistemological priority of universals over particulars: what I called Heavens First versus Experience First Epistemology. As you will recall, one of Plato's arguments for Heavens First Epistemology is the one found in the *Meno*. How can a slave boy come to have true beliefs about the geometrical truths that Socrates reveals he has true beliefs about? The only explanation, claims Plato, is to be given by his Recollection Theory: that the slave boy's immortal soul was merely recollecting its acquaintance with the immaterial forms it had previously been acquainted with in the transcendent world of forms.

We know that Aristotle's *Posterior Analytics* was available to al-Farabi in Arabic translation. The author of *Reconciliation of the opinions of the Two Sages* was quick to make use of it here, and with good reason. *Posterior Analytics* is a work, I take it, on meta-logic. Its object is to discover and explain what logical demonstration or *proof* is—what was then taken to be the most certain form of knowledge. How do mathematical or logical proofs work? For Aristotle, and still to this day perhaps, they (very roughly) work as follows: you take a complex logical or mathematical formula and then break it down to its most basic components (axioms), such that they cannot be broken down any more. These axioms are then said to be self-evident; they require no further proof. We spontaneously, and immediately, *see* (says Aristotle) their self-evidence and indubitability. There is no further proof necessary, for instance, for the proposition that a buffalo is a buffalo: this is *intuitively* obvious, since it comes from a "first principle": the law of non-contradiction that cannot be broken down into more basic propositions, and which is also *intuitively* obvious. But where do these intuitions come from? Ultimately, Aristotle concedes in *Posterior Analytics*: "All teaching and all intellectual learning arises from pre-existing knowledge". The author of *Reconciliation of the opinions of the Two Sages* does not fail to notice how conciliatory that remark is to Plato's theory, and therefore sees in it alone grounds for thinking that Plato and Aristotle were, appearances to the contrary, in fact on the same page.

The author of the *Reconciliation* treatise also addresses what is perhaps the most striking difference between Plato and Aristotle which we also discussed in Chap. 2, regarding *essence*: Plato was thought to identify essence with transcendent, "supersensible" universals—ideas or forms. While Aristotle was thought to identify it with particulars, and that substance was a hylomorphism between essence and matter, here the author of the *Reconciliation* treatise offers this slightly gnomic explanation: the difference can be explained by reference to the context in which both authors discussed the matter. In Plato, he was discussing it in his metaphysical treatises such as the Timeous, whereas Aristotle was discussing it in his *physical* treatises such as the *Categories* or the *Physics*.

The author then makes recourse to the errant work circulating at the time *The Theology of Aristotle* (which we now know was in fact partly Plotinus' *Enneads*) to show how concerned Aristotle was with the transcendent world (the heavens) and that he accepted the notion of an immortal soul. Of course, we cannot use this work nowadays to support this interpretation; but we do know that Aristotle at least in his *Metaphysics* countenanced the idea of a God and of a superlunary world, made up of what he calls the fifth element. And so perhaps there is some scope to ask whether, had he posed the question regarding the essences of what constitute the heavens, he would have come to countenance a position closer to Plato's.

What is more worrying, though, is that the author of the *Reconciliation* treatise stops short of mentioning Aristotle's explanation of the fact that, as he put, "All teaching and all intellectual learning arises from pre-existing knowledge". He goes on to say in the *Posterior Analytics* that this pre-existing knowledge comes from what he calls experience. That is, I come to see a bunch of particulars (let's say a bunch of particular buffalo—James the buffalo, Kate the buffalo, Rowena the buffalo, etc.), and my memories of these buffalo constitute what Aristotle calls experience in this context. From this experience, we tacitly have the universal buffalo: we just need to apply our minds to our intellects to this experience to acquire the universal buffalo.

Perhaps this does not really solve the paradox of the Meno—for we can ask the same question raised there in our own experience. How do we know, when we look to our own experience, what the universal buffalo is, without already (non-t) knowing it? Though perhaps we could also levy this objection to Plato's own theory of recollections. In any case, this would not solve the apparent distance between Plato and Aristotle in terms of what they actually say (if not in terms of what they should have said).

But perhaps we could say that Aristotle's account of universal learning in the *Posterior Analytics* seems to be at odds with what he says about it with respect to the agent intellect in *De Anima*. Here it seems that Aristotle postulates the need for an agent intellect precisely *because* our imagination is incapable of grasping species, universals, essences via sense perception. That all we can get from sense perception are the mere phantasms of buffalo, not the species which they belong to. Perhaps, however, we can interpret things like this: experience of *several* buffalo in some level of potentiality carries with it certain universal(s), but the experience alone does not cause us to apprehend the universal(s). Some other agent then needs to be in place to activate our minds such that it apprehends them.

Emanation and the Active Intellect

One way to blend the works of the "Two Sages" was to argue that really they were arguing for the same treatise (as Porphyry had done in his *That the views of Plato and Aristotle are the same*). Another way was to offer a new theory that used aspects of both. While it is controversial that al-Farabi had engaged in the former project, there is no controversy around the claim that al-Farabi engaged in the latter.

I think the following are the constraints that al-Farabi thought any metaphysics and epistemology must meet (and which he of course inherited from the Greek tradition).

(i) **Meno's Paradox.** [The issue of how we can come to learn (some proposition) that p without already knowing that p].

(ii) **Aristotle's Third Man Argument**. [The problem regarding positing an individual, particular form/perfect instantiation of each of a thing's essence—since that particular perfect instantiation is a particular and so will be subject to a further particular perfect instantiation, and so on ad infinitum].

(iii) **The One Over Many Problem.** [This is the claim that there are abstract entities such as numbers that aren't reducible to particular instantiations. Frege later can be considered to espouse this doctrine in his anti-psychologism about maths and logic.]

So al-Farabi seems to accept all these three things as constraints that a metaphysics and epistemology must meet. In proposing a theory that aims to meet all these things, he can't but attempt to fuse together aspects of Plato and

Aristotle. In other words, none of Plato or Aristotle's theories, on their own, can meet all three constraints. We must either then either argue against one of the constraints, or else propose a new theory that will blend Plato and Aristotle. The theory will necessarily mesh the two, since two of the constraints are Platonic and one is Aristotelian—such that meeting all of them will mean taking on board both Platonic and Aristotelian ideas.

What al-Farabi does here is put together the Emanationist theory of Plotinus with Aristotle's ideas on the agent intellect in *De Anima*. Something like that was attempted by al-Kindi before him, but al-Farabi does so more explicitly and adds a twist, and by so doing is also more explicit about presenting his view as a *new* view, rather than a mere interpretation of the Greeks.

Here is how the system goes. As in the Plotinian system, we start out with the One, the First Principle of all existence. From this immutable One emanates, like a cascading, overflowing fountain, several other layers of existence. For al-Farabi, unlike Plotinus, there are nine other layers of existence, each corresponding to a chain in a hierarchy of heavens. One, intermediary heavenly layer, for instance, corresponds to Jupiter and the lowest one to the Moon. Each of these heavenly layers of existence is said to be spherical and translucent, such that light can pass through it, and corresponds to one of the nine planets. So one can imagine perhaps a shining star, marble-like object at the centre, which is then covered nine times over, like a Russian doll, with layers of translucent spherical objects. The sphere had of course long been associated with, been the symbol of, the heavens; the square was the symbol of the earth. An example of this is the columns at Durham Cathedral, which were designed so that if they were unrolled, as it were, they would form perfect squares—the idea being that by bringing squareness and circularity together you would put in the world a place where the heavenly and the earthly meet.

What is more important in al-Farabi is that each of these layers is made up of immaterial intellect. (We must not think of things like Jupiter and the Moon as material things for al-Farabi.) The first intellect, the One, is pure intellect. It has no external object of thought. It is thought thinking itself, pure intellect. But each intellect that is emanated from the One can have as its object of thought the intellect that is higher up the hierarchy than it; and each yearns to be back to the highest intellect from which it emanated, and after departure from our physical bodies begins its ascent back to unification with the One. The lowest level of intellect, that associated with the Moon, marks the frontier between the superluminal and the world of generation and corruption—this world. From this last intellectual layer, by now quite corrupted when compared with the original source, emanates the material world. I think that these ten layers are meant to explain how the pure intellect, itself immaterial, can emanate the material world. Having several sequences is supposed to help explain how the intellect could have become so corrupt; a little like how a copy of a copy of a copy of a cassette recording is much worse than the original. It is a bit as if the whole universe was once just one thing at a sort of Big Bang point, from which the one divided, and in a series of divisions became less like itself (less fundamentally one) and eventually turned into what we see as the material universe.

How is all this supposed to address the three constraints that al-Farabi sets out?

It addresses Aristotle's **Third Man Argument** like this. What was problematic about the Platonic picture was that it postulated a world of free-standing ideas: forms. But that world is just going to be a more perfect version of our world, inhabited by the perfect human, the perfect buffalo and so on. But then there could be a world that is a more perfect version of *that* world; and so on without end. Al-Farabi's picture has an end, the first cause, the One. And that's because the form and the ideas are not perfect and free standing but rather carried by, thought by, emanated intellects. Indeed, the phrase that al-Farabi uses for the intellect here is Giver of Forms.

Meno's Paradox is addressed like this: the last superluminal intellect at the frontier between our world and the heavens is the active intellect of Aristotle's *De Anima* 3.5. But, and this is the clever bit, the active intellect does not just illuminate our minds (as al-Kindi also held, in the sense that it turns what al-Kindi calls the "potential intellect" into the "acquired intellect"), but also brings form to the material world. So the active intellect switches on the material in our brains to bring about consciousness and the possibility of abstract thought; but it is also the intellect from which the form of the material world emanated. This means it is the intellect that actualises (switches on) our minds that also brings forms to the material world. So it is no surprise that we can know, from the armchair as it were, the form of a material thing (such as its genus) or the principles of mathematics—the indubitable axioms we spoke of earlier—which are the same principles that constitute and shape the fabric of the material world. Because al-Kindi's active intellect does not also give shape to the material world, it cannot explain why the abstract principles that we grasp in thought are the very same principles that govern the material world.

The One Over Many Problem is taken care of head on here, since al-Farabi accepts that there are abstract ideas. But it is just that for him, unlike for Plato, those ideas are not instantiated by perfect objects but rather are carried by emanated intellects.

Some commentators, such as Peter Adamson (2007a, b), have put emphasis on the Peripatetic aspect of al-Farabi's thought, in particular in virtue of the fact that he denies the instantiation of a Platonic world of forms. Others, however, such as Majid Fakhry, have emphasised the fact that al-Farabi makes use of the Plotinian Neo-Platonist schema, and that he is true to the one over many problem, therefore labelling al-Farabi a Neo-Platonist. However, I think it is fair to say, given all of the above, that the Farabian system overrides the Neo-Platonist–Peripatetic distinction.

Concluding Remarks

I am sure that al-Farabi's system looks pretty metaphysically extravagant today, but I hope I have done something to make it look intelligible to modern mindsets. As with Plotinus, there is a genuine question to be answered as to the relation between supersensible universals and our physical universe. Clearly, the theory about the heavens being made of see-through spheres now looks very antiquated—yet the three constraints his system is meant to respect denote issues for which there is not yet anything like a consensus solution. Further, what I take to be al-Farabi's most fundamental contribution lies with his overall meta-philosophical stance underlying this; that is, his move from al-Kindi's Evidentialism to his moderate Evidentialism. At the heart of this move is an interesting kind of epistemological fallibilism in al-Farabi's account of certainty. I have mentioned that he thought the Muʿtazilite theologians could not attain absolute certainty, and as such their method of inquiry was the lesser one over philosophy. This is the standard interpretative line, but I think it needs a minor reinterpretation: it is true that the theologians cannot really get knowledge, but then neither can most philosophers—only the prophets can obtain knowledge worth of absolute certainty. The crucial point, I think, is that the prophets turn out to be *philosophers*—but why? Because philosophy and not theology deals with *necessary* truths—timeless truths that transcend cultures and particular natural languages. We (philosophers) are not prophets, we cannot acquire real knowledge; but we can nonetheless acquire something resembling it. The more we reason like philosophers, the more our knowledge resembles that of the prophets. Yet the more this knowledge resembles that of the prophets, the more we, the subjects of knowledge, are able to communicate our knowledge and will be able to see how this knowledge is applicable in the "real" world.

But why cannot theology deal with timeless truths? The answer, a consequence of al-Farabi's moderate Evidentialism, is that the unique epistemic function of prophecy is to educate the epistemic non-elite to come to have beliefs at least approximating the truth, and it does this via the use of symbolism, rhetoric and allegory. Thus if there is any sense in which theology is different from philosophy it is that the former's and not the latter's object of study is these symbolisms. As we will see, this position ultimately both lands Falsafa in hot waters and is seriously misused in the hands of modern "extremist" thinkers. However, as we will also see in Chap. 8, the view is very fertile and can give us the seeds of a remarkably insightful Islamic response to what is wrong with extremist belief.

Study Questions

- Can we remove some of the metaphysical baggage in al-Farabi's Cosmology-Epistemology, replace it with more modern folk-physics and leave the system intact?
- Does Islamic moderate Evidentialism allow for prophecy to be both independently verified but have a unique epistemic function?

What to Read Next?

- Al-Farabi: *The Perfect State—Mabādi' ārā ahl al madīnat al-fādilah.* Translated by Walzer, R. (1985): *On the Perfect State* (Oxford: Oxford University Press).
- Fahkry, M. (2002) *Al-Fārābī: Founder of Islamic Neoplatonism* (Oxford: Oneworld).

Notes

1. Fakhry (2004, p. 111).
2. Such as Yahyá ibn 'Adī (893–974).
3. The prominence of Evidentialism perhaps inexorably had let to a movement in religious scepticism, in particular the writings of al-Sararkhsi (d. 1096), who called the Prophets "charlatans", and al-Rāzī (854–925).

4. This point is also made by López-Farjeat (2015), inter alia.

5. Matheson (2005), mistakenly I think, claims that for Goldman "dialectical superiority" just comes down to "rhetorical superiority"—but Goldman makes a clear distinction between what he thinks is dialectical superiority and what he (Goldman) calls "additional signs of expertise" that I'm calling (following Matheson) "rhetorical superiority".

6. This focus on certainty may be down to a mistranslation of episteme (the Greek word for knowledge) in the circulating Arabic translation of the *Posterior Analytics*, see Black (2006).

7. As translated in Black (2006, p. 17).

8. Knowledge that one knows.

9. Avicenna's famous 'Flying Man' thought experiment being a case in point here. We will discuss this in Chap. 5.

10. Very roughly *pro toto* reasons are conclusive reasons, while *pro tanto* reasons are not.

11. Translated in Black (2006, p. 27), with some of my own modifications.

12. The issue about whether God can know particulars is a heated one in Islamic philosophy. Al-Ghazali's fatwa at the end of *The Incoherence of the Philosophers* names the belief that God does not know particulars among the beliefs of the Falasifa, determining them as apostates. For discussion of Avicenna's claim that God can know particulars but in a universal way, and whether or not it escapes al-Ghazali's charge, see Adamson (2005). For a discussion of al-Farabi's, and his school's, take on the issue see Adamson (2007a, b).

13. The embedded quote from al-Farabi is from his *Book of Demonstration* Chapter 2, 23. 4–8.

14. Such as being in fake-barn country, full of barn facsimiles, and looking at the only one real barn.

15. He thinks he gets this holism from Aristotle: "If we wish to know the thing for which we ought to labor, we have to know the purpose of man and of the human perfection for which we ought to labor. This is why we are forced to know the purpose of the totality of the world; and we cannot know this without knowing all the parts of the world and their principles—we have to know that *what, how, from what,* and *for what* of the whole world as well as every one of the parts that make up the world" (Al-Farabi, *The Philosophy of Aristotle*, p. 80).

16. Thus al-Farabi says: "If … no use is made for him [the Prophet], the fact that he is no use to others is not his fault but the fault of those who either do not listen or are not of the opinion that they should listen to him" (Al-Farabi, *The Attainment of Happiness*, p. 49).

References

Secondary Sources

Adamson, P. 2005. On Knowledge of Particulars. *Proceedings of the Aristotelian Society* 105 (3): 273–294.

———. 2007a. *Al-Kindī*. Oxford University Press.

———. 2007b. Knowledge of Universals and Particulars in the Baghdad School. *Documenti e Studi Sulla Tradizione Filosofica Medievele* 18: 141–161.

Black, D. 2006. Knowledge ('*ilm*) and Certitude (*yaqīn*) in al-Fārābi's Epistemology. *Arabic Sciences and Philosophy* 16 (1): 11–46.

Deutsch, H. 1990. Real Possibility. *Noûs* 24 (5): 751–755.

Fakhry, M. 2004. *A History of Islamic Philosophy*. Columbia University Press.

Goldman, A. 2001. Experts: Which Ones Should You Trust? *Philosophy and Phenomenological Research* 63 (1): 85–110.

Leaman, O. 2009. *Islamic Philosophy: An Introduction*. Polity Press.

López-Farjeat, L.X. 2015. Al-Ghazālī on Knowledge ('ilm) and Certainty (yaqīn) in al-Munqidh min aḍ-Ḍalāl and inal-Qisṭās al-Mustaqīm. In *Islam and Rationality: The Impact of al-Ghazālī – Papers Collected on His 900th Anniversary*, ed. Georges Tamer. Brill.

Matheson, D. 2005. Conflicting Experts and Dialectical Performance: Adjudication Heuristics for the Layperson. *Argumentation* 19: 145–158.

Prichard, D. 2005. *Epistemic Luck*. Oxford University Press.

5

Avicenna and the Modality of the World

Introduction

We started this book by looking at the philosophical and historical under-pinnings of the Islamic faith and how they gave rise to Muʿtazilite theology, and in turn how that paved the way for the Islamic philosophical project. We then explored al-Kindi's philosophy: we saw how he fused some of the work of Plato and Aristotle; how he acted as rather a salesman for philosophy; how he conceived of the relationship between philosophy and prophecy; and how there was some sense in which he set the scene for the philosophers to follow, in particular with regard to putting together parts of Aristotle's *De Anima* on the active intellect with Aristotle's epistemological/meta-logical work *Posterior Analytics* and with bits of Plotinus' Neo-Platonism. I contend it is the particular way that the Falasifa handled this mix that makes their theories so fascinating. It is also, I suggest, what makes Islamic philosophy more germane to mysticism than is perhaps modern Western philosophy, as we will discuss in Chap. 6. However, this affinity with Islamic (Sufi) mysticism is mostly *doctrinal*— a consequence of a partial espousal of Neo-Platonist doctrine; the philosophical methodology undertaken in Classical Islamic philosophy is mostly Aristotelian, heavily reliant on the use of syllogism and *reductio ad absurdum* to contradiction, as such in sync with the style of con-temporary analytic philosophy. As we saw in Chap. 4, for instance, there is a sense in which al-Farabi is the very first analytical philosopher—emphasising the primacy of logic as an ideal language, and the importance of maths, in philosophical analysis (to illustrate further: al-Farabi thought that all

© The Author(s) 2017
A.R. Booth, *Analytic Islamic Philosophy*, Palgrave Philosophy Today,
https://doi.org/10.1057/978-1-137-54157-4_5

philosophers ought to do a propaedeutic—a preparatory class—in maths before going on to do philosophy). One of the interesting things about al-Farabi was that he, unlike al-Kindi, was forthcoming about the fact that there were points of at least prima facie divergence between Plato and Aristotle. And thus that there was philosophical work *still to do*— namely, that philosophy was not *just* history of philosophy (or interpreting the Greeks) but about actually thinking through the issues a priori and coming up with answers.[1] Again, this is in complete accord with the spirit of contemporary analytic philosophy. However, in al-Farabi's departure from al-Kindi's Evidentialism towards a modulated version of that doctrine, and in his account of absolute certainty (necessarily involving rhetorical and practical ability), his overall methodological commitments can be thought to deviate from that of contemporary analytic philosophy—for the former, unlike the latter, seems allow for the use of allegory as philosophy. However, as I will develop a bit further in Chap. 8, perhaps we can see this as an intermediate position, between the historicism of Western figures such as Martin Heidegger, and those who see analytical philosophy as a continuation of the ideals of the Enlightenment.

In this chapter we will look at by far the most influential of the Islamic philosophers, Abū ʿAlī al-Ḥusayn ibn Sīnā or Avicenna (as he was called by the Latin speaking Scholastics). Throughout this book, I refer to him as Avicenna, since he is so well known under that name. Avicenna takes on the same spirit of doing philosophy as does al-Farabi and is even more explicit about presenting his theories as original theories that depart from Aristotle—in his view for the better, and, again in his view, in a way that vindicates the truth of Islam. His innovations have turned out to be highly influential, and we see in his work some of the very first explicit accounts of how philosophical thought experiments come to have probative force, packaged together with a metaphysics of modality, and possibly the very first philosophical account of self-consciousness. However, although his account of prophesy is slightly different from al-Farabi's—underscored by his new work on modality—he is still an adherent of what I called Islamic moderate Evidentialism. As such, we can see some of his work as lying outside the purview of what we might think is traditional analytic philosophy. Some of his work is in the shape of allegory, and together with his commitments to parts of the Neo-Platonist doctrine, this work becomes extremely influential with the more mystical elements of Islamic thought. We will start looking briefly at his life story, before moving on to explaining some of his fascinating philosophical innovations.

Avicenna: A Very Short Biography

Avicenna was born circa 980 near Bukhara in present-day Uzbekistan. Bukhara was the capital of the Samanids, a Persian dynasty. Avicenna, then, spoke Persian, but of course knew Arabic, and wrote most of his works in Arabic. His father was a well-respected Ismāʿīli scholar (Ismāʿīlism is a branch of Shiite Islam). In his *Autobiography*, Avicenna tells us that he discussed Ismailism with his father's circle of Ismāʿīli scholars, but that he did not subscribe to their views. It has turned out to be controversial whether or not Avicenna was a Sunni or Shiite Muslim, but I will not dwell on the issue here, since his philosophy should stand up to scrutiny regardless.

I think it is fun to think of Avicenna as the Sheldon Cooper of his day. Sheldon Cooper, of course, is a character on the very popular (if perhaps overplayed) TV sitcom the *Big Bang Theory.*

Like Sheldon Cooper, Avicenna is not shy about praising his own intellectual capabilities and achievements. In his autobiography he frequently expresses how proud he is of what he considers to be innovative breakthroughs that he has achieved. Also like Sheldon Cooper, Avicenna had an eidetic memory. He is said to have memorised the entire Koran by the age of ten. He tells us that by that age "I had completed the study of the Koran and a major part of the Arabic letters so much so that people wondered at my attainments."[2] Like al-Farabi, Avicenna had to travel around quite a lot to get patronage from various rulers. He would not then have access to the works of philosophy he was engaging with—but this was not a problem for Avicenna, since he was able to work from those texts via memory alone.

Like Sheldon Cooper, Avicenna puts a lot of emphasis on *independent* thought. As we have already mentioned, Avicenna was keen to present his work as *new* work—not as mere *interpretation* of what had gone before. He was not very forthcoming about acknowledging the influence of work of others on his work. Historically speaking, it is probably significant that Avicenna did not—like al-Farabi before him—belong to a particular school (such as the Baghdad school). Overall he did not seem to see philosophy as a collaborative enterprise—though he does praise al-Farabi's intellectual attainments, and is perhaps more indebted to them that he likes to acknowledge.

Like Sheldon Cooper, Avicenna had a prodigal intelligence. He started learning medicine when he was 16, and apparently mastered what material was then available by the age of 18. His work *The Canon of Medicine* is taken to be a very important work—and was a required textbook in medicine at the universities of Montpellier (in France) and Leuven (in Belgium) as late as 1650. He regards medicine, however, as "easy" and philosophy to be the hard stuff, more worthy of his full attention. No doubt, Sheldon Cooper has a similar attitude in regard to the difference between, say, geology and physics. Most of the philosophy we will look at in this chapter is in his huge compendium *The Healing* (*Al-Shifā*), and in particular his books on metaphysics and psychology.

Unlike Sheldon Cooper, however, Avicenna had a reputation for liking womanising and wine. A lot has been made of this fact (unsurprisingly, by his Islamic detractors). Though it seems that his liking for wine was mainly down to his thinking that a bit of wine was good for medicinal purposes and that it would help him stay up at night such that he could be as remarkably productive as he in fact was. It is well known that he's supposed to have died (in 1037) of (I quote) "having too much sex". One of his students, in another biographical account,[3] tells us that Avicenna had self-prescribed himself to abstain from sex—but that he had been unable to do so. However, the idea that he could have died of "having too much sex" regardless of what he had prescribed for himself has recently been shown to be—to use one of Sheldon Cooper's favourite phrases—complete hokum. A recent article in the journal *Arabic Sciences and Philosophy* by J. Lameer shows the account to have been a sixteenth-century forgery.

Whatever the details of his life, however, it is undoubtedly the case that Avicenna has been one of the most influential philosophers of all time. When the famous Ashʿarite theologian al-Ghazali a century later writes his attack *The Incoherence of the Philosophers* he has almost exclusively Avicenna as his target—the implication being that if you bring down Avicenna, you bring down *all* the philosophers. This should give us some indication as to the esteem in which Avicenna was held. Indeed, the fact that theologians felt the need to seriously refute the work of the philosophers shows how Avicenna much more so that al-Kindi and al-Farabi had managed to put philosophy on the map as a serious contender to be *the* intellectual pursuit of Islam. Averroes, whom we will discuss in Chap. 7, wrote a trenchant response to al-Ghazali's attack—*The Incoherence of the Incoherence*. But here he sought to show that Avicenna had deviated from the true path of Falsafa, in having moved away from the true interpretation of Aristotle. That is, argued Averroes, al-Ghazali's attacks might go against Avicenna, but they leave not a scratch against Falsafa properly conceived as properly Peripatetic philosophy.

But ultimately Averroes was not to leave much of a mark on Islamic philosophy—though he was tremendously influential in Latin medieval Europe. Yet that is probably not to say that al-Ghazali had managed to "kill off" Falsafa and Avicenna's influence. Still to this day, Avicenna is studied in

Muslim universities as a living breathing philosopher—relevant to today.[4] Avicenna is seen really to embody Falsafa—and later thinkers keen to inaugurate a new kind of Islamic philosophy see Avicenna as their central adversary. Avicenna is probably the only philosopher to have made a huge impact not only on the Islamic philosophical tradition, but also on the Jewish and Christian, Western philosophical traditions. And his work, particularly with respect to the innovations he made in modal logic and its relationship to metaphysics, are relevant to the Scholastic metaphysics, to Leibniz, Spinoza, and Descartes, and to the work of more recent contemporary metaphysicians such as Tim Williamson, David Lewis, and E.J. Lowe.

We will discuss Avicenna's metaphilosophy and his take on the relationship between prophesy and philosophy shortly. Let us however first explore his metaphysics, since this very much informs his overall methodological stance.

Essence and Existence

The term "modality" in metaphysics refers to the ways or *modes* in which things may exist, in particular in respect of the following: necessity, contingency, possibility, impossibility. For example, we might think that the *way* in which we exist is that we exist contingently, since we might not have existed. Or we might think that the way in which a prejudice-free world exists is *possibly*, since it *may* come to be even though it does not currently exist. Now, Aristotle's conception of modality is what is sometimes called a frequentist or statistical view of modality.[5]

Necessity$_{\text{frequentist}}$ A state of affairs (or object) x is necessary iff x occurs or exists eternally. It is contingent if it fails to occur or exist eternally.

Possibility$_{\text{frequentist}}$ A state of affairs (or object) x is impossible iff x never occurs or exists. A state of affairs x is possible if it occurs or exists at any time t (where t can denote a future time).

This is rather a "flat" view of modality.[6] I think there are at least two problems with this account. First, we might think that things that have never existed nor will exist *might* have existed, and so are possible. Likewise, we might think that think that some state of affairs that has never occurred nor will ever occur might nevertheless still be *possible*. For instance, we might think that is was *possible* for Jones (a lazy but clever student) at the age of 18 to have attained an 'A' grade at A-Level history had they worked a little harder.[7]

However, once we know it will *never* happen, perhaps the idea that it is *impossible* is not so strange. As Aristotle puts it in his *Metaphysics*: "It is not allowable that it is true to say 'this is possible but it will not be'" (9.4 1047b).[8]

Second, and more importantly, it does not seem to easily fit with Aristotle's account of essential properties and what he calls "accidents", since it tells us what it is for *objects* or *states of affairs* to be necessary/contingent and possible/impossible. We might modify the account such that it deals with properties, however:

P-Necessity_{frequentist} — A property F is necessary of an object a iff F obtains with respect to a eternally. It is contingent if it fails to obtain eternally.

P-Possibility_{frequentist} — A property F is impossible of an object a iff F never obtains with respect to a. A property F is possible of an object a iff F obtains with respect to a at any time t (where t can denote a future time).

The problem with this modified account—with respect to necessity—is that we might think that there are essential properties of things that may perish. For instance, humans have an essential property (being rational, say) even though humans may well become extinct. We can modify the account even further to deal with this.

*P-Necessity_{frequentist} — A property F is necessary of an object a iff F obtains with respect to a so long as a exists. It is contingent if it fails to obtain so long as a exists.

This appears to be a more promising account, but notice that it gives us a *disunified* account with respect to what makes *properties* necessary/contingent and what makes *objects* and *states of affairs* necessary/contingent.

In order to provide a more unified account "taken care of by one science", Avicenna ingeniously reverses the order of explanation. That is, he thinks that we ought to understand modality in terms of essence/accidents and not the other way round.[9] His account looks something like:

Necessity_{Avicenna} — An object a necessarily bears property F iff F is an *essential* property of a.

Possibility_{Avicenna} — It is impossible for an object a to bear properly F iff a's essential properties are incompatible with the obtaining of F with respect to a. It is possible for an object a to bear property F iff a's essential properties are compatible with the obtaining of F with respect to a.

Now, notice how this account still seems to tell us about what it is for *properties* to be modal. It does not tell us about the modality of *objects* and *states of affairs*. This is where Avicenna draws his famous Essence–Existence distinction, holding (surely correctly) that from the fact that *F* is an essential property of *a* nothing follows with respect to whether or not *a* exists.

> It is evident that each thing has a reality proper to it—namely, its quiddity. It is known that the reality proper to each thing is something other than the existence that corresponds to what is affirmed. (Avicenna—*The Healing (Metaphysics)* 1.5 10.25—28

Nevertheless Avicenna, incredibly ingeniously, tries to show that from *this account* of modality (and not from the predication of any individual modal property) we can derive the modality of objects in general, and of every individual object. As such, his account gives us the unified account we were looking for. And, incidentally, it will give us an argument for the existence of God.

The argument goes as follows. The essences of things do not determine whether or not they exist. What does determine whether things exist is whether they are *caused* to exist. So, in and of themselves, the objects in the world *thought of as* the set of all things that exist, exists (in itself) *contingently* since it may not have been caused to exist. Here the *property* of existence is contingent with respect to whether it is rightly predicated on the objects of the world. But we know that there is a universe (set of all things) and not nothing. So we know that something caused the universe to exist. What is the modal status of that cause? Does it exist contingently or necessarily? If it exists contingently, it would have to have been caused by something else, *ad infinitum*—"and if it regresses infinitely, the existence of the possible, with all this, would not have been specified by it. As such, its existence would not have been realised" (*Metaphysics* 1.6 6.38–40). So in order to avoid this regress and so explain why there is something other than nothing we have to get to a cause (an object) that is not contingent by its very essence. So that there is *one* object or one kind of object whose essence *guarantees* its existence—what Avicenna calls the "necessary existent", which he of course means to identify with God.[10]

Now, if (in itself) the set of all objects is contingent *because* it may not have been caused to exist, it follows that the existence of the set of all objects is actually *necessary* (though not in itself but "necessary through another" as Avicenna puts it), since we know that they *have* been caused to exist by a cause that necessarily exist. This means that every individual object *necessarily* exists. This follows from what we in more modern times call the "Converse Barcan Formula":[11] if it is necessary that everything is *F*, then everything is necessarily

F ($\Box \forall x \varphi \rightarrow \forall x \Box \varphi$). In other words, that if it is necessary that everything exists, then every object exists necessarily. And so we have arrived at an account of the modality of objects (and state of affairs, derivatively): if something (or some state of affairs) exists (or obtains) then it exits (or obtains) *necessarily*. If something (or some state of affairs) has been caused not to exist, then it is *impossible* for it to exist.

This is the view that is these days called necessitism. It is nowadays a reasonably popular view among metaphysicians.[12] Whatever its philosophical virtues, however, the view seems to yield an advantage particular to an Islamic (and broadly theistic) context, and Avicenna was quick to pick up on that. A problem facing Falsafa and its commitment to an Aristotlelian epistemology was that it seemed to claim that the best kind of knowledge is knowledge of universals (or necessary truths), as per the definition of "demonstrative proof". Since God's knowledge is the best kind of knowledge, it seems to commit Falsafa to the potentially heretical claim that God cannot know particulars (contingent truths). The advantage of necessitism then is that everything is necessary after all, and so eligible for God's knowledge. This may be what Avicenna means by the claim that "God knows particulars in a universal way".[13]

For all its ingenuity and its many advantages, Avicenna's position does look vulnerable to the following issues. First, I think we can ask whether his essence-existence distinction problematically depends on the idea that only properties admit of modality. This is because we can describe properties as states of affairs: *John's being tall,* or *Amanda's being strong.* Indeed, some have argued that "states of affairs, and only states of affairs, can adopt such modalities"(Reinach 1911, p. 339), such that properties (or objects) cannot be bearers of modal properties. One might retort that the objection is merely verbal: Avicenna can easily reformulate and claim that only states of affairs involving properties can be modal. But that will not really help Avicenna, since actually *all* states of affairs involve properties—note the difference here between the proposition <that there are stars> (which seems to involve no properties) with the state of affairs *the stars' existence* (which does involve properties). However, perhaps Avicenna could reply that all he wants to do is deny that *objects* have modal status in and of themselves. He can admit that *the existence of objects* is a state of affairs, and if the denoted property is a necessary property, objects can necessarily exist. That is different from the claim that objects, qua bare particulars, are necessary—it is the property of *existence* that gives them their modal status. So perhaps what Avicenna is really saying is that the predicate *existence* denotes an accidental and not an essential property in everything except God—only the latter has *existence* essentially. Existence may yet be a necessary property of other objects, but not because of *their* essence—but still it is *essence* that determines their necessity, albeit the essence of *another* object. However, we may still complain that the claim that nothing except God bears the property *existence* essentially is not something that can be established simply by the essence–existence distinction, so construed. For instance, just from the fact that bearing the property redness is essential to something's being red, it does not follow that there is no further essential property to something's being red that guarantees that it exists.

Second, correlatively, we might wonder whether other beings than just God have an essence that guarantees their existence. Or, put differently, if we are minded to identify necessary existents with God(s): why can there be only one God (as per the theology of Islam). Avicenna tackles this issue head on in chapter seven of his first book of the *Metaphysics* of the *Healing* subtitled *That the Necessary Existent is One*. Avicenna here argues as follows: suppose (for *reductio*) that there are *two* necessary existents x, y. If there are, then there must be some property F that explains (causes) the difference between them, such that they are two things and not identical. As such, x's existence *qua* something different from y must be *caused* by that property F (and vice versa with respect to (and vice versa with respect to y). And then x cannot exist (not can y) simply out of its own essence—it is *caused* to exist *qua x different from y* by F. The reasoning is ingenious, but perhaps we can reply by asking whether x *qua necessary existent* needs to be Fx (that is, as an x *different from y*). Put differently, we can think that two objects are identical *qua* bearers of the property of necessary existence, but different *qua* (say) buffalo: one is a very hairy one and the other is not, but both exist necessarily. As buffalo they are different, but as necessary existents they are identical. Further, as with Neo-Platonist Emanationism, the account sits awkwardly with Islamic dogma, in so far as it posits that God as the necessary existent *necessarily* and not out of an act of gratuitous goodness creates the world.

These issues notwithstanding (and perhaps they can be addressed), Avicenna's metaphysical necessitism will yield an interesting modification to al-Farabi's epistemology and account of prophesy.

Avicenna on the Active Intellect and Prophesy

Let us again remind ourselves of the Aristotelian account of the active intellect. Recall that the issue comes about because Aristotle wants to maintain a parallelism between his account of perception and his account of intellection. When we intuit, or conceptually grasp essences, our experience is best described perhaps as an intellectual seeming, an intellectual perception in our mind's *eye*. As we have previously pointed out this idea has been defended in recent years, by the Yale philosopher George Bealer (1996). The contrasting view to the idea that intuitions are like perceptions is that they are like *beliefs* or judgements, or propensities to believe or propensities to judge (Williamson 2007). Bealer asks us to consider, for instance two Müller-Lyer lines.

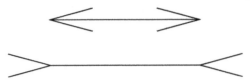

The bottom line *appears* to be the longer line. But the lines are actually exactly the same length—it is a perceptual illusion that the two lines are of a different length. The important point for Bealer here, though, is that once we know that the two lines are of the same length, the perceptual illusion persists—the lines still *appear* to be of different lengths, even though we believe that they are not. So the perception cannot be identical to our beliefs about the lines.

Now, continues Bealer, intuitions have a similar feature. When we intuit that something is the case, the intellectual *seeming* that ensues persists even if it is the case that we come to think that the intuition is leading us astray. Bealer here uses the example naive set theory: it seems intuitive to us to think that any definable collection is a set. But if we have read the work of Bertrand Russell, we know that this seemingly innocent claim leads to contradiction and paradox. So we come to believe that naive set theory is false, but we cannot shake off the intellectual seeming that it is true each time we consider whether any definable collection is a set. In that respect then intuition behaves more like perception, and not like belief.

With this thought in mind, it seems to me that Aristotle's wanting to maintain a parallel between intellection and perception is not indefensible. His account of perception—as we mentioned earlier, a sort of early representationalist account—should also sound relatively defensible to modern ears. Avicenna invents a term for this faculty of intuition in Arabic: *Ḥāds*.[14] And Aristotle's account has this great feature to it that we have not yet mentioned—it seems to answer the sceptical concern about how we can have cognitive access to the external world. The answer is that the phenomenal form of objects gets transmitted through matter and causes our sense-apparatus to *take the form of* the object. In some sense then the perceiver and the object perceived become *one* thing in the act of perception. Thus there is nothing mediating (and so potentially acting as a distortion) between the world and the subject. As we will see shortly, Avicenna develops this thought (and so goes beyond interpreting Aristotle) in interesting ways.

Where Avicenna seems to agree most with Aristotle is that the reason why an active intellect needs to be posited is that when we intellectually grasp universals or essences there is nothing in the world that those abstract objects correspond to. Surely, as al-Farabi also noted, we need to posit these universals to evade Plato's One Over Many problem and not commit ourselves to the kind of rank psychologism that Frege later rallied against. But what is the ontological status of these abstract entities? They clearly do not exist in this world like other kinds of object do. We cannot bump into π, for instance. So what are we grasping when we grasp them? Plato argued that they are transcendent Forms—ideal versions of things in the world. But that still leaves the problem of how those Forms come to cause in us intellectual sensation. And of course we can add to that the famous third man problem. So this is why we need to posit this active intellect—an immortal intellect that is all Forms in actuality and acts as an agent—to switch our minds from merely having the potential to grasp Forms to actually grasping them.

Here two important questions present themselves. And they are questions that came up for al-Kindi and al-Farabi which I think that Avicenna takes up in his *Psychology* book of the Healing.

The first question is this: are *we* not in some sense the *agents* of the change between our potentially grasping and actually grasping an essence? Correlatively, while we might agree that belief is involuntary, our imagination surely voluntary. You can at will decide to imagine that you can fly, in a way that you cannot at will believe that you can fly. So what is the role of the imagination in intellection?

The second question is this: how does Aristotle square this reliance on the active intellect with his emphasis on an empiricist theory of knowledge—namely, that we come to know essences through experience, through our knowledge or particulars?

Avicenna's answers are ingenious. Recall that the forms our sense-organs take when they perceive material objects are mere phantasms or phenomenal forms—the physical *appearance* of a buffalo, for instance. Essences are not imprinted upon us at this stage, since essences need to be grasped intellectually (or at least they are only imprinted upon us as potentialities). We need these experiences, which then get imprinted in memory, in order to *prepare*, says Avicenna, the human intellect such that it is in a state where it is ready to receive the agency of the active intellect Without having the phenomenal impression—the phantasm—of a buffalo or of a house, we cannot ever hope to grasp what the essences are of either buffalo or houses.

But we also, claims Avicenna, need the imagination here to do some preparatory work. We need to be able to imagine a house without a roof or a

reptilian buffalo in order to understand what the essence of a house or a buffalo is. Our imagination, unlike belief, is under our voluntary control and it
is up to us to set up our intellects through our imagination and experience
such that we are able to receive the agency of the intellect, and for us to be able
to see abstract entities and essences. Our imagination and experience act like
the material through which the forms in perception travel (e.g. changes in air
pressure, light etc.) to have a causal effect on us. This is why Avicenna and al-
Farabi denote this as the "*material* intellect". Avicenna here uses the analogy
of light. To illustrate, suppose you want to view the *Mona Lisa* in the Louvre.
You visit the Louvre but the lights are switched off. Before you visited the
Louvre, you did not have the potential to view the *Mona Lisa* easily. Now that
you are in the Louvre, opposite the *Mona Lisa* in the dark, you do have that
potential. All you need is the lights to come on. That is how Avicenna sees the
role of the imagination, setting things up intellectually so that all that you
need in order to intuit the particular object is for the lights of the active intellect to come on. But these lights are on in perpetuity—so all you are responsible for is how you set up your intellect, and whether you have set it up in
such a way that it can receive the forms (analogously, whether you have set
yourself up in the Louvre such that you can see the *Mona Lisa*). That is why it
seems to us that all we need to do in order to grasp essences is to both experience and exercise our faculty of imagination—because once we have done
that correctly we automatically receive the forms. But receiving the forms is
not voluntary—it does not come from us; our true inspiration comes from
the outside.[15]

This marks a departure from al-Kindi's account of the active intellect.
Recall that for al-Kindi, the active intellect actualises the mind from the
state of being properly *potential* to a quasi-potentiality: the acquired intellect. Once the mind has been actualised into an acquired intellect, the
mind can *at will* grasp essences—our minds are the agents of us actually
thinking. But what the account leaves unanswered is how the active intellect actualises the potential intellect such that it is an acquired intellect,
and how it is (given that belief is involuntary) how it is that *we* are the
agents of the final connection with the first intellect (in al-Kindi's termi-
nology). In Avicenna's account it is *us* through our voluntary control of
what we experience and imagine that sets us up to being in a state where
connection with the active intellect is possible and at that point we run out
of voluntary control.

"Re-intuition"

What Avicenna is doing here is using the ideas of Aristotle but innovating in making them more defensible. In a similar vein though, he addresses another problem not addressed by Aristotle. The problem is something like this: suppose that today I intuited that Gettier cases are not cases of knowledge. I intellectually grasp this fact—I can see it with my mind's eye, as it were. But suppose I then fall asleep and stop thinking about it for a few days. A few days later I think about Epistemology and come to "re-intuit" Gettier cases, *at will*. This seems possible. What explains this? Avicenna's answer is that once I have grasped the essence of something, I can at will *retrieve* it from the active intellect. That is, I know how to configure my mind at will such that it will receive the form. This gives Avicenna another reason for why we should posit the active intellect—that it serves as a universal library, or storage space, from which we can download essences and abstract objects. So Avicenna gives the active intellect some further explanatory role than does Aristotle—it explains how we can re-intuit things we have already intuited.

Active Intellect Qua Giver of Forms

Avicenna seems, then, to cherry pick the best bits of philosophy that is available to him and adds bits of his own, much like how the '90s rock band Oasis used to "write" their songs—warping the best bits (as they saw it) of classic rock bands into a new product. Avicenna also cherry picks some parts of al-Farabi in combination with the theory of the active intellect we have just been discussing. Here he borrows al-Farabi's ideas that (a) the active intellect is the carrier or bringer of forms—and this is where the harmonisation of Plato and Aristotle really gets some traction (that is, we still posit forms, universals, so that we do not violate the one over many problem, but we do not posit them qua ideal entities so that we do not fall prey to the third man argument). Further, (b) that the active intellect is *both* what illuminates the abstracta in the human mind *and* is that from which forms are emanated into the natural order. This explains why there is an identity between the forms we intuit from the armchair and the forms that shape and give structure to the natural world. What Avicenna adds to this is that the matter in the world somehow needs to be prepared, like the human mind, such that it is capable of receiving forms—that is why water, for instance, cannot ever be made into a sofa, say (not in its liquid form anyway).

Avicenna, like al-Farabi, also uses this epistemology to give a quasi-naturalistic account of what prophecy is. For Avicenna, prophecy occurs when in particular human minds are so well prepared for receiving the deliverances of the active intellect that they almost receive it too strongly. And so the light shined in by the active intellect overflows and shines a light into what would otherwise seem unconnected and trivial matters. This overflowing makes the prophet better able than ordinary people to explain the complex truths of the world in more simple, ordinary terms. Another reason is tht they then see the connection between things better, are also blessed with some pre-cognitive insight—the prophets can sometimes tell the future.

The prophet, then, not only has perfect *theoretical* knowledge, he also has immense *practical* and *rhetorical* ability—an ability to explain the complex truths of the world in ways that the public can understand, via images and stories. This enables Avicenna, as for al-Farabi, to endorse Islamic moderate Evidentialism and account for prophecy's unique epistemic role, assuming that there are members of the public for whom it is acceptable to come to believe for reasons that will fall short of giving them demonstrative proof and absolute certainty.

Avicenna spends (compared with al-Farabi) little space discussing ethics and political philosophy. He does discuss these subjects, however, in *The Healing (Metaphysics)* where he expounds the al-Farabian idea that the proper political leader is what he calls the "prophet law-giver" amid an Aristotelian account of the human good. Avicenna also gives an account of prophecy in the psychology book of *The Healing*.[16] The main difference between al-Farabi and Avicenna on prophecy, is that for the latter, new knowledge can be the product of prophecy, whereas for the former prophecy can only really facilitate *understanding* knowledge that one already has (and this understanding renders the justified true beliefs items of certain knowledge, since they now satisfy strict KK conditions).[17] The reason for this difference is due to the emphasis Avicenna gives to the role of the imagination in knowledge, and correlatively, both his necessetarianism, and a kind of "priority monism" that follows from it.

Priority monism is the view that there is only *one* truthmaker to all the true propositions there are (assuming that every true proposition has a truthmaker).[18] According to Avicenna, everything that exists is either a necessary existent, or caused by a necessary existent. So everything is explainable by reference to the necessary existent, which (as we saw) Avicenna argued was *one* thing. Since all truths ultimately have the *same* truthmaker, they are all in a sense ultimately connected up. Further, since they are all *necessary*, an incredible faculty of imagination will enable the bearer to work out—a priori —

truths about the actual world (not just about universals). That is, the prophet's ability will enable him to attain knowledge that the ordinary person could not get—his special ability does not just change the *mode* in which the prophet knows (as al-Farabi held). This is also what underwrites the prophet's precognitive insight. These truths may be beyond the ordinary human's ken, but they are not *unknowable* by humans as such. They would be known on the attaining of relevant empirical evidence. This means that prophetic claims are always verifiable, at least in principle, so are not in principle *esoteric*. This, as we will discuss further in Chap. 6, may provide an explanation as to how there can both be proof of prophecy but yet prophecy retain a unique epistemic function (aside from its rhetorical function with respect to the epistemic non-elite). For now, though, I want to discuss some of the other things that Avicenna is famous for: his argument for the immateriality of the soul, and the epistemic role of self-knowledge.

Self-Consciousness and the Flying Man Argument

On the Identity Between Object and Subject in Perception and Intellection

As we mentioned earlier, Avicenna rejected the Aristotelian idea that in perception or intellection the object of knowledge and the subject become the same thing. But the idea had the nice advantage of staving off scepticism about our knowledge of the external world. So Avicenna had better have a good argument against it, and some better way of dealing with scepticism. Fortunately, I think he does go some way towards both those ends.

His argument against the object/subject identity, made in his *Psychology* book of the *Healing*, is really rather simple, for all its surface complexity. Effectively, the thought is simply this: if the form delivered through the matter of the thing perceived turns me into it, then the thing that I have become has a causal history (i.e. me before I turned into the thing perceived) that the thing I have perceived does not share. In other words, if I'm turned into the thing perceived, it's conceptually ruled out that I am identical with what the thing was before I turned into it. On the contrary, we (it and I) have come into existence as something new. As such then, Aristotle cannot have solved the issue with respect to scepticism about our knowledge of the external world—since what we were looking for was an account of how we can know the object of perception qua objects *prior* to their putative transformation in perception.

What is more interesting, however, is Avicenna's own answer to the sceptical problem. And here he really does anticipate Descartes by some 600 years. We do not know for sure whether Descartes read any of the Islamic philosophers, but we can be sure that he read the Scholastic philosophers who did very explicitly make heavy use of them—particularly in the case of Thomas Aquinas. Descartes, of course, tries to dissociate himself from all Scholastic thinkers, clearing the deck (as it were) for his putatively new philosophical method, but this does not mean he did not read Scholastic philosophy, nor that he was not influenced by it. Descartes' certainty and KK requirement on knowledge are already of course in al-Farabi, and what he is most famous for, his use of self-awareness as a means of answering the sceptic and establishing mind–body dualism in his cogito argument, are already in Avicenna (I believe, perhaps controversially), though Avicenna approaches the matter slightly differently.

Avicenna thought that for *ordinary* objects of intellection there is no identity between subject and object. *But* there *is* identity between subject and object in one special case: the case of self-thought, self-awareness. And that is because when you grasp your own thought in reflection, your thinking the thought and the thought *do* share the same history, they *do* share the same properties. So in this reflexive act you can come to have this kind of perfect knowledge where the object and subject of intellection are the same thing. Thus, you can know that there is at least one thing that really exists: you. There can be no illusion about this fact. Descartes came to a similar conclusion: that the only thing that I can know for certain is that I exist; as he famously put it: "I think therefor I am".[19] From a historical point of view though, I think it is interesting to note that Avicenna's work looks like the first place where we see this emphasis on self-awareness which then occupies so much of modern Western philosophy.

What is also interesting is how Avicenna uses the idea of self-awareness to argue for mind–body dualism. Or, more accurately for him, body-soul dualism. For him, like al-Kindi and al-Farabi before him, the soul was immaterial. But he uses a fun thought experiment together with some of the developments he had made in modal logic, and this emphasis of self-awareness to concoct a novel thought experiment designed to at least partly convince us of the truth of the thesis. Avicenna is one of the first philosophers to really recommend the use of thought experiments, and that is because of the role he thought the imagination played in preparing the intellect to receive the agency of the active intellect.

The thought experiment goes like this (prepare your self to be zapped by the active intellect!): the guiding question here is: is the "I" that accompanies all your desires, hopes, dreams, perceptions, intellection—what Kant later called the "transcendental unity of apperception"—that is *you*, in the body or is it in an immaterial soul?

So now imagine that God created you spontaneously in mid air as a grown adult. You are not wearing any clothes and are blindfolded. Your fingers are also configured and spread out in such a way that they cannot touch each other. The point is that you cannot receive any external stimulus. A better, modern way of making the point would be to imagine yourself being brought into existence already as an adult into a sensory deprivation tank. At this point you have had *no* single sensory, physical experience. The question is: is it conceivable that you are nonetheless self-aware? Our intuition—the active intellect zapping us—seems to be that it is conceivable. If it is conceivable, then it is at least metaphysically possible for the "you" of your soul and the body to come apart—that is, for you to exist as a bodiless spirit. This has two important results: that you are *directly aware* of your own existence, and that it is at least conceivable that the "I" is a bodiless spirit.

We should be careful to note that Avicenna is explicit that he does not mean the flying man argument to be read as his giving conclusive proof of body–soul dualism. And that is probably because of what he has said about the concept of modality—that for a proper Aristotelian, modality really concerns investigation into essential properties. We will not know whether the "I" really is a bodiless spirit through *simply* running these imaginative thought experiments. However, by engaging our imagination in this manner, we at least begin to prepare our minds to actually grasp the truth. This is why Avicenna really thinks of this thought-experiment as what he calls a "pointer"— part of the process for preparing the intellect.

Concluding Remarks

As we will see discuss in Chap. 6, Avicenna's identification of God with the necessary existent was to prove difficult to swallow for the many of the Islamic philosophers and theologians who followed Avicenna. The idea that God creates the world necessarily was, in particular, incompatible with the newly dominating (in the late tenth-century Islamic world) Ash'rite theological school. And Avicenna's ideas fanned the ire of the most famous Ash'rite thinker, al-Ghazali, who in his *Incoherence of the Philosophers* ultimately issues a fatwa against many of Avicenna's teachings. Not only that, Avicenna's whole underlying methodology, premised as it was on the Evidentialist idea that prophesy's proof was to be found in reason, was ultimately deemed *kāfir* by al-Ghazali. This is because, as we will discuss, it seems that al-Ghazali was not ultimately satisfied with Avicenna's account of how prophecy could nevertheless be epistemic unique (sophisticated as Avicenna's underpinning account of modality was). In the next chapter we will explore al-Ghazali's competing account of the relationship between philosophy and prophecy, embedded in what we will call: anti-Evidentialism.

Study Questions

- Is Avicenna's account of modality really an improvement over Aristotle's?
- Does Avicenna's account of how prophecy works do better with regards to respecting the epistemic uniqueness of prophecy than does al-Farabi's account?

What to Read Next?

- Goodman, L. 2005: *Avicenna* (Ithaca: Cornell University Press).
- Avicenna: *The Healing (Metaphysics)—Al-Shifā (al-Ilāhiyyāt)* (Translated by Marmura, M.E. 2008: *The Metaphysics of the Healing*) (Provo: Brigham Young University Press). (Book 1).

Notes

1. Though like al-Kindi he *also* follows the Peripatetic and Neo-Platonist tradition of writing commentaries on the works of Plato and Aristotle.
2. In Avicenna's *Autobiography*.
3. Reisman (2013).
4. For example see the prominence of Avicenna (Ibn Sina) in the curriculum at the department of Islamic philosophy of Ankara University: http://divinity.en.ankara.edu.tr/?page_id=449
5. Hintikka (1973). Hintikka also calls this the "principle of plenitude".
6. The more modern view that is rather *de rigueur* in analytic philosophy involves thinking about "possible worlds": some object (or some state of affairs) exists necessarily if it exists (or obtains) in *all* possible worlds, or at least all the *close* possible worlds (worlds that resemble our world); something is possible if it

exists (or obtains) in at least some close possible worlds and something is impossible if it exists (or obtains) in none of them (cf. Lewis 1973).

7. Adamson (2016, chapter 17).

8. Conway (1984) for discussion.

9. Since essence and accident look also like modal properties, the definition is not going to be fully non-circular, a point which Avicenna takes on the chin: "It may also prove difficult for us to make known the state of the necessary, the possible, the impossible through ascertained definition, and we would have to make this known only through a sign" (*Metaphysics* 1.5 22.32–34) and "none of these things can be shown by proof totally devoid of circularity or by the expression of better known things"(*Metaphysics* 1.5 15.18–19).

10. The famous Dutch philosopher Spinoza seems to use this argument for the existence of God too. For discussion see Douglas (2015, chapter 3).

11. Named after the famous philosopher/logician Ruth Barcan Marcus (1921–2012).

12. In particular, see Williamson (2015) who characterizes the proponent on the view as claiming: "The pieces of the puzzle are given, however they are rearranged" (2015, p. 1).

13. See Adamson (2005) for an excellent account of this.

14. Though Avicenna seems to think that this faculty is not available to everyone.

15. As Dag Hasse puts it: "Avicenna appears to combine two incompatible concepts in one doctrine: either the intelligible forms emanate from above or they are abstracted from the data collected by the senses, but not both" Hasse (2001, p. 39). I hope to have shown how Avicenna was successful in doing so.

16. For discussion see McGinnis (2010, chapter 8).

17. As Herbert Davidson puts it: "Avicenna likewise recognizes, and attaches the name prophecy to, knowledge that results when the emanation from the active intellect—or another supernal being—acts on the human imaginative faculty. But as an extension of his view that man receives intelligible thought directly from an emanation of the active intellect, he, unlike Al-Farabi, recognises, and names as prophecy, genuine theoretical knowledge imparted by the active intellect to the human intellect without the human intellect's having to employ standard scientific procedures" (Davidson 1992, p. 117). Fazlur Rahman makes the distinction by calling revelation of new knowledge "intellectual revelation" and revelation bringing understanding to existing knowledge "imaginative revelation" (Rahman 1958, p. 36).

18. For a modern defence of priority monism, see Schaffer (2010). His is a secular version of the thesis, according to which the *one* truthmaker is the world taken as a whole.

19. In his 1637 *Discourse on Method*.

References

Secondary Sources

Adamson, P. 2005. On Knowledge of Particulars. *Proceedings of the Aristotelian Society* 105 (3): 273–294.

———. 2016. *Philosophy in the Islamic World. A History of Philosophy Without Any Gaps.* Vol. 3. Oxford University Press.

Bealer, G. 1996. A Priori Knowledge and the Scope of Philosophy. *Philosophical Studies* 81: 121–142.

Conway, D. 1984. 'It Would Have Happened Already': On One Argument for a First Cause. *Analysis* 44: 159–166.

Davidson, H. 1992. *Alfarabi, Avicenna, and Averroes, on Intellect.* Oxford University Press.

Douglas, A.X. 2015. *Spinoza & Dutch Cartesianism: Philosophy and Theology.* Oxford University Press.

Hasse, D.N. 2001. Avicenna on Abstraction. In *Aspects of Avicenna*, ed. Wisnovsky. Princeton University Press.

Hintikka, J. 1973. *Time and Necessity: Studies in Aristotle's Theory of Modality.* Oxford University Press.

Lewis, D. 1973. *Counterfactuals.* Blackwell.

McGinnis, J. 2010. *Avicenna.* Oxford University Press.

Rahman, F. 1958. *Prophecy in Islam: Philosophy and Orthodoxy.* Allen & Unwin.

Reinach, A. 1911. On the Theory of Normative Judgement. Trans. Barry Smith 1982. *Parts and Moments: Studies in Logic and Formal Ontology.* Philosophia.

Reisman, D.C. 2013. The Life and Times of Avicenna: Patronage and Learning in Medieval Islam. In *Interpreting Avicenna: Critical Essays,* ed. Adamson. Cambridge University Press.

Schaffer, J. 2010. The Least Discerning and Most Promiscuous Truthmaker. *Philosophical Quarterly* 60: 307–324.

Williamson, T. 2007. *The Philosophy of Philosophy.* Blackwell.

Williamson, T. 2015. *Modal Logic as Metaphysics.* Oxford University Press.

6

Anti-evidentialism and Al-Ghazali's Attack on Falsafa

Introduction

Islamic philosophy is often divided into two historical periods: what happened before al-Ghazali (up to and including Avicenna), what Peter Adamson for example calls the "formative period", and what happens afterwards. In Chap. 1, we looked at how the dominance of the Muʿtazilite theological movement contributed towards creating an intellectual environment where Falsafa could flourish. By around 1063, however, this dominance was in trammels, the intellectual environment in the Islamic world at somewhat of a crossroads, and a new theological school was beginning to take dominance. This was the Ashʿarite school we also discussed briefly in Chap. 1. The Ashʿarites' most famous thinker was undoubtedly Abū Ḥāmid Muḥammad al-Ghazālī, who is sometimes referred to as the most important Muslim after Muhammad. As we discussed in Chap. 1, the Ashʿarites' take on the ethics of belief was the antipode to the Muʿtazilites', with their holding what we called anti-Evidentialism. And this anti-Evidentialism also inevitably led to a collision with Falsafa—and nowhere do we see this reflected more than in perhaps al-Ghazali's most famous work, *The Incoherence of the Philosophers (Tahāfut al-Falāsifa)*, which contains, in its last pages, a *fatwa* levied at certain Falsafa teachings and overall philosophical methodological principles. But al-Ghazali's acceptance of anti-Evidentialism was not an un-calibrated one. The issue as to how to discern genuine prophets from counterfeits remained a seriously live one for al-Ghazali, and one that unmodulated anti-Evidentialism could not solve. So, just as I have argued, the central motif of Falsafa was to moderate Evidentialism, al-Ghazali's overall methodological stance was to modulate

© The Author(s) 2017
A.R. Booth, *Analytic Islamic Philosophy*, Palgrave Philosophy Today,
https://doi.org/10.1057/978-1-137-54157-4_6

anti-Evidentialism to finally endorse a position I will call moderate anti-Evidentialism. I think that this position encapsulates his weaving together of the best parts (as he seems them) of Sufi mysticism, Ashʿarite theology, and also (once put in their place) the works of the Falasifa. This of course led to Averroes' famous complaint that al-Ghazali was something of a fair-weather thinker: "a Sufi with the Sufis, an Ashʿarite with the Ashʿarites, and a Philosopher with the Philosophers".[1] But I hope this chapter will demonstrate how ingenious al-Ghazali was in synthesising these positions in his moderate anti-Evidentialism. As usual, we will begin with a few biographical and historical details, before exploring al-Ghazali's methodological commitments in his moderate anti-Evidentialism. Here we will take some time to discuss Sufi themes that come up in his work, and in the philosophical mysticism that becomes very important. Finally we will look at the *fatwa* that al-Ghazali issues and his philosophical case against the three teachings mentioned in it: that the world is pre-eternal, that God does not know particulars, and that there is no bodily resurrection at the Day of Judgement.

Al-Ghazali: A Very Brief Biography

Al-Ghazali was born in 1056 in present-day Iran—so like Avicenna he was Persian. He died on the memorable date of 1111. North-eastern Iran had, at around the time of his birth, seen the persecution of the Ashʿarites. But, by 1063, that persecution had ended. As we discussed in Chap. 1, after Muhammad, the Caliphate had passed from his closest followers to members of his extended family, and then to the Umayyad and Abbasid dynasties. The Arab empire was in disarray by the middle of the eleventh century when the Seljuk Turks (originally from central Asia) came on the scene with a vengeance. The Seljuks at this time conquered Persia, Iraq (capturing Baghdad in 1055), Syria, Palestine, and the Hijaz (including Mecca and Medina). It is probably significant—in terms of the historical influences on al-Ghazali's thought—that it was in part the break-up of the Arab empire during this time that emboldened Christian Europe to embark on its first crusade in 1096. The taking of Jerusalem, for instance, in 1099 by the Christian Knights of the first crusade must have made it seem as if Islam was under fresh and serious attack.

It is not straightforward to explain why Seljuk rulers came to be sympathetic with the Ashʿarite theological movement (as this kind of historical matter never is). But the fact is that they were. Perhaps they too, like the Abbasids before them, were keen to make their dynastic rule culturally distinctive—and in their view superior—to their rivals' and to what there had been before.

They probably wished to see themselves as heralding a new cultural age, better in tune to the true religion. As such, the Ash'arites would have fitted the bill rather well in respect of those ends, if they were indeed their ends. Recall the central difference between what Ash'arite theology and Mu'tazilite theology considered to be the first principle through which we should understand the faith:

Mu'tazilites: God is One. God is Just.
Ash'arites: God has untrammelled, inscrutable omnipotence.

It is important to note here that the Ash'arites did not mean to deny the unity or justice of God. Nor did the Mu'tazilites wish to deny God's untrammelled power. The two theses are not in that sense incompatible. God could be just, indivisible, and all-powerful. What's at issue is a matter of *emphasis*— what is the guiding principle that should colour how we interpret the text, and, in particular, that should determine whether we take a text figuratively or literally. Again, if that principle can be taken from the Koran taken literally, that's surely going to give proponents of that principle a certain dialectical advantage when it comes to the determining which interpretation is the most *Koranic*.

And an interpretation that can *start off* with a literal interpretation is surely going to find it easier to make the case that it is the more interpretation that is more true *to the Koran*.

In any case, for whatever reason, the Seljuk Turks did support the Ash'arite cause. They founded, or supported the founding of, a series of schools called madrasas of Ash'arite theology. Al-Ghazali studied in one of these madrasas in Nishapur (north-eastern Iran). Here he was taught by one of the great Ash'arite theologians, al-Juwaynī (al-Juwaynī had himself been taught by the founder of the Ash'arite movement—Abū al-Ash'arī).

Al-Ghazali later became head of the famous Niẓāmiyya madrasa in Baghdad (in around 1091—shortly before the first crusade) and from here wrote perhaps his most influential work: *The Incoherence of the Philosophers* (around 1095).

The Three Sources and Moderate Anti-Evidentialism

Al-Ghazali's intellectual work drew from three sources:

(a) Ashʿaritism
(b) Falsafa, and in particular logic.
(c) Sufism (mysticism).

Let's begin then by reminding ourselves of the overall contours of Ashʿarite theology, which may explain why al-Ghazali was so drawn to it.

As we have just discussed, the central prima facie difference between Ashʿarite and Muʿtazilite theology is their relative emphases on the power of God, and on the unity and justice of God. As we discussed in Chap. 1, this made Ashʿaritism germane to a kind of Occationalist metaphysics—according to which God is the proximate cause of every event—even though it might not seem to us that it is. There is a passage in the Koran that is meant to support this, where God has arranged the world with regularity to make it easier for us to navigate—but there is no need for the world to be as it is, God could easily have made it otherwise. As we also mentioned, it meant that the Ashʿarites had to invent quite a sophisticated compatiblism concerning free will and determinism, to make room for God's justice.

There may be a more fundamental difference between the two schools of thought that underscores and explains the sundry theological differences. That more fundamental debate concerns this question: do beliefs constitutively aim to represent the world such that correct belief is one that represents the world as correct, and is thus true? Or are beliefs correct or incorrect in virtue of other properties than their being true or false?

As we discussed in Chap. 1, the Muʿtazilites held an occurentist view about the metaphysics of belief, and this led directly to their Evidentialism:

Evidentialism   A subject S's belief that p is justified iff S has sufficient evidence that p.

One of the central advantages of this normative thesis is that it makes it easy to see how one might determine true from counterfeit prophecy—namely, the evidence will tell us, since the true prophet will not utter falsehoods. But the problem, as we have seen, was that Evidentialism has a hard time respecting the epistemic uniqueness of prophecy. This led the Falasifa (al-Farabi and Avicenna) to endorse a modulated kind of Evidentialism:

Islamic Moderate Evidentialism: For *some subjects* S (the epistemic elite) and for all propositions p, S ought to believe that p iff S has sufficient evidence that p.

This meant that for the epistemic non-elite it is permissible (or even required) that one believe on non-epistemic grounds, and on the basis of reasons that will fall short of providing the subject with *demonstrative proof*. That is, they are allowed to believe on the basis of allegory and rhetorical ploys, which are not really indicative of the truth. Prophecy maintains its epistemic uniqueness, under this picture, by providing the epistemic non-elite such non-epistemic reasons for belief.

This issue mirrors a standing debate in meta-ethics: do our moral judgements aim to represent the world (just that they are correct iff they do so veridically (as cognitivists and realists in ethics maintain)? Or are moral judgements just expressions of approval or disapproval toward certain actions or state of affairs? In other words, is what makes moral judgement correct that it veridically represents some moral facts out there in the world, or (as expressivists such as Hume held) are there some other non-truth-related criteria—such as being part of a system to which overall adherence makes us happy, or cohering with religious dogma—by which we determine their correctness?

The alternative doxastic metaphysics, as we mentioned, then might be what one might call a broadly behaviourist or pragmatist conception. According to this conception, to believe that *p* is simply to be disposed to *act* as if *p* is true. And from this picture of what is a belief, we get an accompanying normative account of what makes belief *correct*. This is anti-Evidentialism.

Anti-Evidentialism: S's belief that p is justified iff S has non-epistemic reason to believe that p.

For the Ashʿarites, the relevant non-epistemic reason was a voluntaristic one as one would find in divine command theory. That is, to the question "Why should I believe that p?" the answer is "for all subjects and all propositions: because God *commands it*". God's *will* is ultimately the source of all normativity, with respect to what we ought to do, and what we ought to believe.[2]

But the trouble is, in the context of trying to determine what is the proof of prophecy: how do we determine what is God's *will*? Or, put differently, how do we know that a putative piece of prophetic text really is a prophetic text (the mechanism through which we can know God's will)? This issue is an especially relevant one for Islam, given that it counts among its sources of prophecy not only the Koran as revealed to Muhammad, but also the Hadith—a collection of sayings and accounts of the practices of the Prophet collected after the death of Muhammad. How did we come to determine the accuracy of these accounts?

The traditional (and Hanbalite) view was that the Prophet was to be distinguished by his performing miracles, testimony of which was passed on through tradition *(tawātur)* and, further, by his perfect moral character and behaviour. This issue is especially problematic for the Ash'arites, given their *anti-Evidentialism*, since they had to be forced to reject the traditional view, and in particular the idea that the sign of true prophecy is at least partly to be found in the perfection of the Prophet's character and behaviour. The latter is to admit that there is a source of moral normativity that exists independently of God's will, anathema to the Ash'arite world-view. And, further, the Ash'arite view seems also to have a problem with appealing to miracles, not only because of the inherent difficulties in identifying proper miracles (as opposed to sheer trickery),[3] but also because the appeal to the performance of miracles as a means of verifying the true prophet from the impostor is to appeal to good *evidence* for the veracity of the prophet's claim. And this is to accept that God's will is not the ultimate source of *doxastic* normativity (grounding what we *ought to believe*), and as such to renege on anti-Evidentialism. Perhaps, in view of this, the Ash'arites could restrict their voluntarism to matters concerning the normativity of action, and not extend it to belief. But this generates inconsistencies with other with other Ash'arite doctrines, such as the idea that belief is really an action, or to be evaluated in terms of behaviour or behavioural dispositions, and thus obviating the Ash'arite confrontation with Mu'tazilite theology.

It is this problem that makes later Ash'arite thinkers such as Fahr al-Dīn al-Rāzi (1149–1210) and, especially, the great Imam al-Ghazali (1058–1111) diverge somewhat for the traditional view. I think al-Ghazali's view amounts to what I will call *Moderate Anti-Evidentialism*: the view (as we shall see) that for all propositions p, except one very special proposition, p should be believed because God wills it. As with the general *anti-Evidentialist* line here, the view is that even if God commands us to believe in accord with our evidence, it is—ultimately—God's will that is the source of doxastic normativity. The view here is that one ought to believe this special proposition *just because* the evidence supports it, such that the evidence itself is normative.

Moderate Anti-Evidentialism: For all except one proposition, S ought to believe that p for non-epistemic reasons.

Al-Ghazali's summarises his position very succinctly in this claim of his (in his work *Moderation in Belief*, the title of which also sums up the view he aims to articulate):

The obligation to believe with one's tongue and heart is an act, like other acts, that can be founded on probabilistic evidence. (Al-Ghazali *Moderation in Belief* p. 210)

Two things are going on here, I suggest. The first is that in line with Ashʿarite anti-Evidentialism, the normativity of belief is held to be no different from that of action.

The second is the claim that both obligation to belief and action then *can* be founded on evidence. That is, the having of evidence that p can make it— just on its own—the case that one is obliged to perform certain actions (or have certain beliefs, which are for al-Ghazali a certain kind of action). And this is where we see the influence of (b) Falsafa (above) play a role.

Now, al-Ghazali wants to maintain that prophecy has a unique role, and yet maintain that the legitimacy of the prophets has an evidential base. He attempts to do this, it seems, by holding that a good portion, *though not all* (e.g. not theoretical knowledge about what happens in the afterlife) the *theoretical* claims of prophecy are available by consulting independent evidence. Further, *no* practical knowledge is available independent of knowledge of prophecy. This means that we *can* ascertain the prophet's legitimacy by:

- Finding verisimilitude between the theoretical claims of the prophet and what our evidence indicates;
- Finding that the prophet not only asserts truths, but does so sincerely (his assertions are not true accidently).
- In practical matters, seeing that following the practical rules of the prophet leads to their desired effect, namely to "purify our hearts".[4]

In practical matters, however, what we gain is really *theoretical* knowledge about the effect of the prophet's works. As the prominent contemporary scholar of al-Ghazali Frank Griffel (2004) shows, al-Ghazali's account with respect to the prophet being sincere is heavily based on Avicennan psychology, where different modes of mental representation are enumerated, and sincerity is thought to consist in coherence between what is mentally represented to *A* and what *A* asserts. Once we have verified the prophet's trustworthiness (*ṣidq*) on these evidential grounds, we then ought to believe and act on the basis of what the prophet tells us is the will of God. That is, the source of both the normativity of belief and action is ultimately the will of God.

Now, Griffel thinks that this account neatly gets the Ashʿarite position out of jail, since it "does not violate the [Ashʿarite] principle that there is no normative practical knowledge independent from revelation" (Griffel 2004,

p. 142). However, it seems a bit *ad hoc* to maintain that the Ash'arites thought that only *practical* normativity, and not doxastic normativity, has its ultimate source in revelation. Further, it is clear, as the quote above from *Moderation in Belief* shows, that al-Ghazali wants to (rightly, in my view⁵) conflate doxastic and practical normativity. So I think al-Ghazali's position is really to concede that there is one piece of normative knowledge that can be gained independently from revelation. This normative *blind-spot* is belief in the proposition that the prophet is a genuine prophet. The evidence for this proposition *alone* makes it the case that one *ought* to believe it. But once one believes this proposition, the normativity of *all* other beliefs (as well as actions) is ultimately determined by the will of God. This is the case even if the prophet mandates that one ought to believe in accord with our evidence, since what makes this latter obligation normative is the fact that God wills it—the evidence alone is not normative. This is why I think the position is a kind of *moderate anti-Evidentialism*—it affirms that *all but one* propositions ought to be believed just in case God wills it.

Al-Ghazali famously gives us a "universal rule" for knowing when to interpret the Koran allegorically or literally. And this "universal rule" is part and parcel of what I have called his moderate anti-Evidentialism. He claims in several works that a passage of the Koran—when taken literally—says something that is in plain contradiction to epistemic reason (theoretical knowledge that yields proper certainty

("demonstrative proof"), then it should be taken allegorically. As al-Ghazali puts it in *Moderation in Belief,* a work attempting to moderate the competing claims of reason and prophecy:

> Regarding what reason deems impossible, if it is reported in the revelation, it must be interpreted metaphorically. It is inconceivable that the revelation contains what is conclusively contrary to reason. (p. 210)

The reason it is "inconceivable" that prophecy goes against reason is that revelation's containing propositions contradicting certain theoretical knowledge would put into jeopardy our grounds for believing in the veracity of the prophet. In his *The Incoherence of the Philosophers* he charges the Falasifa with apostasy as regards *some* of their beliefs. These are the Falasifa's beliefs, according to al-Ghazali, that amount to holding that the Koran must be taken allegorically, but where the Falasifa fail to have the demonstrative proof that shows that they should. Al-Ghazali looks to be engaged in what some Philosopher's call "Imminent critique" whereby one shows one's opponent's position to be unstable, or self-defeating.

This amounts to unbelief and apostasy for al-Ghazali, rather than mere mistake, or innovation, and subject to the death penalty, since it hamstrings (under the interpretation just canvassed) the support for the proposition that the prophet is a genuine prophet. Mistakenly claiming that a theoretical truth in the Koran is to be interpreted allegorically and not literally would:

(i) block the possibility of demonstrating that the proposition as literally interpreted is supported by our ordinary non-prophetic evidence; and
(ii) violate the normative principle that we ought to believe (for all propositions bar the proposition that the prophet is legitimate) on the basis of God's will, and not on the evidence alone.

Where does al-Ghazali's avowed Sufism come in, however? I think it concerns the nature of the evidence that is supposed to verify the prophet's legitimacy. Epistemic reason leading to demonstrative proof is not ruled out by, al-Ghazali, but he thinks there is an even more superior form of evidence, the test of which is "the purification of one's heart". And this extra-superior form of evidence can only be attained by engaging in Sufi practise. Let me now say a little bit about Sufism before re-engaging with al-Ghazali's position.

Sufi Mysticism

Sufism seems to predate Islam in so far as there were *mystical thinkers* before the advent of Islam. For example, we know that there were Byzantine mystics and there is a strong sense, as we have discussed already, that Plotinus was more a mystic than a philosopher—though whether these two things are in opposition is very much an open question, especially for the more philosophically minded Sufis that come after al-Ghazali (notably, Ibn al-ʿArabī and the poet Rumi[6]). The term "Sufi" is most commonly interpreted to mean wool, denoting the simple woollen cloak worn by the early Sufis—a symbol of asceticism, and a belief that there is a higher reality that the one found in this world of generation and corruption. Sufis consider their practice to be supererogatory—beyond the call of duty—such that Muslims are not *required* to be Sufis. According to Sufis, in Muslim prayer one's inner (one's private thoughts, roughly) and outer life (one's behaviour) are in harmony with each other and with the Real—that there is no *real* self, only unity with God and with "others". This is an expression of the priority monism we discussed in Chap. 5— that everything is connected through a higher unity—and is given the famous term unity-of-being (*waḥdat-al-wujūd*) by Ibn al-ʿArabī. But Sufis aspire to achieve this symmetry between the inner and the outer at *all times* and not just during prayer. This is obviously no mean feat, the person who attains this is called by Rumi the Perfect Man—and as such is one reason why Sufism is supererogatory.

Central to Sufism is the idea that there truths that are in some sense *ineffable*. Where by "ineffable" is meant something like "beyond theoretical reason", or something that "cannot be put into words".[7] Examples of such truths may include:

- Truths about what things *feel* like, such as what it feels like to see read. To illustrate by way of Frank Jackson's famous thought-experiment,[8] a colour-blind neuroscientist (Mary) with complete knowledge of physics and neuroscience comes to *learn* something new on re-acquiring the ability to see red, and experiencing it for the first time.
- Truths that can only be *shown* not said. For example, the fact that the *Mona Lisa* is a painting is not somehow expressed *in* the painting as part of the pictorial depiction of her. Rather, the picture *shows* the fact that it is a picture in being a picture. Roughly this kind of thought is behind Wittgenstein's famous say-show distinction in his *Tractatus Logico-Philosophicus*.[9]
- Truths about some the *significance* of things, aside from their *semantic value*. We might here compare the difference between the way a young teenager may understand and assent to the proposition <everyone dies> with the manner in which a War veteran may understand and assent to the same proposition.[10]

The idea then is that if there are such ineffable truths, then we cannot reach them through the use of theoretical reason—they cannot be *cognized* but only "tasted".[11] To help understand things we might use Russell's distinction between knowledge by description and knowledge by acquaintance.[12] The former is the sort of knowledge we acquire by learning how a thing is described: I come to know something about Baghdad by learning that it is the capital of Iraq; or a I come to know something about Fatima by learning that she has green eyes. Knowledge by acquaintance is defined negatively: it is the sort of knowledge about something that we *cannot* acquire by learning any description of that thing. Our knowledge of the ineffable, under this picture, is knowledge by acquaintance—it is knowledge that is "tasted". So to taste these truths one must not merely do Philosophy *qua theoretical activity* but also but engage in dance, music, poetry, literature, meditation, love, recitation of God's names, all with the aim to "cleanse one's heart". As we will discuss very briefly in the next chapter, the famous Aleppo philosopher-Mystic Suhrawardī (1154–1191) calls this "Knowledge by Presence".[13]

To give a slightly more complete picture, let me now try to give a broad overview of some of the central quasi-poetic motifs in Sufism: *The One; the Heart; the Curtain and the Mirror; the Circle and the Return.*

The One

At the heart of Sufism—similarly with Neo-Platonism—is the idea that God is One and indivisible (*Tawhīd*). As with Neo-Platonism, this means that nothing can really be said *about God* and all most be passed over in silence. And as with Falsafa the upshot is that God does not really *create* the world (in some gratuitous act of will) but rather we *come* or *emerge* from him, as does the whole world. As such, we were once part of the One, and ultimately deeply long to return to it. Rumi uses the imagery of the wailing reed flute to capture this—the read flute's song being a sad one or yearning[14] to return to the reed it was cut from enabled by the "breath of the merciful" (to use one of Ibn al-ʿArabī 's famous phrases).[15]

The Heart

For Sufis, because we apprehend, ultimate reality through taste rather than theoretically, we come to have knowledge of this ultimate reality through *love* so via the *heart.* We know God when our hearts are "purified"—purified from the shackles of the ego, the sense that we are really distinct individuals. With the ego comes fear, greed, jealousy, pride: these things stand in the way of our knowledge—that is, love —of God.

The Curtain and the Mirror

The ego is often compared to a curtain, concealing God. In order for that curtain to be lifted, we need to "polish" the mirror that is our hearts—remove the rust (the ego) which is preventing the mirror from reflecting. So lifting the curtain we find a reflecting mirror that enables God to know himself. We are created so that God may know himself, and knowing ourselves is ultimately knowing God (knowing himself).

The Circle and the Return

Recall our brief discussion in Chap. 4 that the circle has long been thought of as a symbol of the transcendent, and of what is eternal. For Sufis, if one travels along a circle one will necessarily follow stages: a descent, and an ascent. These symbolize our descent to our world of generation and corruption, and our ascent when we return to communion with God. We do this once our souls are liberated from their bodies or when one's intellect connect with the Active Intellect according to Falsafa, but with Sufism this happens (besides death) through the various Sufi meditative *practices* and the return can symbolize the person carrying them out successful to return and teach the un-initiated, as a *Sheykh*—a Sufi Master.[16]

We can know return to al-Ghazali's account of the proof of prophecy. Very famously, al-Ghazali, while head of the Niẓāmiyya madrasa suffers a sort of existential crisis, whereby he looses the ability to speak. He writes in his autobiography titled *Deliverance from Error*:

> For nearly 6 months [beginning July 1095], I was continuously tossed about between the attractions of worldly desires and the impulses toward eternal life. In that month, the matter ceased to be one of choice and became one of compulsion. Allah impeded my tongue so that I was prevented from lecturing. One particular day I would make an effort to lecture in order to gratify the hearts of my followers, but my tongue would not utter a single word nor could I accomplish anything at all. (Al-Ghazali *Deliverance from Error* p. 50)

The thing that seemed to be troubling him was the notion of *demonstrative proof* and scepticism. As we have discussed already: for Aristotle, it was necessary for something to be properly *demonstrative* that it be the conclusion of a sound and explanatory logical syllogism the middle term of which is a first principle grasped by *noûs*. To simplify, I think we can ask this question: what is a mathematical or logical *proof* for Aristotle? And the answer seems to involve the Foundationalist idea that we should break up complex formulae into their most basic (foundational) constituents, or axioms, that we can just *see* or intuit with our mind's eye and that we cannot doubt. It seems irrational to doubt that 1 + 1 is not three, or doubt the truth of the law of non-contradiction. We just intellectually see that they are *obviously* true. But if, following Aristotle, intellection involves a kind of perception (this intellectual *seeing* with the mind's *eye*), then this sceptical problem presents itself: ordinary perception sometimes deceives us, as when we see a crooked stick in the water, or when we see an oasis in the dessert, when there isn't one. How do we know that my intellectual perceptions are not prone to similar illusions? And if we cannot know that, then how can we know that for any particular intellectual perception that it is not an illusionary one? In short, how can we determine for any instance of intellection whether it is veridical or not?[17]

As we will discuss in more detail shortly, al-Ghazali had questioned whether Avicenna had rightly thought that there was demonstrative proof for the claim that the universe is pre-eternal. But Avicenna thought that he had grasped a first principle in his arguments for, say, the claim that there must be a necessary existent. And he had declared it apostasy—and so subject to the death penalty—for a Muslim to come to believe such a claim. It surely must have crossed his mind then, given the incredibly high-stakes: but what if *mine, al-Ghazali's* intellectual faculty has led me to intellectually see something that is really a mirage? How could al-Ghazali be *absolutely certain* that his intellectual faculty was not deceiving him, as his senses had deceived him previously? In the absence of an immediate answer, al-Ghazali suffers this episode of epistemic angst. He leaves Baghdad and resigns his prestigious post, ambulating around Syria and Palestine for about two years, taking a pilgrimage to Mecca, studying and practising the "Sufi way", the early stages of which seem to resolve the crisis for him:

> This malady was baffling and it lasted nearly two months. During that time I was a skeptic in fact, *but not in utterance and doctrine.* At length Allah most high cured me of that sickness. My soul regained its health and equilibrium and once again I accepted the self-evident data of reason and relied on them with safety and certainty. But that was not achieved by constructing a proof or putting together an argument. On the contrary, it was the effect of a light which Allah cast into my breast. And that light is the key to most knowledge. (Al-Ghazali *Deliverance from Error* p. 11)

So how was it that through Sufism, al-Ghazali was able cure his anxiety-making scepticism? It seems to me that al-Ghazali ingeniously brings together *part* of the Ash'arite doxastic metaphysics with Sufism.[18] So he agrees with Ash'aritism that having an inner representation of the world is not *sufficient* for belief. But he disagrees with them that it is not *necessary.* Otherwise put, a *full* belief that p, where one is certain beyond skeptical doubt that p, requires *more* than just the inner representation of the world. It requires the right kind of non-cognitive engagement with the proposition as well. Recall the difference we mentioned between the *manner* in which a teenager believes the proposition <everyone will eventually die> and the *manner* in which a war veteran does. The teenager and the war veteran's belief have exactly the same propositional (representational) content: <everyone will die>, the difference in their beliefs is something non-cognitive, or non-propositional, it is about the *way* they engage in the proposition, beyond mere assent. We might think, for example, that the teenager does not really understand the *significance* of the truth of the proposition, or we might think that the teenager does not have the requisite concomitant emotions or feelings—feelings that cannot properly be described in propositional form (so hard to put into words). To summarise: full belief does involve propositional content (inner mental representation), but it involves more than that, it involves a non-cognitive, emotional engagement with the proposition that is hard to put to words, that grounds our certainty in the proposition, and without which it ceases really be a *conviction*.

From this doxastic metaphysics (this account of what belief *is*), normative consequences (about what we *ought to believe*) follow. According to al-Ghazali, it is that there is a higher level of demonstration than that attained by Aristotelian syllogistic demonstration—one that goes beyond mathematical proof, and ordinary empirical proof.

> Beyond intellect there is yet another stage. In this another eye is opened, by which he beholds the unseen, what is to be the future,[19] and other things which are beyond the ken of the intellect. (Al-Ghazali *Deliverance from Error* p. 58)

But this demonstration is arrived at non-cognitively, and so only available via a kind of experience that one "tastes" (not cognizes) through one's *heart*. We can assent to true propositions, but we can't truly know them—that is, know them beyond sceptical doubt—without an accompanying non-cognitive engagement with the propositions. And we can *only* engage with propositions in the correct manner—a manner that will assuage any sceptical worries—when we have had the right kind of experience. Experience we can only attain via engagement with Sufi practise.[20]

It is for al-Ghazali ultimately this kind of "evidence" (experience through Sufi practice, and that will lead to the purification of one's heart) that can vindicate the veracity of a prophet's claims. And once we properly know that the prophet was the True Prophet, we can "accept the self-evident data of reason". But the grounds of our acceptance will have changed, in the sense that what makes it the case that we *ought* to believe in line with epistemic reason is that *the Prophet commands it*. And since the belief that the Prophet is the True Prophet has propositional content[21] (albeit necessarily accompanied with non-propositional content), that belief cannot be in opposition to our ordinary evidence. So what the Prophet says cannot be in opposition to epistemic reason, and so the "test" al-Ghazali provides us with for determining when to take the prophet's word literally or metaphorically remains. And, neatly, it also tells us where to moderate any inclinations toward Sufi excess—such as the claim that one has become God—since once we know the prophet is the right prophet, we can with certainty use revelation to guide us as to when our mystical ecstasy is taking us too far.

The obvious complaint is: but how do we know—beyond sceptical doubt—whether we are having real as opposed to facsimile *mystical self-vindicating* experience? For example, people tell us that when we are *really* in love we will "feel it in our bones", but often people think they felt love "in their bones" but end up realising they were mistaken. But note that al-Ghazali here is not seeking to *prove* that there is such a thing as genuine prophecy, or proving that it is necessary. His theory would predict that he cannot do so simply in writing. Rather, he is merely stating the conditions under which he thinks prophecy is possible, given the constraints that it must have a unique role, and that its legitimacy must be ascertainable by humans.[22] As such, holding a kind of exceptionalism in respect of the proof of a prophet's legitimacy need not be considered *ad hoc*.

However, one may wonder whether there is something indeed *ad hoc* about al-Ghazali's *moderate anti-Evidentialism* when combined with his test for determining when revelation is to be treated allegorically. Recall that the test requires us to determine—with certainty—that a given proposition is (logically speaking) worthy of demonstrative proof. It is only when a passage in the Koran is in tension with a demonstratively proven proposition that we may treat that passage metaphorically and not literally. But Sufi experience gives us the grounds for believing that the prophet is genuine, and then the normative grounds for believing in accord with logical demonstration. But this does not—in a non-ad hoc way—tell us whether a particular putative demonstration is beyond sceptical doubt.

The *Fatwa*

As we observed above, at the end of his *The Incoherence of the Philosophers* al-Ghazali famously issues a *fatwa* on the philosophers, or, more preciously, on three of the philosophers' teachings—as well as their overall methodological stance. By "philosophers" it is important to add that al-Ghazali actually means Avicenna. Some contemporary scholars (notably Frank Griffel) think it is important to note that it is a mistake to translate *Tahāfut* as "incoherence" as it usually is.[23] Primarily, I think the word is translated like that to bring out the fact that al-Ghazali aimed to show that he was taking on the philosophers on their own terms—that their teachings failed to live up to their own criteria—in other words, that he wasn't merely going to beg the question against them. However, the translation also makes it seem as if al-Ghazali was aiming to reject philosophy wholesale. And this, according to scholars such as Griffel, does not seem to have been his intention (although I think we should make some important caveats to this, as I will shortly discuss); his explicit intention was to draw up the overall contours of what Islamic science should be all about, and thus what can be considered consistent with proper Islamic science and what cannot be. Philosophy is then to be situated within Islamic science—some of it turns out to be useful and legitimate (i.e. in accord with Islamic science) and some of it turns out not to be. We should wholeheartedly embrace, according to al-Ghazali, philosophy as conceived as consistent with his rules, but we should reject philosophy in so far as it departs from them. The word *Tahāfut*, suggests Griffel, is better translated as "tripping up"—this captures better al-Ghazali's aims to merely show where the philosophers have gone wrong, not to reject the whole enterprise of philosophy. Nevertheless, it is also important not to lose sight of how much al-Ghazali disagrees with the *overall* methodological principles of Falsafa, and that he does aim to replace them with what I called his moderate anti-Evidentialism.

What is striking is the force with which al-Ghazali thinks we should reject Falsafa practised incorrectly. It is worth looking at the whole *fatwa* that occurs at the end of his *The Incoherence of the Philosophers*[24]:

> If someone asks: "Now that you have discussed in detail the teachings of these [philosophers], do you [also] say decisively that they hold unbelief {kufr} and that the killing of someone who upholds their convictions is obligatory?" "We answer: Pronouncing them as unbelievers must be done in three questions. One of the is the question of the world's pre-eternity and their saying that the substances are all pre-eternal. The second is their statement that God's knowledge does not encompass the temporally created particulars among individual [existents]. The third is their denial of the resurrection of bodies and assembly of bodies [on Judgement Day]".
>
> These three teachings do not agree with Islam in any way. Whoever holds them [also] holds that prophets utter falsehoods and that they said whatever they have said in order to promote the public benefit, [meaning that the prophets] use symbols for the multitude of people in order to make them understand. Such [a position] is manifest unbelief which none of the various groups of Muslims[25] ever held. (Al-Ghazali *The Incoherence of the Philosophers* 21.1–12)

As can be seen from the above, it looks like al-Ghazali has a problem with particularly *three* theses countenanced by the philosophers (that is, really, Avicenna). The three theses are (in his words):

1. The question of the world's pre-eternity and their saying that the substances are all pre-eternal.
2. Their statement that God's knowledge does not encompass the temporally created particulars among individual (existents).
3. The third is their denial of the resurrection of bodies and assembly of bodies (on Judgement Day).

As we have noted already, al-Ghazali's point is to show that, using the methods of Falsafa, the three theses have not been established. That is, he claims to have given us *philosophical* reason to reject them. Since they fly in the face of the literal meaning of the Koran, and there is no reason to take the Koran metaphorically, they should be taken to be instances of plain unbelief. Further, for *Muslims* to believe any of these claims amounts to *apostasy*—since it would be effectively to renounce Islam; and apostasy is punishable by the death in *Sharia* law.[26] Let's now consider briefly consider al-Ghazali's philosophical case for the denial of the three theses (I shall consider them again in light of Averroes' defence in Chap. 7) before we discuss again al-Ghazali's rejection of the epistemological and meta-philosophical commitments of Falsafa (which in my view is the important thing for al-Ghazali).

The Pre-eternity of the World

Recall that Aristotle thinks that the world (or the universe) could not have had a beginning (it is pre-eternal) because denying that it is pre-eternal is to say, as per impossible, that something can be generated from nothing. This is sometimes referred to as the *ex nihilo argument*. As we discussed in Chap. 3, al-Kindi very much distanced himself from this position, and in his *On First Philosophy* rendered arguments for the claim that the world was created and was finite. Avicenna, however, seems to re-commit Falsafa to this Aristotelian line—this is why we can take al-Ghazali's ire to be directed particularly at Avicenna (and indirectly at al-Farabi, given how much Avicenna's doctrines depend and are a development of the latter's views). As we saw Chap. 5, Avicenna's commitment to a *necessary existent* seem to have the corollary that the world is pre-eternal—the world *necessarily* is caused to exist by a being whose essence guarantees that it always exists. So, for Avicenna, to deny the pre-eternity of the world is to deny, as per impossible, that there is a necessary existent—that there is something other than nothing. And we cannot be deceived about the fact that there is something other than nothing as shown by the flying man argument and the epistemically privileged position of self-knowledge. If we are infallibly aware of ourselves then we are infallibly aware that there is something other than nothing.

Al-Ghazali has effectively two responses to Avicenna's position.

First, he argues that in order for God to be the *cause* of the world's existence, he must be the *agent* of the change between the world existing potentially and actually. And, further, appearances to the contrary, *agency* implies arbitrary *choice*. And as such, since the world has an agent, it could not be *necessitated* to exist.

Second, he argues against Avicenna's necessitism. Anticipating the work of British Empiricist David Hume (1711–1776) on causation, he argues that there is no such thing really as *necessity*. In this he is true to his Ash'aritism—in that the latter is committed to occationalism: the idea that God is the direct, proximate cause of everything that obtains or exists.

In the first response above, al-Ghazali makes a plausible suggestion about the idea that free agency implies arbitrary choice. He gives an intriguing example about a hungry man who has to choose between two equally delicious dates:

> Suppose there are two similar dates in front of a man who has a strong desire for them, but who is unable to take them both. Surely he will take one of them through a quality in him the nature of which is to differentiate between two similar things... Everyone, therefore, who studies, in the human mind the divine, real working of the act of choice, must necessarily admit a quality the nature of which is to differentiate between two similar things. (Al-Ghazali *The Incoherence of the Philosophers* 1 46.28–38)

The point here is that freedom must be compatible with arbitrary choice (this going against Kant's famous antimony of freedom[27]). This is because it is ludicrous to suppose that the man in the above scenario is somehow forever *blocked* into inaction because there is no reason to choose one date over the other. People in such situations do as a matter fact end up eating one of the dates. And that can only be possible if free choice can be arbitrary (law-less, or done for no reason). This appears to be a very plausible thought.[28] However, even if this is granted to al-Ghazali, we can simply reply, on behalf of Avicenna, that from the fact that God *could* have created the World arbitrarily, it does not follow that He did. Further, al-Ghazali seems to equivocate on two senses of the concept *agency*: one involving choice (as per "Jimmy was the agent of his own demise"), and the other compatible with the lack of choice (as per "citric acid is the active agent in *Ariel* detergent").[29]

More promising is his second line of response above. Here he buttressed his case with the interesting use of a concept actually introduced by Avicenna: estimation *(wahm)*. "Estimation" denotes a faculty whereby humans (and animals) create a misleading impression of things that they find impossible to resist. Hume later identified something very similar, which we termed something like a "brute psychological inclination" or "brute psychological fact". The point here is that though it may be psychologically irresistible for us to come to believe that things are thus and so *necessarily* (in Hume's case that there is a "necessary connection" between a cause and its effect) there cannot be such necessity. It may be helpful to recall here our discussion in Chap. 5 of our being unable to shake off the intellectual *seeming* that naive set theory is true, even once we know that it is not. In any case, that necessity cannot be observed seems to follow from God's *omnipotence*—which as you will recall is the principle which has lexical and interpretative priority in Ash'arite theology. If God is all-powerful then is cannot be that mammals are *necessarily* warm-blooded (even if it may be irresistible for us to think that they are), since God has it in his power (he is all-powerful) to make it the case that they are not. Further, can we actually observe the *necessity*? It seems we cannot.

The trouble here, of course, is that al-Ghazali's commitment to the interpretative priority given to God's omnipotence (or the kind of empiricism required for the observation point to have probative value) is something that Avicenna is required to accept. And something similar holds for al-Ghazali's response to the other bad theses with respect to:

God's Knowledge of Particulars and the Resurrection of Bodies

Recall the issue of whether God can know particulars, or contingent things. The problem is that under Aristotelian epistemology demonstrative proof is the only thing that can yield absolute certainty, and as such yields the best kind of knowledge available. Avicenna responded, as we discussed in Chap. 5, with the claim that his necessitism obviates the problem. That is, since Avicenna claims that everything that exists, exists *necessarily* (such that modality permeates everything) he can also claim that God can know everything that exists, that God knows particulars but "in a universal way". The al-Ghazali of the *Tahāfut* responds again with the point about rejecting necessitism. But since this depends on his giving interpretive priority to God's Omnipotence—

as per Ash'arite theology—then it looks question-begging against Avicenna. The al-Ghazali of the *Deliverance* (the Sufi al-Ghazali), however, could respond by denying the superiority of demonstrative proof. But here two issues present themselves: first, how can al-Ghazali establish *theoretically* the point without undermining the very claim? The claim would be self-defeating, in other words. Second, as we have already discussed while discussing the Sufi element in al-Ghazali's moderate anti-Evidentialism: is mystically attained higher proof required, or even available, for propositions other than the proposition that the Prophet is the true Prophet? If it is, then moderate anti-Evidentialism seems to collapse into a kind of classical Evidentialism—except with a finessed understanding of what are our (sceptic defying) epistemic reasons.

On the resurrection of bodies, the core of what al-Ghazali says is that in our mortal lifetimes we cannot derive empirical knowledge of the divine spheres, the heavens, and of what happens in the after-life—and so we must trust what we are told about such matters in Revelation. Especially since, as Muslims, we already *know* that the Prophet is the genuine Prophet (and seal of the Prophets). Again, however, this relies on a kind of empiricism and a view of logic (very much resembling Rudolph Carnap's) that some have labelled "syntactic", and one where Avicenna's innovations in modal logic are rejected in favour of the frequentist account we discussed in Chap. 5.

Al-Ghazali Against Moderate Evidentialism

Whilst we might think that al-Ghazali's attack on the three teachings is less than conclusive, I think it is worth remembering that in the very last paragraph of the *Incoherence of the Philosophers* he does accuse the *overall* methodology of Falsafa to be to blame, to recall:

> Whoever holds them [also] holds that prophets utter falsehoods and that they said whatever they have said in order to promote the public benefit, [meaning that the prophets] use symbols for the multitude of people in order to make them understand.

This appears to be a straight attack on the idea that the epistemic uniqueness of prophecy lies in the fact that prophecy may contain allegories, or rhetorical devices to educate the non-epistemic elite ("to make them understand"). And this of course is central to the Falasifa's endorsement of what we called Islamic moderate Evidentialism.

Al-Ghazali's main complaint seems to be that the idea that the prophet may engage in allegory or mythology (just in order to get the masses to understand) is to make the heretical claim that the True Prophet is a liar: that "prophets utter falsehoods".[30] As we will discuss in Chap. 7, however, it is in fact far from obvious that reasons that do not belong in the register of demonstrative proof, therefore fail to be *epistemic* (truth indicating) reasons.

Nevertheless, we may think that al-Ghazali has a point when we note that Avicenna at least was very explicit that the fact that the public has been spun a 'noble lie' must be concealed to them, on pain of the allegory failing to be effective:

> Nor is it proper for any human to reveal that he possesses knowledge that he is hiding from the commonality. Indeed, he must never permit any reference to this. Rather, he should let them know of God's majesty and greatness through symbols and similitudes derived from things that, for them, are majestic and great, adding this much: that He has never an equal, not a partner, not anyone like Him. Similarly, he must instill in them the belief in the resurrection in a manner that they can conceive and in which their souls will find rest. He must tell them about the [eternal] bliss and misery in parables derived from what they can comprehend and conceive. (Avicenna *Metaphysics*, *The Healing* 10, 2 6.17–25)

This seems to imply that the prophet, qua ideal political leader, must by "hiding knowledge from the communality" be less than honest with it. And I think we can ask on al-Ghazali's behalf whether the prophet (qua prophet) has any special abilities that ensure that the public will stay unapprised of the knowledge he is hiding—special abilities Avicenna will surely find hard not to describe in such a way as they appear ugly and unfit for the prophet. And if he does not have such abilities, then what happens when—perhaps accidentally—the communality does get wind of the fact that they have been lied to? Will it make a difference to them that the lie is a "noble" lie, or will they perforce loose their faith in experts and the elite? We will return to these issues in Chap. 8.

Concluding Remarks

In Chap. 1, we raised the point that one of the possible advantages of Mu'tazilite theology's being the state-sponsored theology of the Abbasids was that it disabled a strong confrontation between Sunni and Shiite Islam. A corollary of the Mu'tazilite occurentist metaphysics of belief is that belief is essentially private, such that one's behaviour alone cannot indicate what one believes. This was reflected by the official jurists under the Abbasids, who ruled that so long as one declared oneself a Muslim one could not be prosecuted for apostasy. The Hanbalite—non-occurentist—doxastic metaphysics, on the other hand, does not have that happy corollary. At first blush, it seems that al-Ghazali has sided with the non-occurentist view on this issue, given that he thinks that someone who thinks like Avicenna (who explicitly never renounced Islam, and considered himself a good Muslim) should be castigated with death. It is partly this seeming that has caused many to assert the claim that al-Ghazali ultimately "killed off" Falsafa—at least in the Islamic East (i.e. not in Islamic Spain and North Africa). Although it has recently become *de rigueur* for scholars to dismiss this claim, and for good reason,[31] I will nonetheless end with one further reason to be sceptical of it by way of conclusion. For I think we can read al-Ghazali's *fatwa* to be telling us that to endorse "Islamic" moderate Evidentialism *just is* to disown Islam. It is to tell us that the prophet is a liar, and so not the genuine prophet the *Shahāda* would have him be. And that it is *because* the Falasifa endorsed Islamic moderate Evidentialism that they came to have the three errant doctrines we mentioned. The departure from Muʿtazilite classical Evidentialism also signals a departure from what any Islamic sect or Islamic school of theology ever held. So the belief that really deserves punishment by death is the belief in Islamic moderate Evidentialism. As such, al-Ghazali need not have endorsed a behaviourist doxastic metaphysics.[32] So it remains an open question whether his moderate anti-Evidentialism eventually must collapse into a (a mystical) *kind* of Evidentialism, where all beliefs—in order to be fully justified—need to be somehow underpinned by mystical experience. If that is the case, however, the determinants of correct belief will be a very private matter, and to the extent where we can question whether Islam could in theory have any political role at all.

Study Questions

- Is al-Ghazali right in thinking that belief cannot be evaluated merely in terms of whether or not it is true?
- Does al-Ghazali really endorse a moderate anti-Evidentialism or *mystical* kind of classical (non-moderated) Evidentialism?

What to Read Next?

- Ali, Z. 2013: *Faith, Philosophy, and the Reflective Muslim* (London: Palgrave Macmillan).

- Al-Ghazali: *Deliverance from Error—al-Munqidh min al-Dalāl* (Translated by Watt, M.W. 2012: *Al-Ghazali: Deliverance from Error and the Beginning of Guidance*) (Kuala Lumpur: Islamic Book Trust).

Notes

1. Adamson (2016, p. 153).
2. Recall how this accords with the Ashʿarites' response to the *Euthyphro* dilemma we discussed in Chap. 1.
3. Footnote of Avicenna and al-Ghazali on miracles. Both think they are possible (analogue of mind–body problem, though for al-Ghazali, the prophet can change the essential properties, not just the accidents, of material things) but not easy to identify. Griffel (2004, p. 115).
4. "Convince yourself that [Muhammad (Peace be upon him) is in the highest grades of the prophetic calling] by trying out what he said about the influence of devotional practices on the purification of the heart." Al-Ghazali *Deliverance from Error* p. 62.
5. For a modern defence of this claim, see Rinard (forthcoming).
6. Though there is a sense in which Rumi was an *anti*-philosopher. However, so is the case for Wittgenstein.
7. See Jonas (2016) for detailed discussion.
8. See Jackson (1986).
9. According to Edmonds and Eidinow's (2001) biography, Wittgenstein used to read poetry, with his back turned to the audience, at meetings of the Vienna Circle.
10. For an account of how something like this idea is (very, very roughly) at the heart of Heidegger's philosophy, see Sheehan (2015).
11. There is a Sufi saying that says: "he who tastes, knows".
12. Russell (1912).
13. See his *Philosophy of Illumination*.
14. For Rumi this yearning can take an erotic aspect. He takes this from the famous female eighth-century Sufi mystic *Rabīʿa*.
15. Ibn al-ʿArabī, incidentally, famously spent some time studying under al-Ghazali.
16. This partly accounts for the famous 'Whirling' of the Meveldi Order (the Whirling Dervishes) in a ceremony called *Sema*. The ceremony abounds with circle symbolism.
17. "Do you not expect that you reliance on intellectual truths will fare like your reliance on sense-perception?" Al-Ghazali, *Deliverance from Error,* p. 9.

18. Although I should say that it has been notoriously difficult to say exactly what his overall take on prophecy was. For instance, in his well-known book on prophecy in Islam, Fazlur Rahman writes: "Al-Ghazālī is a most difficult author, if not an outright impossible one, to understand in any coherent manner" (Rahman 1958, p. 94).

19. This seems to suggest that this faculty (that gives us higher-level demonstration) is the faculty of prophetic judgement, such that what the prophet has in abundance, ordinary people also have (but less of). He also seems at times to equate this faculty with what occurs to us in *dreams*—following a tradition (also found in Falsafa that dreams are premonitory states, and to that degree'prophetic).

20. "Now this is a mystical 'state' which is realised in immediate experience by those who walk in the way leading to it." Al-Ghazali, *Deliverance from Error*, p. 55.

21. Even for al-Ghazali's strongly Ash'arite mentor al-Juwaynī, belief that p already could consist of a propensity to utter (silently) to oneself that p in certain situations, as he calls it: "interior speech in the self" (cf. Griffel 2004, p. 134). This makes the view look like a precursor to what Erik Schwitzgebel has called "Liberal Dispositionalism" (a hybrid between behaviourism and occurentism): Schwitzgebel (2002).

22. I have not here discussed his attempt to prove the necessity of prophecy: see his *Fayṣal al-Tafriqa*, which again seems to follow Avicenna: Griffel (2004).

23. See also Adamson (2016, p. 147).

24. A *fatwa* according to Islamic law is a legal response to a question issued by an actual or possible enquirer.

25. Sometimes translated as "Islamic sects", which I think would indicate that al-Ghazali means here schools of Islamic theology.

26. I will say more about the reasons for the difference between apostasy and unbelief in Chap. 8.

27. See Kant's (1785) *Groundwork to a Metaphysics of Morals*.

28. Though, as we will see in Chap. 7, Averroes has some interesting things to say in response.

29. Actually, al-Ghazali anticipates the objection in Discussion 3 of his *Tahāfut*: "...it is evident to the mind that what is a cause for a think divides into that which is voluntary and that which is not...[To this we] answer: All this is by way of metaphor. Real action is that which comes about only through will. Proof of this is that, if we suppose that a temporal event depends on another for its occurrence on two things, one voluntary and the other not, reason relates the act to the voluntary." (*Tahāfut* 3 18–31 p. 58). This seems to be an interesting denial of the libertarian conception of free will (which looks like Frankfurt's trolley cases against the principle of alternative possibilities): that if a putatively voluntary action was actually over-determined by a non-voli-

tional cause, then that action was not after all voluntary. Recall from Chap. 1, that the Ash 'arites were compatibilists about freedom of the will.

However, even if al-Ghazali is right about this, it would just show that we have a predilection to favour the explanation involving volition when there are competing explanations. It would not show that all causation is volition.
30. Griffel (2004).
31. For discussion, see especially Griffel (2009).
32. Hence: "…you should refrain from accusing any group of unbelief and from spreading rumours about the people of Islam—even if they differ in their ways—as long as they firmly confess that there is no god but God and Muhammad is His messenger, as long as they hold this true and do not contradict it. Unbelief is the accusation that something that comes from the Prophet—peace and prayers be upon him—is wrong. Belief is to consider him true and truthful in everything that he does." From his *Fayṣal al-Tafriqa* 134.4–7 (cited in Griffel 2009, p. 106).

References

Secondary Sources

Adamson, P. 2016. *Philosophy in the Islamic World. A History of Philosophy Without Any Gaps.* Vol. 3. Oxford University Press.

Edmonds, D., and J. Eidinow. 2001. *Wittgenstein's Poker.* Faber & Faber.

Griffel, F. 2004. Al-Ghazālī's Concept of Prophecy: The Introduction of Avicennan Psychology into Ashʿarite Theology. *Arabic Sciences and Philosophy* 14: 101–144.

Griffel, F. 2009. *Al-Ghazālī's Philosophical Theology.* Oxford University Press.

Jackson, F. 1986. What Mary Didn't Know. *Journal of Philosophy* 83: 291–295.

Jonas, S. 2016. *Ineffability and Its Metaphysics.* Palgrave Macmillan.

Kant, I. 1785 [2005]. *Groundwork for the Metaphysics of Morals.* Routledge.

Rahman, F. 1958. *Prophecy in Islam: Philosophy and Orthodoxy.* Allen & Unwin.

Rinard, S. forthcoming. No Exception for Belief. *Philosophy and Phenomenological Research.*

Russell, B. 1912. In *The Problems of Philosophy*, ed. Skorupski. 2001 edn. Oxford University Press.

Schwitzgebel, E. 2002. A Phenomenal, Dispositionalist Account of Belief. *Noûs* 36: 249–275.

Sheehan, T. 2015. *Making Sense of Heidegger: A Paradigm Shift.* Rowman and Littlefield.

7

The Philosophers Strike Back: Averroes and Islamic Philosophy After al-Ghazali

Introduction

In Chap. 6 we discussed al-Ghazali and his attack on Falsafa, especially in his work *The Incoherence of the Philosophers*—the three theses held by the Falasifa which al-Ghazali thought to be especially problematic, as well as the underlying Islamic moderate Evidentialism. We also discussed how his rise to prominence was partly explained historically by the advent of Turkish, Seljuk dominance in the Middle East, and the Seljuk rulers' receptivity towards Ashʿarite theology. This, you will recall, emphasises the untrammelled power of God, and as such can claim dialectical superiority over Muʿtazilite theology when it comes to being more faithful to the literal word of the Koran. That can perhaps explain the Seljuk affinity toward Ashʿaritism—the Seljuks being keen to establish themselves as the harbingers of new cultural order, more in tune, they could try to claim, with the true faith.

We did not really mention earlier, however, that the Seljuks did not take control of Muslim Spain, the al-Andaluz region. This is significant. It was from Muslim Spain that Ashʿarite theology, and al-Ghazali's attack on philosophy, was most explicitly resisted. Indeed, the twelfth century saw the cultural centre of gravity move from the Muslim East to the Muslim West. This was partly down to the fact that the Muslim East faced some disarray in dealing with the crusades and the break-up of the Abbasid empire, but partly also, I think, because of some other historical contingencies that we will shortly take a look at. But it was from Muslim Spain that the Islamic philosopher who was to have by far the most influence on European thought came from.

© The Author(s) 2017
A.R. Booth, *Analytic Islamic Philosophy*, Palgrave Philosophy Today,
https://doi.org/10.1057/978-1-137-54157-4_7

This philosopher is Ibn Rushd, or Averroes as he is called in Latin. Looking at his work will take up much of this chapter.

Averroes wrote a response to al-Ghazali's *Tahāfut al-Falāsifa*, called *Tahāfut al-Tahāfut*—the "incoherence of the incoherence"; in Latin it was translated as *Destructio Destructionum* (the Destruction of the Destruction). Here he argues that many of al-Ghazali's philosophical claims are themselves unstable; that they do not measure up to al-Ghazali's own criteria of adequacy, and fail to show that the key theses of Falsafa, nor their underlying methodological principle (what we called Islamic moderate Evidentialism), fall short of demonstrative proof. But in a sense he agrees with al-Ghazali that his opponent—Avicenna—had gone astray. What he does not agree with is the inference that because Avicenna has gone wrong, that the whole practice of philosophy is in some way defective. Avicenna has gone wrong, claims Averroes, but only because he has departed significantly from Aristotle. A philosophy truer to Aristotelian principles would be immune from al-Ghazali's attack. That's not to say that Averroes denies the three claims that al-Ghazali had identified as unbelief. Rather, he thinks that Avicenna's reasons for holding those claims—even though they are true—are incorrect.

In this chapter, we will briefly look at Averroes' defence of the three theses against al-Ghazali's attack, and then in more detail discuss Averroes' defence of the Falasifas' guiding meta-philosophy: Islamic moderate Evidentialism. We will then discuss some of the thinkers from the Islamic world who follow Averroes and al-Ghazali, especially those for whom some version of Evidentialism either explicitly or implicitly plays a huge role (thus "destroying" the (already now unpopular) claim that al-Ghazali had really "killed off" Falsafa—since my claim is that adherence to some aspects of Evidentialism is the unifying motif of Falsafa). First, though, let us take a brief biographical tour of the life of this chapter's central protagonist.

Averroes: A Very Brief Biography

Averroes was born in Cordoba in modern Spain in 1126. He was born into an influential family of lawyers who had supported, and were prominent within, the Almoravid regime. The Umayyad caliphate in Spain had collapsed in 1031 under pressure from the Almoravids from Morocco, who took over. Later, in 1147, the Almohads vanquished the Almoravids. The Almohads were a very interesting dynasty. Their revolt was led by one Ibn Tumart, who was considered to be a "Mahdi" or a "spiritual redeemer"/"messiah". He himself claimed to be a descendant of the Prophet Muhammad, though that claim is now generally thought to be untrue. Ibn Tumart spent some time studying with al-Ghazali in Baghdad, and indeed seems to have been friends with him. It is reported that he was with al-Ghazali when the news came to him that the Almoravids had burnt one of Ibn Tumart's works, and also that al-Ghazali urged him to return to the Muslim West to put the Almoravids in their place.[1]

Ibn Tumart's theology departed somewhat from Ash'aritism. Indeed, he set up a new theological school, to be known as "al-Muwwahidun" (those who believe in the unity of God). Like the Mu'tazilite theology, the new theology emphasised this central belief in the unity of God, and considered some of the anthropomorphic tendencies in Ash'aritism to be tantamount to polytheism. The Almohads also believed that the essence and existence of God could be established via the use of reason alone. So it's not difficult to see how Almohad theology's dominance in Spain could create the conditions under which philosophy was taken seriously.

Once Ibn Tumart had died in 1139, the caliphate in the Muslim West went to Caliph al Mu'min. Averroes travelled to Marrakesh to meet him, and apparently the caliph was so impressed that he gave him his patronage. What seemed to have been important to the caliph was that he himself had found the work of Aristotle hard to understand, and Averroes was good at explaining it. This in a way set up Averroes' legacy. He wrote a number of commentaries on Aristotle's works with the purpose of trying to explain them in simple terms. Averroes' writings were widely circulated in Latin Europe as undergraduate textbooks on Aristotle, and were so well received that no less a figure than St Thomas Aquinas referred to Averroes simply as "The Commentator".

As we will discuss further later in this chapter, Averroes became very well known and influential in the Latin West. Some go so far as to say that his ideas were crucial to the development of the Renaissance. He was not, however, so influential among his contemporaries in the Muslim East. We will explore why that was later on, but for now I shall mention one partly historical explanation. This is that shortly after Averroes died in 1198 the Almohad dynasty began to break up, and the Muslims lost much of Spain (by the mid-thirteenth century the Almohads had lost Spain to the Spanish *Reconquista*). With the death of the Almohad dynasty came the death of Almohad theology.

The Almohads had at times been very progressive. It is said that the period they ruled in was unique in history, because Spain was a place where Muslims, Jews and Christians could co-exist peacefully. Towards the end of his life, however, Averroes was driven into exile by the then caliph (al-Mansur) to what was then a predominantly Jewish village, Lucena. This was taken to be something of a humiliation for Averroes, but the fact that he came into contact with Jewish thinkers during this time helped him to gain a great deal of influence among the Jewish intellectual community, and this in part helped to expedite the later translation of his work into Latin.

Averroes died in 1198, in Marrakesh. Whilst his legacy, made famous by St Thomas Aquinas, was that of a commentator on the works of Aristotle, he also produced works with the aim of defending Falsafa as an Aristotelian enterprise, both in creed and overall methodology, within the Muslim context. This was in the light of the rising tide of Ash'arite dominance in the Muslim East, and in response to al-Ghazali's attack; his *Incoherence of the Incoherence* being the most notable example of this in terms of specific philosophical theses, and his *Decisive Treatise* in terms of his defence of Falsafa's methodological commitments, Islamic moderate Evidentialism. This last enterprise in particular took him some distance away from Aristotle's teachings, if strictly construed, since he was in the business—in a way that Aristotle was not—of *explicitly* investigating the relationship between reason and revelation, and defending the practice of philosophy in an Islamic context. But first let's discuss some of his work on defending what he thinks are properly Aristotelian theses from al-Ghazali's criticisms. In *Incoherence of the Incoherence* Averroes deals with a lot of Ghazali's arguments (al-Ghazali had marshalled some twenty arguments against the philosophers), but here we will only look at the arguments most relevant to the three most controversial theses examined in the last chapter. As we discussed, since al-Ghazali was trying to show that the philosopher's claims fell short of demonstrative proof (and so fell short of their own criteria of adequacy), he gave what he took to be *philosophical* arguments against Falsafa. Averroes' line is typically that though they may hit the target when measured against Avicenna's case for these claims, they do not hit home when the case is rendered along properly Aristotelian lines. Let's begin by discussing the issue that takes up most of al-Ghazali's energy, regarding the (pre-)eternity of the world.

The Modality and Pre-eternity of the World Revisited

Recall that Avicenna (following Aristotle) thought that the world was pre-eternal—that it did not have a beginning and has always existed. But, unlike Aristotle, Avicenna thought this because all things that are actual do not bear *existence* as an essential property, and since we know that there is a world, there must be a "necessary existent" (God) who has brought the world into being.

As we discussed in the last chapter, al-Ghazali thought this idea was problematic for a number of different reasons. One of the primary reasons concerned his questioning of what Avicenna could mean by God having "brought" the world into being. Since Avicenna thinks that God's "bringing" the world into existence (giving it the property *existence*) makes it the case that everything that exists exists necessarily (as per Avicenna's "necessitism"), it must be that God *necessitates* that existence (necessarily "causes" it or it necessarily "emanates" from him). This means, for al-Ghazali, that it cannot have been a *volitional* bringing about, since voluntary choice involves *the capacity to have done otherwise*. This obviously goes against Ash'arite theology, but, claims al-Ghazali, it is also *philosophically* problematic, since "bringing things about" ("agency") is something that always involves volition. Non-agential causation for al-Ghazali (anticipating Hume) is otherwise merely recorded regularity ("metaphorical" agency, as he puts it), and observed regularity *cannot* explain why there is a world and not nothing (since the regularity is here the very thing that needs explaining). The only real causation is agent-causation, and so if God creates the world he must do so as a volitional agent (*fa'il*)—this is of course of a piece with al-Ghazali's commitment to Ash'arite occasionalism (the claim that God is the proximate cause of every event). Further, al-Ghazali aimed to show us how God's gratuitously *willing* the world into existence can resist counter-examples (as per his famous dates example).

Averroes' general strategy in response to al-Ghazali is a tripartite one. He aims to:

(i) Resist al-Ghazali's conception of God's bringing the world into existence as overly anthropomorphic, and so potentially heretical itself.
(ii) Show how al-Ghazali's case for making sense of God's *willing* the world into existence falls short.
(iii) Deny Avicenna's account of modality, and hold it responsible for any vulnerability on the part of al-Ghazali's attack.

Let's take the first part of Averroes' strategy first. One might have expected Averroes to argue that thinking of God as a voluntary agent is already to anthropomorphise him, and not pay due heed to the difference between him and us. Instead, however, Averroes proceeds by noting what must surely be a striking difference between God's will and our, human, will: that God is omnipotent and humans are not. And, as such, the idea that in order for God to have *willed* the universe into existence it must have been possible for him to *have done otherwise* is surely nonsensical, given that the execution of God's will faces no obstacles. Thus, al-Ghazali's claim that if God caused the world *necessarily* then God cannot have created the world voluntarily depends on a limited, human conception of the will.

Now, one may wonder whether al-Ghazali is in fact committed to the principle of alternative possibilities, given the Ash'arite compatibilism we discussed in Chap. 1. Further, as we discussed in Chap. 6, al-Ghazali seemed to come up with a good counter-example to the principle of alternative possibilities: that when an event has both an external cause and a volitional cause, we tend to attribute (nonetheless) the event's occurring to the volitional cause:

> Real action is that which comes about only through will. Proof of this is that, if we suppose that a temporal event depends on another for its occurrence on two things, one voluntary and the other not, reason relates the act to the voluntary. (Al-Ghazali *The Incoherence of the Philosophers* 3 18–31, p. 58)

Al-Ghazali seems to be saying here that, for instance, if your intention to drive on the left is over-determined by some external cause (such as a mechanism put into your car by someone), your driving on the left is nonetheless voluntary. But the problem for al-Ghazali is that this then undermines his case for thinking that if the world could not but have been created, it is therefore not intentionally created. And if al-Ghazali replies that *God's will* is subject to something like the principle of alternative possibilities, because there are no obstacles to the implementation of God's will, that is just going to be grist to Averroes' mill: since God is all-powerful, what God intends *necessarily* obtains.

This leads us straight into the second part of Averroes' strategy contra al-Ghazali. Al-Ghazali faced the issue of how God can create a non-eternal world outside time.

Al-Ghazali asks, what's really wrong with this idea? God exists alone at one stage, then suddenly decides to create the world, and creates it, therefore no longer exists alone. Just as I might be hungry and decide to create a delicious meal for myself, then go ahead and create a delicious meal for myself. There seems to be nothing mysterious going on here. Al-Ghazali raises this to dismiss two potential problems; and Averroes wants to say that al-Ghazali's solution to each of the problems does not work.

The two problems are these:

(i) It makes God's will look arbitrary. Why does he all of a sudden choose to make the world?

(ii) If God is all knowing and eternal, there must have been a time where he
had not yet created the world but knew that he was going to create it later.
At that time *t*, why doesn't God create the world at *t*?

Al-Ghazali's response to (ii) is to say this: does not the idea of delayed decisions make perfect sense—as when a man decides to divorce his wife but waits
until he catches her in adultery to do so? But the problem here, as Averroes
mentioned and we have already discussed, is that the reason that we delay our
actions until after decisions have been made is that there are practical obstacles to the causal efficacy of our decisions. In other words, we delay because
there is something that stops our being able to make the world as we want it
now, but that obstacle will be removed in changed circumstances. But God
can have no such obstacle. He can remove all obstacles by a sheer act of will.
So why should he delay his decisions?

Al-Ghazali's response to (i) is more promising, and perhaps can also be
taken to help (ii) as well. Here he uses the example we discussed in Chap. 6
regarding someone who has to choose between two equally delicious dates.
Does the fact that the dates are identical forever prevent the person from
choosing between the dates? Obviously not. So, al-Ghazali infers, choice must
involve "finding a difference where there isn't one". If we humans can do it,
surely God can too.

Averroes responds, incisively, by saying that the choice the man has in this
situation is actually not a choice between two identical dates, but the choice
between eating and not eating/having the desire unfulfilled. He chooses to eat
a date, in contrast with not eating at all. But he does *not* choose to eat the
right date as opposed to the left date. Choosing to eat the right date is merely
arbitrary, and not really a *choice* as such.

Let us finally turn to the final part of Averroes' strategy, which is trickier to
explain. Here, Averroes' target is first Avicenna's account of modality, which as
you will recall from Chap. 5, is presented as an improvement over Aristotle's
"frequentist" view. Recall our characterisation of Aristotle's view:

Necessity_{frequentist}   A state of affairs (or object) x is necessary iff x occurs or
exists eternally. It is contingent if it fails to occur or exist
eternally.

Possibility_{frequentist}   A state of affairs (or object) x is impossible iff x never
occurs or exists. A state of affairs x is possible if it occurs or
exists at any time t (where t can denote a future time).

And our characterisation of what Avicenna puts in its place:

Necessity_{Avicenna}   An object a necessarily bears property F iff F is an *essential* property of a.

Possibility_{Avicenna}   It is impossible for an object a to bear properly F iff a's essential properties are incompatible with the obtaining of F with respect to a. It is possible for an object a to bear property F iff a's essential properties are compatible with the obtaining of F with respect to a.

Now, both of these accounts are supposed to be accounts of what modality *is*. And Averroes raises the question concerning the epistemology of modality—of how we *know* modal properties. And it seems that Averroes' objection to Avicenna's account of what modality is is that it would make the following account of the epistemology of modality fully adequate: what is conceivable is a guide to what is possible, since possibility entails conceivability. And what is inconceivable is a guide to what is impossible, since inconceivability entails impossibility. So, to illustrate this crudely, since it is impossible to conceive of a round square, we may rule something about the world: that such things are impossible. Or, since it is possible to conceive of a blue square, we may rule that blue squares are possible.[2] Averroes quotes al-Ghazali as actually endorsing this:

> anything whose existence the intellect supposes, provided no obstacle presents itself to the supposition, we call possible and, if there is such an obstacle, we call it impossible and, if we suppose that it cannot be supposed not to be we call it necessary. These are rational judgements which need no real existent which they might qualify. (Averroes—quoting al-Ghazali *Incoherence of the Incoherence* 102)

Now, the issue for Averroes is, I think, that if Avicenna was right about the metaphysics of modality, then conceivability is a good epistemology of modality. But (he will show) it is not. So we should conclude that Avicenna's cannot be the right account of modality (rather, the proper Aristotelian one is). The premise that conceivability gives us a good epistemology of modality if Avicenna is right about what modality *is*, is fairly straightforward since it is surely true that there is no essential property of an object that it is conceivable for that object not to bear and yet not be that object. For instance, we cannot conceive of a house (qua *house*) that does not provide shelter, and so we can rule that it is an essential property of a house that it provides shelter. The premise that conceivability is not actually a good guide to modality rests on Averroes' making a distinction between what these days we would call "real" possibility and mere metaphysical or logical possibility; the idea here being that what may move you to research the cure for cancer may be that you think there is a possibility *in this world* that a cure can be found, as opposed to the conceptual (metaphysical) possibility that it can be found *in some possible world*. Similarly, one might imagine that there are truths that, given the constitution of this world, are *necessary* in *this* world, or at a particular time, but not in all possible worlds, or at all times (Deutsch 1990). Averroes keeps insisting that the important (and true Aristotlelian) modal notion is "*real* possibility". Therefore the fact that we can imagine a cure for cancer—such that it is logically possible—does not tell us anything about whether it is *really* possible for humans in this world to find one. Thus it makes sense to think (along the frequentist lines on modality) that if we *know* that as a matter of fact I will never become a good singer (no matter if I try hard) it is right to say that it is impossible for me to become a good singer, even if it may be logically possible that I become (we can conceive of a world where I am) a good singer. Averroes then blames Avicenna's errant account of modality to allow for a cleavage to open up between modality in the (real) world and modal concepts as grasped by intellects. And it is this opening up that allows al-Ghazali to ask the empirical, sceptical question: where in the world (and not just the mind) are these modal properties? Where, in observation, is the necessary connection between a cause and effect? And this ultimately allows al-Ghazali to maintain that proper agency cannot be about material cause and effect, but God's *volitional* agency. Once we return to the proper Aristotelian account of modality, none of this is possible. As Averroes puts it:

> possibility is a universal which has individuals outside the mind like all other universals, and knowledge is not knowledge of the universal concept, but it is a knowledge of individuals in a universal way which the mind attains in the case of the individuals, when it abstracts from them one common nature (Averroes *Incoherence of the Incoherence* 110)

Put differently, Averroes is affirming what in Chap. 2 we called "Experience First Epistemology": that we know universals *through* our knowledge of particulars and not the other way around. So the ultimate guide to modal concepts must be *the world* and not what it is that we can conceived—to think otherwise is to revert to a non-Aristotelian picture.

The Resurrection of the Flesh and God's Knowledge of Particulars Revisited

As we discussed in Chap. 6, al-Ghazali's objections to philosophy regarding the notions of bodily resurrection and God's knowledge of particulars seem predicated on his scepticism about modal notions, and so of causation yielding more than mere regularity (or "constant conjunction" as Hume put it). God's *will* for al-Ghazali is ultimately the only real agent. Avicenna's "necessitism" must therefore be false: it is not the case that if something exists it exists necessarily, since its existence is actually a function of God's free will, and God can decide to change his mind. The claim that the world (and all the objects within it) exists *modally* (as per Avicenna's necessitism) allowed Avicenna to maintain that God knows universals but in a "universal way". So to reject necessitism is to rob Avicenna of the means by which to account for how God can know particulars. Further, al-Ghazali points out just how out of keeping is the idea that God *cannot* know particulars, as we see in this passage quoted by Averroes:

> this principle implies that God cannot know whether Zaid obeys or disobeys him, since God cannot know any new occurrences that happen to Zaid, as he does not know the individual Zaid ... he cannot know that Zaid becomes a heretic or a true believer, for he can only know the unbelief and the belief of man in general, not as instantiated into individuals. God can even not know Muhammad's proclaiming himself a prophet at the time that he did. (Averroes *Incoherence of the Incoherence* 457)

For Averroes, what is important is that God's knowledge can *be about our world*, rather than about some free-floating ideas. According to him, God's knowledge is unlike ours in that his knowledge of universals need not be arrived at by abstracting from particulars. *But*, given that our knowledge of universals (abstracted from particulars) is knowledge of the same *object* as God's knowledge, God's knowledge is in a way connected to particulars.

> If, for instance, knowledge of Zaid's coming reaches the prophet through a communication of God, the reason why the actual happening is congruous with the knowledge is nothing but the fact that the nature of the actual existent is a consequence of the eternal knowledge, for knowledge *qua* knowledge can only refer to something which has an actualised nature. (Averroes *Incoherence of the Incoherence* 532)

Put differently, since the sorts of necessary and possible propositions that God knows are about "real" (and not merely metaphysical) possibility, these propositions are about the *world*. It is this that allows God to be able to predict, for instance, what Zaid will do.[3]

On the resurrection of bodies, an issue that al-Ghazali raises that we did not discuss in Chap. 6, it seems inconsistent, given the philosophers' avowed endorsement of Aristotle's hylomorphism, to think that the soul survives death qua *form* but does not exist *before* it took its physical form. If the soul (qua) form requires matter to exist (as per Aristotle's hylomorphism) then it should either cease to exist on the perishing of the body, or else to exist through different matter before and after its earthly sojourn. Averroes seems to simply accept al-Ghazali's criticism, and disavows Avicenna:

> I do not know any philosopher who said that the soul has a beginning in the true sense of the word, and is thereafter everlasting except—as Ghazali relates— Avicenna. All other philosophers agree that in their temporal existence they are related to and connected with the bodily possibilities, which receive this connexion like the possibilities which subsist in mirrors for their connexion with the rays of the sun. (Averroes *Incoherence of the Incoherence* 107)

Again, for Averroes, the kind of possibility that a proper Aristotelian philosopher is interested in is *real* possibility. And Averroes seems to take the quite radical view for the time that actually not only is there no bodily resurrection, but also no resurrection of individual souls. One may exist following death, but not as an individual (material) intellect, but as part of the active intellect (which Averroes calls the *universal intellect*). But this just seems to be a concession to al-Ghazali, except to say that actually Falsafa is more heretical than even al-Ghazali had supposed! Here, in the very last section of *Incoherence of the Incoherence*, Averroes responds:

> But the philosophers in particular, as is only natural, regard this doctrine as most important and believe in it most, and the reason is that it is conducive to an order amongst men on which man's being, as man, depends and through which he can attain the greatest happiness proper to him. (Averroes *Incoherence of the Incoherence* 581)

What Averroes seems to be saying here is that one should believe in the resurrection of the flesh but for *non-epistemic* reasons, here *practical reasons* to do with the utility of believing in it, bringing happiness for the many. So here we see Averroes commit himself to moderate Evidentialism. I turn now to his defence of this doctrine.

Averroes' *Decisive* Defence of Islamic Moderate Evidentialism

In his other most famous work, *The Decisive Treatise on the Harmony of Philosophy and Religion*, Averroes sets out to defend the distinctive meta-philosophy of Falsafa: Islamic moderate Evidentialism. He does this too in parts of other works, including in parts of his *Incoherence of the Incoherence*. Recall that the main difference between al-Farabi and Avicenna on prophecy is that for the latter new knowledge can be the product of prophecy, whereas for the former prophecy can only really facilitate *understanding* knowledge that one already has (and this understanding renders justified true beliefs in items of certain knowledge, since they now satisfy strict K-K conditions).[4] Averroes, I think, consistently and vehemently denies this Avicennan innovation, and this is of a piece with his general claim that Avicennan innovation is responsible for any of al-Ghazali's criticisms of Falsafa hitting their target.

It looks as if there is a discrepancy, however, between what Averroes thinks in his earlier works (in particular his *Epitome of the Parva Naturalia*) and what he expounds in his later works (in particular in his *Incoherence of the Incoherence*). In the *Epitome* Averroes quite explicitly denies that prophecy can deliver new theoretical knowledge, and nor can it give anyone a figurative representation of theoretical truths and so furnish the prophet with any special rhetorical ability. Nor can prophecy deliver us with rules for human behaviour that lead to *eudemonia* (the Greek for Aristotle's notion of human good, consistent with our function); indeed, prophecy's function is limited to giving certain humans the ability sometimes to predict the future. In *Incoherence of the Incoherence*, however, Averroes explicitly says that "a religion through intellect alone would necessarily be inferior to religions derived from intellect and revelation" and that "knowledge received from revelation comes to perfect the branches of knowledge of the intellect" (*Incoherence of the Incoherence*, p. 584). Further, he repeatedly says that certain knowledge cannot be attained by some persons "either because of inborn nature, habit, or lack of the means of study" and thus that for them "God has coined images and likenesses of things ... that can only [otherwise] be learned by demonstration [through the use of theoretical science, broadly speaking]" (*Decisive Treatise*, p. 59). This discrepancy has in turn resulted in there being a number of interpretations in regard to what Averroes thought was the proper relationship between philosophy and religion, and thus his broader view on the normative conditions on belief. Philosophers such as Leo Strauss and Ralph Lerner (Lerner 1974 is a work dedicated to Leo Strauss) think that Averroes is really a kind of proto-secularist who thinks that revelation is of very limited value, but that he was unable to make the case for this explicitly—and that if one reads him closely enough one can see that he communicates this esoterically in his writings. Erwin Rosenthal (Rosenthal 1958) on the other hand seems to think that for Averroes Sharia law trumps any claim of reason; Oliver Leaman (1980, 1988) maintains a kind of Kindian vision of Averroes, where reason and faith are both equally efficacious, but different, paths to the same truth; Herbert Davidson also takes a quasi- Straussian line,[5] and thinks that the term "prophet" for Averroes really denotes "nothing than the human author of Scripture; and the term *revelation* would mean a high level of philosophic knowledge" (Davidson 1992, p. 351). The prophet on this reading is really a philosopher, who methodically works out "coolly and deliberately" (and not through an inspired imaginative faculty) how best to present his philosophical knowledge into language more suitable for those untrained in, or simply unable to do, philosophy.

I think the confusion can be solved instead by taking Averroes to be replying to the last words of al-Ghazali's *The Incoherence of the Philosophers*, that to think that the unique epistemic function of prophecy is to communicate (demonstrative) knowledge through allegory and symbolism to those who are unable to do philosophy is to claim "that prophets utter falsehoods", tantamount to the heretical claim that the prophet is a liar.

The central thought that Averroes has in defence of Falsafa is that it may be true that when one believes that *p* on the basis of a rhetorical ploy or on the basis of an allegory, one's reasons fall short of demonstrative proof (the best kind of epistemic reason). But this does not mean that one does not believe for *epistemic reasons*—reasons conducive to the attainment of true belief. Here we do find (*pace* Leaman's interpretation above) the Kindian idea we discussed in Chap. 3, a *teleological* (goal-based) account of the epistemic; the epistemic being that which is conducive to our attaining true beliefs. But Averroes, and he follows al-Farabi's demarcation here, thinks that there are better and worse *kinds* of epistemic reason (so heading in a way towards the lesson in Plato's *Meno* that knowledge is more valuable than mere true belief), those delivered (in descending order of strength) by the following methods:

(i) Demonstrative proof.
(ii) Dialectical reasoning
(iii) Rhetorical devices such as the use of allegory.

As al-Farabi had noted earlier it was not the case that Aristotle considered only demonstration to be a proper part of logic—dialectics and rhetoric were also considered to be part of his *Organon* (the collection of all Aristotle's logical works).

I have not said much about dialectical reasoning, so let me do so now before moving on. When one engages in such reasoning, one starts not from *first principles* (indubitable truths) but with "common notions", what we are all (or what it seems to a person that we are all) inclined to believe. As Averroes puts it, dialectical reasoning "does not reach the level of demonstrative proof. For its premises are common notion, and common notions come close to being equivocal, whereas demonstrative premises are directed toward things belonging to the same kind" (*Incoherence of the Incoherence* 5). Sometimes, however, there are situations where demonstration is the wrong method to use (even if it is the only method that yields proper certainty). To illustrate this with a slightly trite example: suppose you are trying to persuade a climate change denier in a cafe that climate change is actually happening today. Surely, the best method of persuasion is to present the latest article in *Science* or *Nature* on the subject: the average person in a cafe is highly unlikely to understand the article, and if they could they would be unlikely to have the false belief they do. So it is probably better to use analogies (rhetoric) and start out with investigating what they believe, then showing them how some of their beliefs are inconsistent and so need internal revision, until we get finally to the revision of the climate change denier's belief.

For Averroes, notably, theology must be all about dialectical reasoning, since it begins with premises that are "common notions" within theology, and does not attempt to prove these premises beyond doubt. Nevertheless, theology does not necessarily contradict philosophy in so being, since dialectical reasons (like rhetorical reasons) can be *epistemic* (lead to the truth) as of course for philosophical (demonstrative) reasoning; and as he famously puts it in the *Decisive Treatise* "truth cannot contradict truth".[6] Similarly, then, so long as an allegory is effectively used to get people to believe the truth, then the use of allegory provides epistemic reason to believe. And, for Averroes, since we know that Muhammad's prophecy is bound to be an effective tool to get people to believe the truth (if that is what part of its function is), then we know that it provides us in so doing with epistemic reason, and so cannot ultimately be in tension with philosophy. Further, this in fact shows that philosophy should be the ultimate arbitrator of religious disputes (Averroes was also a Jurist, and this was offered as a position in *Fiqh*—Islamic jurisprudence—too), since the truths dealt with by the theologian must then be the same truths dealt with by the philosophers, only arrived at by less lofty means and so worthy of less certainty.

As we will pick up again in the next chapter, we may perhaps want to insist here on behalf of al-Ghazali that this contradicts the fact that an allegory must be occulted to the public in order for it to be effective. But let's for now discuss another, closely related, aspect of Islamic moderate Evidentialism that we have not yet explored, implicit in al-Ghazali's criticism that the prophets "said whatever they have said in order to promote the public benefit". Since if Averroes is right that dialectics and rhetoric provide epistemic reason, then his position seems to revert back to a kind of 'classical' al-Kindian Evidentialism: there are no non-epistemic reasons for belief. For Averroes, Avicenna and al-Farabi, prophecy also had a *practical* purpose: that believing what is in prophecy will lead to us to happiness, and collective human perfection. We do need some Aristotelian assumptions (as found in the *Nicomachean Ethics*) to work as background assumptions, namely [**naturalism**] human good is human perfection in accord with human function and nature, such that knowing human nature is necessary for knowing the good; [**particularism**] there are no *rules* for working out what one ought to do (consistent with the good) for any individual case. This is a matter for **practical wisdom** (Greek: *phronesis*), the bearer of which can intuit how to apply general moral knowledge to particular situations, and which can only be attained through experience. Now we, as humans, are prone to lack *phronesis* when the knowledge we seek to practically implement falls short of proper certainty (attained from demonstration) and many of us lack the capacity for it. But, because there are no general moral rules available to us, *we* must know about human nature, such that we can then gain *phronesis*. In other words, we cannot act in accordance with good simply by following a set of laws that would ensure that we did, so we need to have at least something resembling knowledge of human nature. Since no human can attain certain knowledge of human nature, this explains the need for prophecy, qua rhetorical device for teaching us moral truths that we would not otherwise believe. But since the knowledge we gain in this way is far from reaching the level required for certain knowledge, putting it into practice will not really amount to proper, infallible *phronesis*, such that weakness of the will (Greek: *akrasia*) becomes possible for us. This gives prophecy a further role: to give us a manual about how to live such that we are in control of our desires. The rules the manual gives us, however, can only function *in tandem* with the theoretical knowledge it teaches, such that—in isolation from certain bits of theoretical knowledge—they cannot be taken to constitute generalist moral laws.

Now, al-Ghazali levies an interesting objection to the idea that we must believe in the things in revelation for *practical* reason. Note, though, that he does not thereby think that we should believe them from *epistemic* reason, but that we must believe them for voluntaristic reasons: because God *wills* it. The objection again really resembles Hume's famous *sensible knave* issue for an account of morality whereby one ought to act morally because having morality (as a system of laws of conduct) is in the interest of the communality. If Hume's sensible knave knows that morality *in toto* (as a whole) will survive some minor violation of its laws, then the sensible knave will have *no reason* to resist committing the immoral act (Hume's 1777 *An Enquiry into the Principles of Morals* 9.22–25). [7] In other words, if I think that the only reason in order to have a system of traffic is that it is in general for the masses to have one, if I know the system of traffic will survive my breaking the speed limit this one time, then what moral reason do I have to refrain from breaking it? Al-Ghazali raises this in his *Deliverance from Error* in the context of philosophers who call themselves Muslim, but who fail to really believe the things commanded by prophecy. Here he has Avicenna firmly in mind (you will recall our mentioning how Avicenna liked sex and wine), but says of the Falasifa *in general*:

> These are the people who show politeness to Islam. Often you see one of them reading the Koran, attending the Friday worship and praising the sacred Law. Nevertheless he does not refrain from drinking wine and from various wicked and immoral practices! ...he is then asked, 'And why then do you drink wine?' and he replies, 'Wine is forbidden only because it leads to enmity and hatred; I am sufficiently wise to guard against that, and so I take wine to make my mind more lively'. (p. 69)

> The man who verbally professes belief in prophecy, but equates the prescriptions of the revealed scriptures with (philosophical) wisdom, really disbelieves in prophecy. (p. 75)

The point here being that if you believe that one should believe in prophecy for the practical reason that having a system of laws as those prescribed in revelation is good for the communality, then the normativity of prophecy will be vulnerable to sensible knave-type challenges—in this case, the very real case of Avicenna's (rationally) drinking wine, despite knowing that it is forbidden by Sharia law. This is then a *reductio* of the idea that the inherent normativity of prophecy is practical, and thus of the idea that there can be *practical* reasons to believe in prophecy.

But in the philosophers' defence, as Averroes argues, the *practical* function of prophecy ultimately derives from an *epistemic* deficiency. If we were all capable of demonstrative proof, we would not fall foul of *akrasia*. We would have attained that level of certainty about what is good that our minds could not be changed, that we cannot waver—in other words, that we do not lose our resolve. Thus, we can follow Averroes' thought for him: if we come to know via demonstration the truths about human nature and the good, then we are indeed exempt, as Avicenna was, to some of the laws—in other words, exempt from believing certain things in the Koran (such as that God sits on a throne) literally. Thus we have a *principled* reason for exemption, and Islamic moderate Evidentialism survives without a scratch.

The central difference, then, it seems to me, between al-Farabi and Averroes, is that for the latter ordinary humans (that is, non-prophets) *can* attain the best kind of knowledge (the philosophers can do so), while for al-Farabi only the prophets can attain proper certainty. This means that al-Farabi can better account for revelation's unique function than can Averroes. For the latter, prophecy can at best give us practical knowledge about how to best live our lives (and as such there may be beliefs that are justified via pragmatic and not epistemic reason, if having those beliefs are constitutive for someone to have the requisite ability), but this is knowledge that is in principle available to everyone, albeit with toil, through experience. That Averroes' position fails to maintain prophecy's complete uniqueness (as per Davidson's contention above) explains why several theorists have taken him to be a more extreme Evidentialist than he actually was.

This interpretation chimes together well, I think, with what Averroes says about the unity of truth, and his well-known claim in his *Decisive Treatise* that "truth does not contradict truth", or more completely:

> Now since this religion is true and summons to the study which leads to knowledge of the Truth, we the Muslim community know definitely that demonstrative study does not lead to [conclusions] conflicting with what Scripture has given us; for truth does not oppose truth but accords with it and bears witness to it. (Averroes *Decisive Treatise*, p. 50)

The reason that philosophical truth and prophecy are in accord, or as Averroes puts it that "demonstrative truth and scriptural truth cannot conflict", is that the former is either the truth arrived at through rhetorical or dialectical methods (which nonetheless yield *epistemic* reason, or else it is practical knowledge gained through inspiration (through dreams or heightened faculty of imagination). When the subject matter of scripture is theoretical truths, then these are either apparently in accord with theoretical truths known through philosophy or they are not. If scripture looks to be in apparent contradiction with demonstrative truth (philosophy), we must conclude that the work of scripture is to be understood allegorically, since it too is the very product of philosophy. And the reason there is a need for scripture to be parsed allegorically at times "lies in the diversity of people's natural capacities and the difference of their innate dispositions with regard to assent" (*Decisive Treatise*, p. 51). This is why in his *Middle Commentary on Aristotle's Categories* he claims that ordinary language predication on God's properties are neither necessarily equivocal or univocal with respect to religious language predication on God's properties. Because religious language can be allegorical, it may simply be what he calls (from Aristotle) *pro hens* equivocal with respect to ordinary language.[8] When, on the other hand, scripture gives us practical knowledge, that is, commandments on how to live our lives:

> …the situation is different … everyone holds that the truth about these should be disclosed to all people alike and to establish the occurrence of unanimity about them we consider it sufficient that the question [at issue] should have been widely discussed and that no report of controversy about it should have been handed down. (Averroes *Decisive Treatise*, p. 53)

In other words, Averroes is saying that provided we have no reason to doubt the veracity of the claim of inspiration or of clairvoyant dreaming,[9] because these give us practical pieces of knowledge and so cannot in principle contradict items of theoretical knowledge, then there can be no further controversy about them. Practical knowledge depicted in revealed texts may *look* like (has the guise of) theoretical knowledge, but really it is not. Memorising a manual on how to swim is not to know-how to swim.[10]

So, ultimately, in order to respond to al-Ghazali's complaints about Islamic moderate Evidentialism, Averroes had to concede somewhat on the unique epistemic role of prophecy as compared to doing philosophy. But this ultimately led him not to question the Islamic credentials of Falsafa but rather to the conclusion that Falsafa had thus to be the best (indeed the only) way of understanding the Koran. As they say, one person's *modus ponens* is another's *modus tollens*!

Averroeism and the Rise of Islamic Modernism and Neo-Islamic Moderate Evidentialism

Averroes' work had a great impact on the intellectual scene in Western Europe, particularly towards the end of the thirteenth century, and in the fifteenth century during the Renaissance. In the first iteration, as we have already mentioned, St Thomas Aquinas (1225–1274) seemed so impressed by Averroes' commentaries on Aristotle that he simply called him "The Commentator". Until then there had been comparatively little Aristotle on the Latin scholastic curriculum at the medieval universities, and Averroes' commentaries were translated into Latin to help with educating students in line with the newly regained enthusiasm in Europe for Aristotelian thought. But Aquinas was careful to distinguish between the Aristotle preserved by Averroes and the innovations that Averroes had brought in. These innovations looked particularly heretical to a medieval Christian audience: they were the doctrine that there was no personal (or bodily) survival after death, and the Islamic moderate Evidentialism that underpinned Averroes' ideas on the issue as to why people should believe that there was survival after death even if it was literally taken as false. As we discussed in Chap. 4, Aquinas's version of moderate Evidentialism made it the case that ultimately *faith* was the ultimate arbiter of religious disputes. When our evidence as to a proposition is inconclusive, such as to enable a dispute, we should believe not for epistemic reasons but in line with *faith*.[11] This is of course the reverse of what Averroes believed—that disputes should ultimately be settled by philosophy. And Aquinas attempts to refute, on philosophical grounds, Averroes' account according to which (literally) taken there can be no survival after death of the individual person qua *material* intellect. However, others in the thirteenth century (such as Siger de Brabant, Dante, and Boethius of Dacia),[12] were more taken with Averroes' heterodox views. In particular, Siger de Brabant interpreted Averroes' Islamic moderate Evidentialism (not that he used this label) as a "theory of double truth", whereby the claims of religion and reason could be contradictory at no rational detriment to either. De Brabant's rendering of Averroes caused the latter to be condemned at the University of Paris in 1270 (de Brabant had been attached to the Faculty of Arts there). This "theory of double truth" resonated later with the thinkers of the Renaissance (especially in Florence and Padua), who were also revisiting some of the ancient Sceptics such as Sextus Empiricus. In Rafael's *School of Athens* that we talked about in Chap. 2, Averroes is depicted—his inclusion symbolising him as one of the protagonists of civilised thinking.[13]

However, Averroes was to have little influence in the Islamic East in the centuries immediately following his death. There are probably many reasons for this, not least that Avicenna had begun to be canonical among philosophically minded thinkers there and was more easily amalgamated than was Averroes with the kind of Mysticism that al-Ghazali had ultimately recommended. And as such Avicenna was taken much more seriously by the then emerging "Illuminationist" (*Ishraqui*) school of Islamic philosophy—a merging of Mysticism and Avicennan Falsafa. The foremost proponent of the Illuminationist school was Suhrawardi (d. 1191), after whose *The Philosophy of Illumination* the school is named. This work was said to have been completed on 16 September 1186, a day that coincided with a rare alignment of planets—one of the many fantastic (and slightly other-worldly) details of Suhrawardi's life.[14] Very briefly, Suhrawardi noted a distinction made by the Falasifa between the transcendent world and the material world, and that (as per their Neoplatonism) thought that the relationship between the two was one of emanation—where at the last stage of emanation, matter (suitably prepared) becomes ensouled by intellects. Suhrawardi replaces this with a central distinction between Light and Dark. Instead of the One at the centre of everything there is the 'Light of Lights', from which literally shine different lights and of different orders—a vertical order and a horizontal order (these lights are real lights, though not exactly like the physical lights in our world). When these lights "meet" darknesses (or "barriers"),[15] something like the shape of our physical world begins to appear and the lights are caused to refract and so bring about this horizontal order of lights, which corresponds—for Suhrawardi—to Plato's forms, what Suhrawardi calls "the archetypes of the talismans". It is unclear whether Suhrawardi thinks there is a *philosophical* argument for these claims, but has rather arrived at them through spiritual acquaintance; through what he calls the "path of intuition". He seems to think there are two ways of getting knowledge, via the "path of intuition" and via the "path of inquiry", which corresponds to theoretical knowledge, or what we called in Chap. 6 "knowledge by description". He thinks that it is possible to master *both* paths: this will yield the "perfect philosopher", the person who should be a political ruler, and the perfect version of which is the Prophet Muhammad. Significantly, Suhrawardi explicitly portrays his Philosophy of Illumination, a synthesis of Mysticism and Falsafa, as being a distinctly *Eastern* philosophy, more in accord with the Philosophy of the Buddha than with Peripatetic philosophy. Suhrawardi's ideas were (most famously) developed by the Safavid, Shiite thinker Mulla Sadra (1571–1640)—Shiite Islam was in the ascendant during the rule of the Safavids in Persia 1501–1736—who is to this day taught in the famous Qom madrasa in Iran. Very briefly, Mulla Sadra thought that Suhrawardi made a mistake in thinking that existence is something that exists only in the mind, not the actual world: for Surhawardi all there is is an interplay between light and dark, and we interpret this as things existing or not existing in our minds. Mulla Sadra calls this (slightly misleadingly) the thesis of the "primacy of essence" (misleading since Suhrawardi thought that essence also exists only in the mind), and proposes the doctrine of the "primacy of existence". Existence is the unanalysable variable that underpins everything, and interestingly (for Mulla Sadra) can come in *degrees*: things can exist more or less intensely (in a similar manner to which lights can shine with varying degrees of intensity). It is this variation of existence that we (in our minds) interpret as variation in the essences of things. Mulla Sadra's philosophy seems to have been very politically influential in today's Iran, and Ayatollah Khomeini (the first Supreme Leader of the Islamic Republic of Iran, following the 1979 revolution) is said to have been deeply influenced by his thought. The thesis of the "primacy of existence" looks on the surface similar to the modern European Existentialist slogan that "existence precedes essence"; and some have taken this affinity to underscore the dangerous, totalitarian aspects of the Existentialist father Martin Heidegger,[16] together with the fact that certain thinkers of the Iranian Revolution drew a more explicit inspiration from with his work, and especially its criticisms of Modernity. However, following Shehaan (2014), it seems to me that when Heidegger talks about *Being* he is really talking about something slightly different than Mulla Sadra, exclusively about the significance (beyond the semantic or pragmatic value) of things.

Another reason why Averroes' ideas did not get much purchase immediately in the Islamic East is that in the latter we see the beginnings of an ascendance of a neo-Hanbalism, especially during the time of the Mongol invasions, the Mongols having taken Baghdad in 1258. This was especially the case with Ibn Taymiyyah (1263–1328). In works such as *Against the Logicians* he angrily attempts to refute the philosophers, including al-Ghazali, thinking that it is impossible for the Koran ever to contradict reason (as in al-Ghazali's "universal rule"); in other words, one ought to read revealed texts *literally*, as Ibn Hanbal had recommended. He was especially concerned with how Falsafa and *Kalām* had fused in the wake of al-Ghazali to create a new widely practised theology, and thought that Islam must return to its roots (especially given the threat from the Mongols) and emulate the practice of the Rightly Guided Caliphs—the *Salaf.* Most importantly, however, Ibn Taymiyyah reprises the Hanbalite *behaviourist* doxastic metaphysics, according to which belief p is nothing other than acting or being disposed to act in a particular way. And from this metaphysics, the normative doctrine follows that to have correct belief is to behave, or be disposed to behave, correctly. This means, to describe it as Wittgenstein might have put it, that belief is not *private*—and this has the very significant corollary that we may more easily evaluate whether someone has a given belief than if belief were an essentially private, occurrent, mental state. So in a stance that is to have modern significance, Taymiyyah rules that the Mongol rulers (given their actions) were *not Muslims* even though they had explicitly converted to Islam. Other thinkers in the Muslim East, however (such as Fahr al-Dīn al-Rāzi (1149–1210), followed the Ash'arite way of thinking and further developed al-Ghazali's thought. Logic is, to this day, taught as an essential component of the traditional curriculum at the madrasas. Others such as Nasīr al-Dīn Tūsī (1201–1274) defended and developed Avicennan philosophy, and yet others such as Abu'l-Barakāt al-Baghdādī (1080–1165) engaged with (and were critical of) Avicenna's philosophy, but from a philosophical point of view.[17] Indeed, Ibn Taymiyyah's work had little impact on his contemporaries, and he died in a Mamluk prison at the Citadel of Damascus in 1328.[18] However, Ibn Taymiyyah's work and overall stance was taken up much later by Muhammad ibn al-Wahhab (1703–1792), who with Muhammad ibn Saud (d. 1765) founded the precursor of the modern state of Saudi Arabia in 1744 (the Emirate of Diriya). The official *fiqh* of this state was to be, and continues to be, Hanbalite.

So we do not see many thinkers tackling Averroes until we get to the late nineteenth century. At this time the Ottoman Empire (which had once been one of the great empires, under Sultan Suleiman the Magnificent 1520–1566) had gone into a decline, and was referred to as the "sick man of Europe". In this context we see the beginnings of what is called Islamic Modernism, the central idea being that the Islamic world is in need of serious political and socio-economic reform; it needs to *modernise*, in short (hence 'Modernism'). But the thinkers that called for this, at least in the first instance, Jamāl al-Dīn al-Afghānī (1836–1897) and Muhammad 'Abduh (1849–1905) (in Egypt), and Muhammed Iqbal (1877–1938) in British India, called for reform by *turning back* and recovering what they saw as Islam's proper intellectual heritage. For this reason they are also sometimes considered, like Ibn Taymiyahh and Ibn al-Wahhab, to be *Salafists*—they aim to reform by recovering the past.[19] But the central difference is that the Modernist movement interprets the original Islam (and the one practised by the *Salaf*) to be in tune with broadly Evidentialist ideas that we saw espoused by Mu'tazilite theologians and the Falasifa. Al-Afghānī in particular is very emphatic about reappropriating the work of Averroes here, and that the ideas of Ash'arite thinkers as al-Ghazali had led the Muslim world into accepting a kind of fatalism (recall the Ash'arite commitment to Occationalism; the idea that God is the proximate cause of every event) that is in tension with the reformist spirit of the Prophet Muhammad, and ultimately responsible for a kind of meekness in the face of ribald European colonialism. In Muhammad 'Abuh we see the idea that through Averroes and on inheriting Evidentialism Europe became civilised once again, such that he is famously said to have said:

I went to the West and saw Islam, but no Muslims; I got back to the East and saw Muslims but no Islam.[20]

The idea, starkly put, is that it was the West that was (at the end of the nineteenth century) reaping the intellectual fruits of the Islamic golden age, and that the Islamic world had become degenerate precisely because it had moved away from its true quiddity, as expressed in a commitment to Evidentialism. We see this sentiment in more contemporary writers such as Mohammed ʿAbed al-Jabri (1935–2010), who want the Islamic world to reappropriate Averroes (seen to be more committed to Evidentialism than Avicenna):

We, post-Averroes Arabs, have lived on clinging to the Avicennan moment after Ghazali granted it currency within "Islam". As for Europeans, they went on to live the very history that we had exited, because they knew how to appropriate Averroes and how to keep living the Averroes moment to this day. (Al-Jabri 1996, p. 124)

A commitment to Evidentialism is found in al-Afghānī too:

This religion enjoins its adepts to seek a demonstrative basis for the fundamentals of belief. Hence it is always addresses reason and bases its ordinances upon it. Its texts clearly state that human felicity is the product of reason and insight, and that misery and perdition are the outcome of ignorance, disregard or reason, and the extinction of the light of reason.—*Refutation of the Materialists*.

But in Iqbal we see, despite an attack on William James's fideism (and other, this time Islamic, fideists), Iqbal's moderating Evidentialism. He claims, for example, that:

Purely metaphysical arguments, however, cannot give us a positive belief in personal immortality. (*The Reconstruction of Religious Thought in Islam*, p. 111)

However, his kind of moderate Evidentialism seems more in tune with Western moderate Evidentialism (as per Aquinas) than what we called Islamic moderate Evidentialism:

In the evaluation of religion, philosophy must recognize the central position of religion and has no other alternative but to admit it as something focal in the process of reflective synthesis. Nor is there any reason to suppose that thought and intuition are essentially opposed to each other. They spring up from the same root and complement each other. The one grasps Reality piecemeal, the other grasps in its wholeness. The one fixes its gaze on the eternal, the other on the temporal aspect of Reality. (*The Reconstruction of Religious Thought in Islam*, p. 3)

Unlike in Averroes (and Avicenna and al-Farabi), then, we do not find the idea that an epistemic non-elite are subject to different doxastic norms than the elite, until we reach slightly more "radical" thinkers in political Islam; in particular Sayyid Qutb (1906–1966), whose work we will return to in the next chapter.

Concluding Remarks

We have explored here some of Averroes' ingenious rejoinders to al-Ghazali's clever arguments against some of Avicenna's teachings. Whilst these rejoinders are premised on disavowing Avicennan innovation on Aristotle, and in particular Avicenna's new account of modality, they are also premised, as we saw, on an overall methodological principle shared with Avicenna: Islamic moderate Evidentialism. The *moderate* part of Averroes' legacy did not robustly live on in medieval Europe, unless we interpret the Latin Averroeists' "theory of double truth" as a kind of commitment to it. Typically, however, Averroeism seems to have come to symbolise in Europe a denial of personal resurrection and a *proto* scientistic (secular) attitude. This image of Averroes has then very much influenced the manner in which thinkers of the Islamic Modernist Movement have sought to use his ideas in order to revive modern Islam, again with little emphasis on the *moderate* aspect of his Evidentialism. Perhaps that was because there are unanswered questions about the idea that an epistemic elite can legitimately make use of symbols and rhetoric to educate the masses, in a way that does not legitimise the idea that the elite can lie to the public, and in a way that would be immune from being patronised by an epistemic elite with totalitarian, or otherwise subjugating, intent. These are the central questions underpinning our next, and final, chapter.

Study Questions

- How can al-Ghazali claim that it is unbelief to claim that one ought to believe that p because believing it will lead to your happiness, but claim that the proof of prophecy is that following it will lead to the "purification of the heart"?

- What might happen when the public accidentally come to realise that their religious beliefs are not literal truths, but based on mythologies told by an epistemic elite?

What to Read Next?

- Averroes: *The Decisive Treatise—Kiqtab Fasl al-Maqal* Translated by Hourani, G. F. (1961): *Averroes: On the Harmony of Religion and Philosophy* (Gibb Memorial Trust).
- Leaman, O. (1988): *Averroes and his Philosophy* (Curzon Press).
- Kedourie, E. (2014): *Afghani and 'Abduh: An Essay on Religious Unbelief and Political Activism in Modern Islam* (Routledge).

Notes

1. Griffel (2004).
2. This is a view that Saul Kripke seems to share in his famous (1980) *Naming & Necessity*. See Strohminger and Yli-Vakkuri (forthcoming) for an overview of contemporary views about the epistemology of modality.
3. Leaman (1988) seems to suggest that Averroes is an early kind of what we would nowadays call "semantic externalism"—the idea that as Hilary Putnam famously put it "meaning ain't in the head" (Putnam 1973).
4. As Herbert Davidson puts it: "Avicenna likewise recognizes, and attaches the name prophecy to, knowledge that results when the emanation from the active intellect—or another supernal being—acts on the human imaginative faculty. But as an extension of his view that man receives intelligible thought directly from an emanation of the active intellect, he, unlike Alfarabi, recognizes, and names as prophecy, genuine theoretical knowledge imparted by the active intellect to the human intellect without the human intellect's having to employ standard scientific procedures" (Davidson 1992, p. 117). Fazlur Rahman makes the distinction by calling revelation of new knowledge "intellectual revelation" and revelation bringing understanding to existing knowledge "imaginative revelation" (Rahman 1958, p. 36).
5. I'll say more about this "Straussian" line and Leo Strauss's political philosophy later in this chapter.
6. As Van den Bergh (2008, p. xxxv) puts it in his translator's introduction to the *Tahafut*: "There are three possible views. A Sceptical view that religion is opium for the people, held by certain Greek rationalists; the view that religion

expresses Absolute Truth; and the intermediate view, held by Averroes, that the religious conceptions are the symbols of a higher philosophical truth, symbols which have to be taken for reality itself by the non-philosophers".

7. "a sensible knave ... may think that an act of iniquity ... will make a considerable addition to his fortune, without causing any considerable breach in the social union ... That honesty is the best policy, may be a good general rule, but is liable to many exceptions: and he, it may perhaps be thought, conducts himself with most wisdom, who observes the general rule, and takes advantage of all the exceptions."

8. That is, neither fully equivocal, but not univocal, but rather "pointing toward" the same thing. For more on *pro hens* equivocals, especially as taken by Aristotle, see Shields (1999) (he calls the underlying notion "core-dependent homonymy").

9. "true visions include premonitions of particular events due to occur in future time ... this warning foreknowledge comes to people in their sleep from the eternal Knowledge which *orders and rules* the universe" (*Decisive Treatise*, p. 55) (my emphasis, to highlight the practical nature of such knowledge for Averroes).

10. Anscombe (1957).

11. This is why St Thomas is sometimes referred to as a *fideist*.

12. For a helpful account of the doctrines of the various Latin Averroeists and how their views can be considered to constitute a unified view, see Marebon (2007).

13. Though he is depicted as rather a solitary figure (not involved in discussion as are most the others) and takes the pose of someone who is doing more *listening* than commenting.

14. For more see Walbridge (2004).

15. These can be substantial or accidental (these latter being what he calls "talismans").

16. For a circumspect take on the influence of Nazism on Heidegger's thought see O'Brien (2016).

17. There is a real wealth of undigested, untranslated philosophical work in the Islamic world between this immediate post-al-Ghazali period and the last moments of the Ottoman Empire. We are living in exciting times where this material is beginning to be more widely understood, especially by thinkers in the West.

18. The Mamluks' Empire (1250–1517) spanned, at its greatest moment, Egypt, parts of North Africa and the Levant.

19. This has been the line of other radical reformers; for instance on feminist reform, the sociologist Fatema Mernissi (1940–2015) has argued that an empowerment of women will come hand in hand with a recovery of Islam's original teachings (Marnissi 2011). Other feminist writers such as Ayaan Hirsi Ali have been much more critical of Islamic (traditional or otherwise) attitudes towards women. And there have of course been more non-theistic versions of Evidentialist reform movements, such as those of the "Young

Turks", who paved the way towards the establishment of the modern Turkish *secular* state.

20. Apparently in 1888 on having returned from France, as reported here: https://www.foreignpolicyjournal.com/2011/07/02/democracy-religion-and-moral-values-a-road-map-toward-political-transformation-in-egypt/.

References

Secondary Sources

Anscombe, G.E.M. 1957. *Intention.* Blackwell.

Al-Jabri, M. 1996. *Arab-Islamic Philosophy: A Contemporary Critique*, Middle East Monography Series. CMES.

Davidson, H. 1992. *Alfarabi, Avicenna, and Averroes, on Intellect.* Oxford University Press.

Deutsch, H. 1990. Real Possibility. *Noûs* 24 (5): 751–755.

Griffel, F. 2004. Al-Ghazālī's Concept of Prophecy: The Introduction of Avicennan Psychology into Ash'arite Theology. *Arabic Sciences and Philosophy* 14: 101–144.

Kripke, S. 1980. *Naming & Necessity.* Blackwell.

Leaman, O. 1980. Ibn Rushd on Happiness and Philosophy. *Studia Islamica* 52: 167–181.

———. 1988. *Averroes and His Philosophy.* Curzon Press.

Lerner, B. 1974. Introduction. Trans. *Averroes on Plato's Republic.* Cornell University Press.

Marebon, J. 2007. Latin Averroism. In *Islamic Crosspollinations. Interactions in the Medieval Middle East*, ed. Anna Akasoy, James Montgomery, and Peter Porman. Gibbs Memorial Trust.

Marnissi, F. 2011. *Beyond the Veil.* Saqi Books.

Putnam, H. 1973. Meaning and Reference. *Journal of Philosophy* 70: 699–711.

Rahman, F. 1958. *Prophecy in Islam: Philosophy and Orthodoxy.* Allen & Unwin.

Rosenthal, E.I.J. 1958. *Political Thought in Medieval Islam.* Cambridge University Press.

Shields, C. 1999. *Order in Multiplicity: Homonymy in the Philosophy of Aristotle.* Oxford University Press.

Shehaan, T. 2014. *Making Sense of Heidgger: A Paradigm Shift.* Rowman and Littlefield.

Strohminger, M., and Yli-Vakkuri. forthcoming. The Epistemology of Modality. *Philosophy Compass.*

Van den Bergh, S. 2008. Introduction. In *Averroes: Tahafut al Tahafut.* Gibb Memorial Trust.

Walbridge, J. 2004. Suhrawardī and Illuminationism. In *The Cambridge Companion to Arabic Philosophy*, ed. Adamson and Taylor. Cambridge University Press.

8

Islamic Philosophy and Politics

Introduction

In the previous chapter we discussed Averroes' defence of Falsafa in light of al-Ghazali's critique. We discussed his defence of some of the specific doctrines endorsed by the Falasifa as well as the overall methodology of Islamic moderate Evidentialism. In essence, where things in Revelation are to be taken metaphorically, they cannot be lies, since they are to be believed for *epistemic* reason (albeit weaker epistemic reason than yielded by philosophical demonstration) and so cannot be really in tension with philosophy. Where propositions in revelation are to be believed for *practical* reason, the correctness conditions for belief are such that they are of a different order to the epistemic conditions of philosophy, so cannot contradict philosophy there either. We also had a look at how Averroeist philosophy was appropriated by various groups throughout history, and ended with the thought that the way in which Averroes fully *moderated* his Evidentialism, actually broadly in line with al-Farabi and Avicenna, made him look, and be taken to be, more of a (classical, al-Kindian) Evidentialist than he actually was; so that we do not really see Islamic moderate Evidentialism properly picked up (though in a different guise, and not in that name) by more modern, seemingly "radical" thinkers such as Sayyid Qutb.[1] Qutb has very misleadingly even been labelled "the Philosopher of Terror" by American journalists and, as I hope to show, this is partly because of a strange (and uneasy) fusion of Qutb's ideas and Hanbalite ideas concerning the determinants of correct belief espoused by some of the radicals (such as Ayman al-Zawahiri and Osama Bin Laden—the founders of al-Qaeda) that aimed to put Qutb's theories into practice.

© The Author(s) 2017
A.R. Booth, *Analytic Islamic Philosophy*, Palgrave Philosophy Today,
https://doi.org/10.1057/978-1-137-54157-4_8

In this chapter, I want to return to explore further the political dimension of Islamic moderate Evidentialism, especially through the writings of the philosopher who tackled this most explicitly—al-Farabi. I then want to explore how, in light of some of the questions with which we ended the last chapter, some of these ideas are germane to what in Marxist and Critical Theory circles is known as "Ideology Critique", first in the writings of post-colonial theorist **Edward Said (1935–2003)**,[2] and then in Qutb's writings in his reformulated concept of *Jāhilīyah* (*al-Jāhilīyah* being originally the Koranic term for "ignorance"—the time preceding the Koranic Revelation). I will end by taking a look at how we might interpret al-Farabi's writings such that Islamic moderate Evidentialism may resist some of the criticisms levied, and such that it gives us what I consider to be a very fruitful working definition of what is extremist belief and what is uniquely wrong with it.

The Prophet Law-Maker, Allegory and Rhetoric

To more fully appreciate al-Farabi's political philosophy, let us compare it with that of Plato. Very briefly, Plato's theory as found in the *Republic* is as follows. Underlying everything is a psychological theory about the way the human soul is constituted. Plato held what is often called a "tripartite theory of the soul" according to which the soul is essentially constituted of three parts: a rational part, an appetitive part and a spirited part. In the *Phaedo*, Plato compares the rational element of the soul to the charioteer steering a chariot of two horses: in order for the chariot to move in a harmonious way, the charioteer must steer the two otherwise wild beasts in the same direction. But without the horses the chariot would not move at all. The appetitive part is said to correspond to our bellies, to our desires and inclinations; the spirited part to our hearts, to our emotions such as courage and fear: it is both our spirited and appetitive natures that move us into action. We are our best selves when the three components of the soul are acting in unison or in harmony: we feel fear towards things we rationally think are fearful and so desire to avoid them, for example. A soul divided upon itself leads to weakness of the will—*akrasia*—and to otherwise unhealthy action. Interestingly, it seems that Plato held that virtue is a kind of knowledge, along with what is known as a "guise of the good" thesis: that if you desire that *p*, you de facto *believe* that *p* is desirable, good (and if you fear that *p*, you de facto believe that *p* is something to be feared). This is what explains the irrationality of the differing parts of the self to be at war with each other, since it would involve straightforward contradiction: both believing that *p* and not-*p*.[3] This means that actually really *knowing* (so being certain) that *p* makes it impossible for you to experience weakness of the will, since you cannot *know p* and not-*p*—this is why the rational element must be ultimately at the helm.

Now, in the *Republic* Plato expresses the view that there is a parallelism between the constitution of the soul and the constitution of the human collective: the state.[4] So the state comprises essentially three parts too, which are going to correspond to the three parts of the soul. In lieu of the rational part, we have the Philosopher Kings; standing proxy for the appetitive part we have the Workers (an economic class); corresponding to the spirited side we have the Guardians (defenders of the state). A virtuous, proper-functioning state is a harmonious state, just as a virtuous non-akratic human soul is a harmonious one (underscored by knowledge). So just as the rational element needs to be at the helm of the three parts to ensure harmony, so must the Philosopher Kings be the rulers of the state. Importantly, especially with respect to Islamic moderate Evidentialism, Plato seems to suggest that the real theory that underpins this theory of government (the one above that I have hugely simplified) will be beyond most people's comprehension, since it is after all a *philosophical* theory and only some people are capable of doing philosophy. And so he thinks that in order to encourage belief or aid comprehension, people should be told a "noble myth": roughly that the Philosopher Kings are born with a piece of gold in their hearts, the Guardians with a piece of silver and the Workers with a piece of silver. So Plato seems to be advocating for the use of mythologies in order to either (or both) (a) get people to believe things that will lead to good consequences (the flourishing of the group) and (b) get people to believe something at least approximating the truth. As we discussed in Chap. 2, it looks as if Plato was advocating for the use of allegory in Socrates' way of persuading Meno of his view (that the recollection "theory" is in fact allegorical), and the whole point of Plato's works being in *dialogue* form must have been to do with his countenancing the use of dialectical methods. Yet the use of dialectical methods and allegory might be seen to provide us with *practical* reason, as argued by Averroes: it seems that if the end of engaging in these practices is something like what is denoted in (a), then they cannot provide us with *epistemic* reasons for belief, but rather *practical* reasons. I'll come back to the importance of this shortly. For now let us explore al-Farabi's take on it.

For al-Farabi, Plato's account of leadership looked incomplete at best and contradictory at worst. For if it is vital for the harmony of the state that the rulers keep the masses on board with "noble myths", then it cannot be those who are adept at *theoretical* reason alone who ought to be in charge. The rulers will need to have practical and rhetorical skill (in line with (a) and (b)) above. This is why for al-Farabi the prophet must be the ideal political ruler. And his theory is an elegant one because his account of absolute certainty (which we discussed in Chap. 5) has the following corollaries: that only the prophet can be fully certain, and that the prophet's state of certainty necessarily comes with great rhetorical and practical skills. For al-Farabi there are essentially two kinds of virtues (the practical virtues and the theoretical (purely epistemic) virtues). In the state of the prophet's perfect certainty these virtues are in complete harmony (he is even the perfect Warrior/Guardian—hence the great conquests at the time of Muhammad). However, for everyone else these virtues are scattered and dispersed among the community. And, here he follows Plato, the community (the state) flourishes only if these virtues are brought into harmony, and it is only prophetic leadership that can bring this about. Below is an illustration:

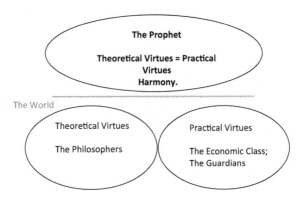

What matters for al-Farabi is the question of what happens when there is no existing prophet to take the helm. But let us now return to the question of the legitimate use of "noble myths" by governments. The Chicago-based philosopher Leo Strauss (1899–1973) was very much influenced by what we have been calling Islamic moderate Evidentialism (though he does not call it by that name). He argues that modern political liberalism (as a product of Enlightenment Evidentialism) will contain the seeds of its own destruction if it does not embrace what he thinks is a more sophisticated conception of political philosophy endorsed by the "ancients", al-Farabi being included among their number. That is, unless the modern liberal epistemic elite (the intelligentsia) become prepared to moderate their avowed Evidentialism, and engage in rhetorical and dialectical methods,[5] the public will become more and more alienated by the elite, unable to really grasp their underlying motives and philosophy, and this will inevitably lead to the public's overthrowing of the liberal political world order.[6] However, the idea that the ruling elite should engage in these methods comes with its own problems. As we have already discussed, al-Ghazali thought this idea sacrilegious, since it would mean that

Revelation was effectively a lie. Averroes responds by saying that, if part of the purpose of these noble myths is to educate the people, then allegory actually provides us with *epistemic* reason to believe (albeit less good epistemic reason than that provided by demonstration). However, I think we can ask whether that is enough for the circulation of these myths not to be considered to be purposefully misleading, if not outright lying. This is brought out by asking whether the public would still believe them were they told that they were actually myths, merely allegories for the actual truth that they are not intelligent enough to understand. It seems pretty clear that the myths can only be effective—qua mechanism to get people to believe something—if the fact that they are myths is *concealed* from them, and that they are all the more effective if they appear to be obvious truths to the public; the more obvious, the more effective. Recall Avicenna on the matter:

> Nor is it proper for any human to reveal that he possesses knowledge that he is hiding from the commonality. Indeed, he must never permit any reference to this. Rather, he should let them know of God's majesty and greatness through symbols and similitudes derived from things that, for them, are majestic and great, adding this much: that He has never an equal, not a partner, not anyone like Him. Similarly, he must instil in them the belief in the resurrection in a manner that they can conceive and in which their souls will find rest. He must tell them about the [eternal] bliss and misery in parables derived from what they can comprehend and conceive. (Avicenna *Metaphysics, The Healing* 10, 2 6.17–25)

It's hard to think that circulating these myths is not in some way deceitful if one must be at pains to never reveal what one "is hiding from the communality". Further, there is the issue of propositions in Revelation that, according to Averroes, we are not to believe for epistemic reasons but for practical reasons, since these propositions are not even *metaphors* for an actually true proposition (or set of propositions). This, you will recall, was the case for our reasons for believing in any manner of personal afterlife (bodily or otherwise): we ought to believe it because of the practical benefit believing it has—it will lead us to acting in accord with virtue, and so the flourishing of the human collective. This is presumably why the Prophet Prince is called the "Prophet Lawmaker" by Avicenna.

But the problem is that, as we discussed in Chap. 6, we seem not to be able to believe at will—having the intention to believe that *p* seems impotent where we have evidence that not *p* is the case. We cannot seem to engender belief just by considering our practical reasons. The intellect for Falsafa is passive *until* it is activated by an *external* agency. Further, as per Averroes' denial of the Ash'arite view on normativity, evidence is normative: having sufficient evidence that *p* automatically gives us all things considered *reason* to believe that *p*. To illustrate: even though I may have reason to want to stay ignorant with respect to how *Star Wars: The Last Jedi* will end, once I have acquired evidence about this (say by seeing a preview on Facebook) I thereby *ought* to believe in line with my evidence, despite my having strong *practical reasons* for not doing so. As the contemporary philosopher Mark Kelly puts it, "one cannot *immunize* against the possibility of acquiring reasons for belief by not caring about the relevant subject matter" (Kelly 2003, p. 628). If this is right, then I think that it will have to be the case that the non-elite will have to have the fact that the real (or "objective" or as it is sometimes put *ex ante*) *practical* reason for the belief will have to be concealed to them, and the reason *for which* they believe (the *ex post*) reason will have to seem to them to be an *epistemic* reason. Put more simply, the non-elite will think that the reason that justifies their belief in personal survival after death is epistemic, but the actual reason that justifies the belief is practical: they believe it because they think it is true, but what actually justifies the belief is that believing it leads to good consequences (in the same way in which believing that I might recover from an illness, despite the evidence, might make it more likely that I will recover).

There are at least two problems with this view: the first is that it violates the requirement for what is these days called *the basing relation*. Put simply, the requirement states that in order for S's belief that *p* to be justified for reason *R*, *R* must be the reason *for which* S believes that *p*. So if the reason that justifies my belief is different to the reason I actually hold the belief for, then my belief cannot be justified. Second, it's hard to see how the view does not in some sense involve countenancing a deception of the public, since the practical reasons that *justify* one's beliefs in such propositions would have to be occulted from one. Finally, more broadly, it is surely the case that the political regime or leader who is circulating these noble myths will find it difficult to completely *ensure* that the public do not know that they are myths, and if they do, it seems reasonable to suppose—as per Avicenna—that trust in the elite will evaporate and the political regime will come under threat. And anyway, is there any way for the public to know that these myths are being used for benign and not insidious ends? What is the difference between noble myths and perverse ideology? To answer these questions, let us now turn to exploring the notion of ideology in a pejorative sense (in the way Marx and contemporary critical theorists mean it), and how Muslim writers such as Edward Said and Sayyid Qutb have taken it.

Ideology, Propaganda, Colonialism

Ideology in the pejorative sense above is analogous to a kind of propaganda: the illicit use, by those in power, of a mechanism with the function of persuading people to have false beliefs, beliefs which will somehow legitimise and support a social structure that enables those in power to continue to wield power.[7] A theory of ideology in this sense:

> is a program of criticism of the beliefs, attitudes, and wants of the agents in a particular society. This research program is initiated by the observation that agents in the society are deluded about themselves, their position, or their interests … The basic use of the term 'ideology' is '(ideological) delusion' or '(ideologically) false consciousness'. (Geuss 1981, p. 12)

What is meant by "false consciousness" is that to enough people in a society it will appear to them that p, but p is false, and it would not appear to them that p were it not for the obtaining of the malicious ideology. The idea of an ideology in this pejorative sense was most famously introduced by Karl Marx in his classic 1932 paper (written with Engels) "The German Ideology" and developed most recently by Jurgen Habermas (b. 1929) and his Frankfurt School of Critical Theory, by contemporary philosophers of language such as Sally Haslanger and Jason Stanley, and by critical race theorists such as Tommie Shelby. However, in their avowal of the use of religion by an elite as a means to both educate the public and get them to act in ways that are ultimately in their interests *in such a way that the myths cannot be made apparent to them*, the Falasifa seem to have discussing a very similar phenomenon. The public's belief in, say, the resurrection of the flesh will appear to them to be true, and as such it will be a delusion *deliberately* orchestrated by the ruling elite. There are, however, two important points of difference between what the Falasifa advocated and what contemporary theorists mean by ideology in a pejorative sense.

The first is that according to most accounts, an ideology is a "false ideology" only if it (a) "contains a false belief to the effect that the particular interest of some subgroup is in the general interest of the group as a whole" (Geuss 1981, p. 14) and (b) as having a certain kind of history (or "genealogy")—as a system of belief constructed as "collective rationalisations", "i.e. as systems of beliefs and attitudes accepted by the agents for the reasons which they could not acknowledge" (Geuss 1981, p. 20).[8] On (b), for example, Jason Stanley (2016) characterises "ideological belief" as belief that is immune to counter-evidence, because of its being intimately connected to one's identity—because one cannot change one's identity easily, one cannot drop a belief constitutive of that identity even when one has overwhelming evidence against it. Ideology Falsafa-style is supposed to be beneficial for the whole group as a whole, and is supposed to be *purposefully* implanted into communities' doxastic lives by the epistemic ruling elite—the reasons for which they not only are cognisant of, but think fully justify the implant. I think it is fully plausible to question whether the desideratum denoted in (b) is really necessary for an ideology's being an insidious one—since one could easily image a powerful community with insidious ends *in full consciousness* implanting an ideology on a community,[9] or alternatively a powerful community *taking* itself to be implanting an ideology for good reasons, but it turning out as an unforeseen consequence that the implant leads to domination over a community of people. Further, in Critical Theory there also exists the concept of an ideology in a *positive* sense, the classic example being in what Lenin proposes in his 1901 political pamphlet *What is to be Done?*, in which he calls on party intellectuals—a "vanguard"—to get the "labour movement to elaborate an independent ideology for itself", one that will properly serve their interests. Falsafa-style ideology on this account then seems to be a *positive* ideology, even in Marxist terms; this especially when we bear in mind this important point made by Geuss:

> A political order suitable for the maximal development of the capitalist mode of production was created in the English Civil Wars by members of the incipient bourgeoisie in the course of pursuing various religious fantasies. The more the members of the bourgeoisie know about the true nature of capitalist society, the less effective they will be in the class struggle, because the more hopeless they will realise their situation will be in the long run. So the bourgeoisie, paradoxically enough, has an interest in being self-deceived. If, then, the distinction between ideology in the pejorative sense and ideology in the positive sense is not as sharp as one might have hoped, this is partly a reflection of the fact that historically satisfaction of one's interests and oppression, pursuit of a sense of identity and false consciousness have been all but inextricably linked. (Geuss 1981, p. 25)

Falsafa-style ideology is ideology that is meant to be in the service of the idea that the non-elite have an interest in being self-deceived, though the explanation for this, as we have already discussed, has to do with people's *epistemic* limitations—as concomitant susceptibility to weakness of the will—and not with any contingent historical facts. I will address the issue of whether the Falasifa are entitled to this account of the normativity of belief in the section that follows. For now, let's look at how certain more contemporary Islamic philosophers have used some of these ideas about ideology.

The two theorists whom I think use these concepts most notably are Sayyid Qutb and Edward Said. Edward Said's 1978 book *Orientalism* was a very serious intellectual achievement, and has been one of the most influential books of all time, pretty much marking the advent of what is these days called "Post-Colonial Theory". To simplify hugely, Said was interested in the way that *intellectuals* studied the Islamic world, and the 'scientific' narratives they presented to the world—"Orientalism" being now (thanks to Said) an old fashioned term to describe the work done in what is now called Middle Eastern/North Africa Studies or Islamic Studies. Said argued that these narratives (probably unconsciously) were actually *colonial* instruments of control, ultimately depicting the "Orient" as "homogeneous", "weak", "feminine", mysterious", as something "radically *other*" prone to mysticism, fatalism and irrationalism, and as ultimately something to be "possessed" and "dominated".

> I doubt if it is controversial, for example, to say that an Englishman in India, or Egypt, in the later nineteenth century, took an interest in those countries, which was never far from their status, in his mind, as British colonies. To say this may seem quite different from saying that all academic knowledge about India and Egypt is somehow tinged and impressed with, violated by, the gross political fact—and yet *that is what I am saying* in this study of Orientalism. (Said, *Orientalism*, p. 5)

In other words, these narratives were operating as ideologies to subtly justify a colonialist world view. The fact that they were presented as *scientific* and so as beyond argument just explains how they are effective—since the whole point of an ideology (as we saw from our discussion of Falsafa-style ideology) is that it *seems* that there is good *epistemic* reason to believe it, where in fact there is none. Otherwise, given that belief is not receptive to practical reasons, we would not be able to believe them. To successfully overcome colonialism, argued Said, it would therefore be necessary to overcome this concomitant ideology.

This idea that pejorative-sense ideology was one of the most powerful (because underhand) weapons of colonialism was one that heavily influenced Sayyid Qutb. Qutb was particularly concerned with a kind of cultural ideology, which propelled Western values at the expense of Islam's and would allow the West to keep control and subjugate the Islamic world via proxies—or puppet dictators (such as the later assassinated President of Egypt Anwar Sadat (1918–1981)). Qutb wanted to give this ideology idea more explicitly

Islamic clothes and called it *Jāhilīyah*. In order for the Islamic world to be truly free of its colonial shackles it must then confront this ideology and replace it with a new one, and it must do so through an epistemic elite, a "vanguard" that will lead the masses. As we will discuss shortly, I think that in fact Qutb's overall theory resembles modern liberal theory (as defended by John Rawls), but I think that the way in which Qutb uses the theory of ideology brings to light some of the flaws (and thus potential solutions) of what we have in this book been calling Islamic moderate Evidentialism. This is because the fact that one is under a particular spell of *Jāhilīyah* could mean that one might be under the *illusion* that one is really a Muslim but may not actually be one. And this throws up again—even within an Evidentialist framework—the idea that someone could declare themselves a Muslim and yet really be an apostate, and so that legally speaking it is not enough to do the former in order to escape the charge of apostasy. This of course opens up the possibility for a Koranic justification of killing leaders who declare themselves Muslim but are only doing so out of false consciousness. This, to more extreme groups, meant that there was a connection to be drawn between the work of Sayyid Qutb and the literalist Hanbalite Ibn Taymiyyah. And so even today we see the likes of the leaders of al-Qaeda pledge inspiration from the works of *both* men, as if they were in intellectual harmony when they are not. Put differently, what happens to Qutb's work shows just how easily the ideas in Islamic moderate Evidentialism can be put to bad work, and it needs theoretical checks in order to prevent this. I will now move to discuss how I think al-Farabi's work has at least the seeds to show us how to do this.

Doxastic Normativity, Human Perfection, and the Utopian City-State

One might think that if one espouses Evidentialism one thereby also espouses the Normativity of Evidence thesis, understood as the claim that evidence alone can generate *reasons* for belief: that having evidence that there are x number of pebbles on Brighton beach gives all subjects (all things considered) *reason* to believe that there are x number of pebbles on Brighton beach. However, I do not think Evidentialists need to commit themselves to the Normativity of Evidence thesis (so construed), since they may think that what makes it the case that one ought always to believe in accord with the evidence is some *further* fact. For instance, even modern-day Evidentialists (as we discussed briefly in Chap. 1) defend their thesis via something about what a belief *is*—namely belief is a mental state which *essentially* has evidence as its correctness conditions. If *this* fact did not obtain, then evidence would not be normative—so the evidence alone cannot carry all the normative weight. Alternatively, an Evidentialist can claim (perhaps more in line with what William Clifford had in mind) that one ought to believe in line with our evidence, because only by doing so can we satisfy certain of our *moral* or *pragmatic* ends (if we do not believe in accord with the evidence, as per Clifford's famous neglectful sea-captain, we are *immoral*). I think that al-Farabi's account of normativity looks to be *teleological* in character, and this for doxastic normativity as well as for the normativity of action. Put differently, al-Farabi thinks that right belief, and right action, must be determined by considering what is *good* belief and *good* action. We are obliged to do and believe what is in accord with our human perfection. Good belief and good action are then, following Aristotle, thought of in terms of what is the function of humankind. In the final analysis, satisfying our ends, our unique function qua human, is what will make us happy, what constitutes the good life for such creatures as us. This leads al-Farabi to give us an account of what constitutes our realising our unique end, our human perfection. He does this most explicitly in his *The Attainment of Happiness*, but broaches the subject in many of his other works. And, in my reading, *The Conditions of Certainty* is also ultimately an answer to this question. This is because, if I am right, al-Farabi sets out to give an account of what he takes to be not only *theoretical* perfection—what is the best cognitive state a human can be in—but also what it is that marks out prophets from ordinary humans. The prophet is to be distinguished from the ordinary person by her vastly superior faculty of imagination. And this enhanced faculty enables her not only to achieve the best kind of certainty available (bar God's certainty) but also gives her the best kind of practical knowledge available—she better than anyone knows how to transform the ideal into the real. Indeed, it is the very property that enables her practical knowledge that enables her certainty—her certainty is a composite of both practical and theoretical perfection—such that in the prophet the theoretical and practical virtues are inextricably unified. Since the prophet is human perfection realised, we must take it that human perfection is a composite of both theoretical and practical perfection. As far as this perfection is concerned, then, there cannot be a fragmentation between our epistemic and practical ends. There cannot be, in other words, a uniquely epistemic end determining what it is that we ought to believe.

In contemporary epistemology, the received view is a teleological one,[10] where doxastic normativity is thought to be a function of our having specifically *epistemic* ends, usually held to be the twin ends of believing truths and avoiding falsehoods. Selim Berker (2013) has recently complained that this view about the normativity of belief suffers from failing to respect what he calls the "unity of the proposition"—an analogue of a familiar problem facing teleological theories in ethics (that utilitarianism violates the unity of the person) (cf. Smart and Williams 1973). According to Berker, the epistemic teleologist will have to accept unacceptable trade-offs, as when someone in virtue of believing an obviously false proposition will make it the case that she believes lots of true propositions. The teleologist seems forced to accept that S's belief in this false proposition is *epistemically* justified, even though S knows it to be false. Berker thinks this is grossly counter-intuitive.[11] What seems to be counter-intuitive, however, is specifically that the belief is *epistemically* justified, or rational. It is not at all clear to me that it is counter-intuitive to think that it is justified, if we are judging it from a pragmatic, moral or perhaps an *all things considered* perspective. According to many contemporary Evidentialists, there is no *all things considered* perspective when it comes to belief. There is, for these epistemologists, no such thing as just plain ought to believe (Feldman 2000; Kelly 2003),[12] only ought to believe relative to some perspective or another—and this underscores their commitment to the normativity of evidence. This seems to me to be the opposite view to al-Farabi's, where the ultimate human end is an inexorable *mix* of the epistemic and the practical, such that there can only be obligation *sans phrase*. On this version of doxastic teleology Berker's objection has less bite: we can accept that it is odd to think that belief in a known falsehood is *epistemically* justified, since it is not so obviously odd to think that it is *all things considered* justified, depending on what is at stake in the particular case. Further, al-Farabi's account gives us the standard by which to commensurate competing epistemic and practical claims on either belief or action—what is most in accord with human perfection as embodied by the prophet's perfect certainty.

Now, this helps us also with the issue mentioned earlier with respect to Islamic moderate Evidentialism's violation of the requirement of the *basing relation*. The objective *ex ante* reasons are the prophet's reasons, and these are *not* purely epistemic—they are *all things considered* reasons that encapsulate all the different kinds of reason there are. Our *ex post* reasons are not—cannot be—the prophet's reasons, so in that sense al-Farabi's epistemology violates the basing requirement, strictly speaking. However, perhaps it does so in a benign way, since it's not as if, in al-Farabi's epistemology, the reasons for which non-prophets (the non-elite) hold their beliefs (the *ex post* reasons) are of a totally different order than the prophet's *ex ante* reasons. That is, our reasons are sometimes practical, sometimes moral, sometimes epistemic; the prophets' always *all things considered* (where all the relevant things are practical, moral and epistemic reasons). So our reasons are the same as the prophets', but not as good because fragmented. And the fact that for al-Farabi *only* the prophet is a rightful member of the epistemic-elite means that it is *not* the case that the public's reasons will somehow be different from the intelligentsia's. Philosophers too have to believe that there is an afterlife, and for moral reasons. The point that only the Prophet is a member of this elite group is what I think ultimately puts those brakes on Islamic moderate Evidentialism that we discussed with reference to Qutb above. And it also gives us the resources for an account of what extremism is and what's wrong with it from within Falsafa.

To see this, let's begin by recapitulating the connection between politics and prophecy that I think al-Farabi makes. Absolute certainty can only be had by those, at least on earth where there exists the possibility of being in sceptical scenarios, who have a superior faculty of imagination, and so can understand why they know first principles grasped by intellectual intuition. Only those with this power can satisfy al-Farabi's sixth condition on certainty. Given the connection he has made between superior imaginative faculties and prophecy, it is natural to conclude that the only people who can attain this perfect level of certainty are prophets. As such, the very property that enables the prophet to attain certainty is also the very property that gives the prophet certain practical abilities—the ability to explain difficult ideas to the public and the ability to know how to put abstract ideas into practice, to realise the ideal. This has certain important corollaries: that human perfection, as exemplified by the prophet's condition of certainty, is a composite of both *practical* and *theoretical* perfection; that the prophet is the ideal political leader.[13] But it also means that *only the prophet* can attain this level of perfection, at least in this world, and at least qua single individual—since only the prophet has the requisite "superior nature". What then becomes important for al-Farabi is how we can attain a level of perfection that most resembles it. And just as he uses the ideal of absolute certainty to identify the various different gradations of justified belief (levels of certainty), he uses the ideal of the prophet as human perfection to identify the various gradations of human perfection as found on earth.

We see al-Farabi do this explicitly in his work *The Attainment of Happiness* where, having given an account of human perfection (qua composite of theoretical and practical perfection), al-Farabi turns to the issue of how this ideal can be realised in more than just an individual Prophet:

> This, then, is theoretical perfection. As you see, it comprises knowledge of the four kinds of things by which the citizens of cities and nations attain supreme

happiness. What still remains is that these [virtues] be realized and have actual existence in nations and cities while conforming to the account of them given by the theoretical affairs. (al-Farabi *The Attainment of Happiness*, p. 25)

Notice that a-Farabi talks about "cities and nations" and not just one individual city-state. This is because the ideal ruler for al-Farabi—the prophet—has final jurisdiction over not only a given city-state, but a much wider community of people. Presumably here he has the Muslim community (*umma*) in mind. In al-Farabi's words, the ruler "is the first sovereign of the excellent city, he is the sovereign of the excellent nation, and the sovereign of the universal state" (al-Farabi *The Perfect State*, p. 247). This immediately raises the question of how cities or nations should be governed when the prophet is absent: he cannot govern every city at once. This is so even while the prophet is alive, and of course is even more pressing when he is not. So there are two questions that I think al-Farabi wants to try to answer in his political works: first, how does the prophet realise happiness on earth?; and second, how do we organise things politically when the prophet is absent, or there is no extant prophet? Of course, the second question is going to be informed by the first for al-Farabi, since he thinks we should try to replicate as best we can the model the prophet gives us. But the situation related to the second question is of course the situation that humans will find themselves in most of the time—and as such, in answering this second question, we can see al-Farabi departing from "ideal theory" though in a way where the ideal informs the real (since he thinks the answer to the first question must inform the second). Now, the practical and theoretical virtues as found in the prophet are unified and this is why al-Farabi insists that the words he has used for "philosopher" and "ruler" are co-extensive: "So let it be clear to you that the idea of the Philosopher, Supreme Ruler, Prince, Legislator, and *Imam* is but a single idea" (al-Farabi *The Attainment of Happiness*, p. 47).[14] But the virtues then fragment when they are not in their perfect state, as embodied by the prophet. This elegantly mirrors his emanationist cosmology, where progressive emanation from the First Cause involves less and less unity. Hence we have al-Farabi say:

Those which are from the very outset provided with all the essentials of their existence are made to imitate the First (Cause) and its aim from their very outset, and hence enjoy eternal bliss and hold the highest ranks; but those which are not provided from the outset with all the essentials of their existence, are provided with a faculty by which they move toward the expected attainment of those essentials and will then be able to follow the aim of the First (Cause). The excellent city ought to be arranged in the same way: all its parts ought to imitate in their actions the aim of their first ruler according to their rank. (al-Farabi *The Perfect State*, p. 239)

So the prophet cannot lead the people over whom he has jurisdiction towards happiness in the same way that he is happy—he cannot make them *that* perfect. But he can lead them towards being as happy as it is possible for them to be, make them "imitate" (resemble as closely as possible) his state. But, and this is crucial, in no other human state than hers are the virtues necessary for human happiness properly unified. In our ordinary, less than perfect state, these virtues lie fragmented. And they cannot be put back together again by any *single* individual, other than the prophet. But they *can* be put together as an emergent property, when the individuals embodying the various virtues are working together in harmony.[15] This is why, according to al-Farabi, humans must be part of a community in order to be truly happy: "for an isolated individual cannot achieve all the perfections by himself and without the aid of many other individuals. It is the innate disposition of every man to join another human being or other men in the labour he ought to perform: this is the condition of every single man" (al-Farabi *The Attainment of Happiness*, p. 23).[16] Arguably, al-Farabi could mean here that by being part of this emergent property, by joining others in the pursuit of happiness, human beings transcend their physical presence. This would harmonise the twin ideas that human perfection requires practical perfection, and that human perfection requires transcendence from the physical. However, I cannot find a very explicit endorsement of this view in any of his extant writings.

In any case, what is explicitly al-Farabi's concern is how the prophet can best lead people towards happiness, given that humans are prone to *akrasia* and that they cannot attain perfection working alone. To this there one must add another Aristotelian background assumption—one I mentioned in the last chapter—[particularism] there are no *rules* for working out what one ought to do (consistent with the good) for any individual case: this is a matter for practical wisdom (Greek: *phronesis*; Arabic: *Ta'aqqul*), the bearer of which can intuit how to apply general moral knowledge to particular situations, and can only be attained through experience. For al-Farabi, we are imperfect creatures and so are prone to lack *phronesis*. Only the prophet with his superior capacities is able to really have infallible *phronesis*—partly because only he has proper certainty about human nature, and partly because only he has the requisite practical knowledge about how things are best carried out. Further, because there are no general moral rules available to us, *we* must know about human nature, such that we can then gain *phronesis*. In other words, we cannot act in accordance with good simply by following a set of laws that would ensure that we did, so we need to have at least something resembling knowledge of human nature. This is why we need prophecy, thought of as a rhetorical device for teaching us moral truths that we would not otherwise believe. But our knowledge of human nature must fall short of absolute certainty, for the non-perfect philosopher and those who have moral beliefs acquired by rhetorical device, and this makes *akrasia* possible: we can waver, since we are not sure of our moral opinions come what may. For us, doubts can creep in, and we can lose our moral resolve. This, as I mentioned, gives prophecy a further role; to give us a manual as to how to live such that we are in control of our desires. The rules the manual gives us on how to live, however, can only function *in tandem* with the theoretical knowledge it teaches, such that—in isolation from certain bits of theoretical knowledge—they cannot be taken to constitute generalist moral laws. And this is further the case because these rules will work best if others are following them too. That is, the prophet gives us rules as to how to behave as individuals, and following these rules enables us to reach our full flowering only when our neighbours are following them too.

In his *The Attainment of Happiness* al-Farabi tells us that in order to ensure that a community—city-state or nation—works in harmony there ought to be instituted in each community three departments whose purpose is to educate both the public and future rulers in three different ways. The departments correspond to what al-Farabi thinks are the two different ways in which the theoretical and the practical virtues can be "realised" in nations and cities: "There are two primary methods of realizing them: instruction and the formation of character" (p. 35). Those who comprise the group associated with "instruction" are "those who should preserve the theoretical sciences". And this last group, along with "the *imams* and princes" is made up of those who should receive the instruction relevant to this group, and then the "the princes among them will be placed in subordinate offices and promoted gradually through the ranks until they are fifty years old" (p. 35). The second group concerns realising practical virtue, the formation of character. The second group is split between those teaching what al-Farabi calls "popular theoretical science" and "image-making theoretical science" (p. 39). The object of the former science is effectively the same truths attained through demonstrative proof, but they are believed on the basis of persuasive rhetoric, not philosophical argument and logic. The object of the latter is the art of persuasive rhetoric itself. All the people of a nation or city—including those not fit for political office—are to receive training in the former science, whereas only the princes and those who are later to be the teachers of this science are to be instructed in the latter. Because "compulsion" is sometimes requisite in the learning either of these sciences, both are associated with the "craft of war": "The prince needs the most powerful skill for forming the character of others with their consent and the most powerful skill for forming their character by compulsion. The latter is the craft of war: that is, the faculty that enables him to excel in organising and leading armies … to conquer the nations and cities that do not submit to doing what will procure them that happiness for whose acquisition man is made" (p. 37). Finally, the third group will preserve and teach the knowledge of how the latter three more general sciences are applicable to a very particular group of people. Thus what this group teaches is variable, depending on what nation or city one is in: "There will be as many of these extracted sciences as there are nations, each containing everything by which a particular nation becomes perfect and happy" (p. 40). Al-Farabi at times seems to equate these "extracted sciences" to religion; which is why he draws the inference in a different work that "therefore it is possible that excellent nations and excellent cities exist whose religions differ, although they have as their goal one and the same felicity and the very same aims" (al-Farabi, *The Perfect State*, p. 281).

The idea here is that the "First Leader"—clearly the prophet, though we are never told so explicitly—is to set up these three institutions/communities. One reason why we ought to think that this "First Leader" is the prophet is brought to light on consideration of the status of the preceding claim (that the First Leader is to set up these three institutions): is it meant to be a normative, *de jure* claim, or a descriptive de facto one? If the latter, we must worry about on whose authority we are supposed to accept it; particularly since only this First Leader will have the theoretical and practical knowledge requisite to be able to adequately make this sort of normative judgement. So if we take al-Farabi's claim *de jure*, then we must also take him (al-Farabi) to be this First Leader. I am not sure anything al-Farabi says explicitly rules out the idea that he thought of himself in those terms, but I suggest it is really rather more likely that he did not. Instead, it is probably that he is here tentatively suggesting that trying to build these institutions is what the prophet did among his circle de facto, while at the same time giving us some rationale for why he did; and the rationale is that communities of people require a leader. This follows from the interpretation I gave earlier as to how for al-Farabi the practical and theoretical virtues are united *only* in the prophet, but that human felicity finds its perfection in their union. A leader is requisite to help bring these virtues together when they lie in their fragmented state, scattered among humankind. The leader does not correspond to the rational part of the human soul as it does in Plato, but rather a state where the virtues are united. Because of this, al-Farabi takes it that there must be leaders whose virtue and perfection resemble those of the prophet, but fall somewhat short. That is, since each community must have its own leader, and the First Leader cannot be the local leader for every community, the need for a "Second Prince" becomes salient, as it does when we are in a state where there is no longer a First Leader. This is why, of course, the First Leader must create the aforementioned three institutions. The Princes following the First never match the First in terms of human perfection. For this reason, these secondary leaders must be habituated and brought up to fulfil their function, and kept in check by the departments—they cannot wield absolute power, nor are their judgements to be taken to constitute absolute certainty.

The Imperfect Cities, Democracy and Liberalism

According to al-Farabi, the First Leader must kick-start a political process, as explained at the end of the last section. Provided we identify the First Leader with the prophet, this means that there cannot be a virtuous city-state *before* the time of the prophet. However, rather obviously, we can live in a time where there is no prophet, and al-Farabi concedes that there can be a time where there is no one suitable to take on the principality, either of a particular city-state or the agglomeration of all city-states. This means that city-states (again, specific ones or the set of all city-states) can, if this happens for too long, degenerate into becoming less than virtuous city-states. Just as he carefully enumerates the various sub-par conditions of certainty, and the various progressively less unified emanated spheres of existence, al-Farabi gives us a hierarchy of the various conditions a city-state can be in when it is less than virtuous. That is, when its components—corresponding to the theoretical and practical virtues—are either inexistent or are not in proper harmony. We are told in both *The Political Regime* and *The Perfect State* that city-states can fail to be virtuous by being immoral, ignorant or errant. Roughly speaking, al-Farabi seems to hold that the difference between the immoral and ignorant cities is rooted in his motivational externalism—the citizens of the former having knowledge of virtue but failing to conduct their affairs in accord with that knowledge, where the citizens of the ignorant cities merely do not know what virtue is or, more precisely, have no "representation" of virtue and have no beliefs about what it is. The citizens of the errant city then have such a representation, but it is an incorrect one.

It is in this context that al-Farabi discusses the democratic city-state. However, here we find an apparent tension in that in *The Political Regime* he seems to say that the timocratic city "is the best among the ignorant cities" (section 97) but later claims that the democratic city is "the most admirable and happy" (section 115) among the ignorant cities. Muhammad Ali Khalidi (2003) has diagnosed the problem roughly as follows: al-Farabi evaluated sub-par city-states here with respect to two differing criteria. The first criterion concerns how closely a city-state resembles the virtuous state, and the second how easily it can be converted into becoming virtuous. The democratic city fares better pitted against the timocratic on the second criterion and worse on the other. According to Khalidi, there are three reasons why al-Farabi thinks that the democratic city fares better than a timocracy relative to the second criterion. First, that "it contains within itself certain microcosms of the virtuous city" (Khalidi 2003, p. 388), such that even though the democratic city is not as a whole virtuous, it contains smaller constellations of people or "miniature cities" that are. Second, and relatedly, the fact that these miniature virtuous cities exist within the democratic city will make the latter more easily transformed into a virtuous one. "Though Farabi does not tell us how this might actually be done, his emphasis on virtuous communities, and indeed virtuous philosophers, naturally suggests a lobbying group for the virtuous within the democratic city" (Khalidi 2003, p. 390). Khalidi's third reason is that al-Farabi would have considered the democratic city to be in better accord than the timocratic as regards the "official ideology of the Islamic *umma*, which regarded ethnic diversity as a virtue and deemed religious affiliation to trump cultural affiliation", and as such to have in general terms been more germane—than, say, Plato—to the possibility of cultural pluralism.

I think this picture cannot be quite right, however. This is because there cannot be a way for cities, once they have fully degenerated into unvirtuous cities (the three institutions having been dismantled) to be "transformed" into virtuous city-states, not unless God sends us another prophet (or an older prophet reappears). That is, a First Leader needs to kick-start the process again. Notice that Khalidi in the quote above admits that al-Farabi does not himself tell us "how this might actually be done". So I suggest we need another explanation as to why al-Farabi seems conflicted as to whether the timocratic or democratic city is the best among the ignorant cities. Khalidi is right, however, in thinking that al-Farabi emphasises the existence of virtuous microcosms within the democratic city. The democratic city is happy, then, in so far as it contains communities of people who are living in proper harmony. This happens accidentally (since the institutions bringing the different virtues together will not exist in a democracy) but is a final, or intrinsic, good; it is not an instrumental one. While some of its parts may be virtuous, when taken as a whole, the democratic city is less like the ideally virtuous city than the timocratic. This alone may be enough to explain al-Farabi's seeming ambivalence. But when one factors in the third of Khalidi's reasons for thinking that the democratic city is the best among the non-ideal cities, then I think that we should conclude that *all things considered* al-Farabi thought that the democratic city trumps the timocratic one.

What I think is extremely interesting in al-Farabi's political theory so construed is that it ultimately makes him an advocate of a kind of liberalism (though this liberalism will resemble something more like anarchism, or anarcho-socialism,[17] than our modern notion suggests).

> The democratic city is the city in which every one of its inhabitants are equal to one another, and their traditional law is that no human being is superior to another in anything at all. Its inhabitants are free to do what they like. One [inhabitant] has authority over another or over someone else only insofar as he does what heightens that person's freedom.
>
> Thus there arise among them many moral habits, many endeavours, many desires, and taking pleasure in countless things. Its inhabitants consist of countless similar and dissimilar groups. In this city are brought together those [associations] that were kept separate in all those [other] cities—the vile and the venerable ones. Rulerships come about through any chance one of the rest of those things we have mentioned. The public, which does not have what the rulers have, has authority over those who are said to be their rulers. The one who rules them does so only by the will of the ruled, and their rulers are subject to the passions of the ruled. If their situation is examined closely, it turns out that in truth there is no ruler among them, and no ruled. (*The Political Regime* 113)

If his account of sub-optimal politics is parallel to his account of sub-demonstrative, full certainty, his politics are not utopian like Plato's. For most of us, who are not prophets, we need to concern ourselves with something lesser than absolute certainty. Similarly, for most of us, who are not living during a time of prophecy, and when the three institutions that the prophet prescribed seem absent in any formal sense, then we need to concern ourselves with something lesser than how to construct a virtuous state. But this does *not* make him an advocate of "realism" or non-ideal theory. The prophet's perfection embodied in his state of certainty informs not only what the ideal state should be, but how human happiness is possible *outside* a virtuous political regime. And this is achieved by effectively not regulating the state *at all*. By not doing so, the probability is that "microcities" will emerge and will organically harmonise the virtues such that they resemble the prophet's state of certainty (a state in which the virtues exist united). As I mentioned, I'm not sure that this means al-Farabi is espousing liberalism and democracy as conceived by us today. Khalidi himself expresses concern about whether our notion of democracy maps on to either al-Farabi's or Plato's: "it may be argued that the centrally salient feature of the democratic regime, in Plato as in Farabi, is freedom rather than majority rule, equal participation in the political process, or any other main features that we associate with democracy in the twenty-first century" (Khalidi 2003, p. 394). But I think it would be equally anachronistic to consider al-Farabi's and the ancient notion of "freedom" to correspond to something like, say, a Rawlsian account of Liberalism where the mechanisms of state somehow *guarantee* these freedoms. [18] And this is why in the Platonic account, at least, "democracy" must necessarily lead to anarchy. But if this is true, and al-Farabi's political philosophy is effectively to endorse a kind of anarcho-socialism, then the following question emerges: what is the role of Islam here? Is al-Farabi's political philosophy ultimately an admission that Islam has no role in the politics of a non-prophetic era? I think that the al-Farabian answer lies in the role the ideal plays in determining non-deal theory. Al-Farabi has tried to give an account of the prophet's political supremacy, why it is legitimate, and why political regimes that lie in the immediate wake of the prophet are virtues regimes. For al-Farabi Islam has a role here, clearly. But it also has a role in the state of ignorance, since knowing its true role comes with knowing that the least bad way for humans to attain happiness is in a "democracy" and in a state where it does not have sovereignty over all.

An alternative way of answering the question is to claim that Islam in a political incarnation is the mechanism that serves the role of *guaranteeing* certain important human rights. This, I think, is ultimately the view of Sayyed Qutb, despite—as we discussed—his having been much maligned by the Western press as the "Philosopher of Terror".[19] We can see this in the following passage:

> It is not the intention of Islam to force its beliefs on people, but Islam is not merely 'belief'. As we have pointed out, Islam is a declaration of the freedom of man from servitude to other men. Thus it strives from the beginning to abolish all those systems and governments which are based on the rule of man over men and the servitude of one human being to another. When Islam releases people from this political pressure and presents to them its spiritual message, appealing to their reason, it gives them complete freedom to accept or not to accept its beliefs ... in an Islamic system there is room for all kinds of people to follow their own beliefs, while obeying the laws of the country which are themselves based on the Divine authority. (Sayyed Qutb *Milestones*, p. 61)

The idea here is that Islam is the guarantor of freedom, and freedom of belief especially. This follows the famous Koranic edict that:

There is no compulsion in religion. (Koran 2:256)

Just as the liberal state is supposed to guarantee these freedoms, so in Qutb's theory is an *Islamic* state properly conceived.[20] Why then is Qutb critical of the West, which under Liberal eyes also sees itself as occupying exactly this role? His answer can be seen in this passage:

There can be no decent life if every individual seeks to enjoy his absolute freedom without limit. Such behaviour is guaranteed to destroy both the society and the very individuals. Society has a higher interest which must limit the freedom of the individual, and it is in the individual's own interest to have definite limits to his enjoyment of freedom so that he does not get carried away by his instincts, desires, and pleasures to the point of destruction, and also so that his freedom does not clash with the freedom of others, resulting in endless quarrels, turning freedom into a torment and a hell, and arresting the growth and perfection of life in the interests of a shortsighted individualism. This is what has happened with the "freedom" of the capitalist system. (Sayyed Qutb, *Zilal* vol. 2)

The disagreement then between Qutb and Western "capitalist" liberalism is not that one is anti-tolerance and freedom and the other is not. Rather, it is a disagreement about the limits to freedom. And both Qutb's political Islam and Western liberalism agree that there must be limits. As John Rawls puts it in *A Theory of Justice*: "Justice does not require that men stand idly by while others destroy the basis of their existence" (p. 192). This is why apostasy is supposed to be considered a crime worthy of capital punishment, since to disown Islam so construed is to violate the human rights of people *in the knowledge* that one is so doing, and that it is wrong to do so.[21]

But the very fact that the disagreement about what constitutes the *limitations* of freedom brings to the foreground a serious problem with Liberalism as a political system installed to *guarantee* human freedom. And this is ultimately an epistemological problem. It is an epistemological problem because it raises the question of how we can possibly resolve the disagreement. What common, neutral, higher-order epistemic standards can we appeal to in order to dissolve it? It is very hard to see that there can be any such standards for us, fallible human creatures. But if there are not then it looks as if the justification of any of our beliefs needs to be thought of in the deontic terms of permissibility, not obligation and requirement. That is, S's having a justified belief that p will not rule out the possibility of another subject's S*'s having a justified belief in not-p, even where S and S* share the same evidence and have similar cognitive abilities—given that S* might endorse radically different higher-order standards as to how one might evaluate one's first order evidence. As far as I am concerned, this means that one can never be justified in having full certainty in one's credence regarding any proposition.[22]

In Leo Strauss's view, it seems, the Falasifa held a unified idea (at least in so far as Averroes and al-Farabi are concerned) that true knowledge can only be had be a certain epistemic elite (the philosophers). This includes knowledge regarding human nature, and as such (given their Aristotelian commitments) knowledge of what one ought to do. The philosophers must then avail themselves of rhetorical skills, and cease to confine themselves exclusively to their theoretical pursuits. This is especially salient in Strauss (1959), where he explicitly gives al-Farabi the view that there is a difference to be had between the "way of Plato" (where rhetorical skill is considered important) and the "way of Socrates" (where *theoria* (theoretical knowledge) is all that counts); the absence of Socrates in Plato's *Laws* is claimed to vindicate this. But for Strauss, the very fact that the literal truth about human nature is beyond most humans' cognitive capacities is something that the epistemic elite need to conceal from the masses. In advocating this, the Falasifa, in Strauss's interpretation, seem to *ex hypothesi* also advocate a demagoguery of sorts. And this is exactly what al-Ghazali had found so problematic about Falsafa's moderate Evidentialism. I hope I have made the case that this view is mistaken, at least in so far as al-Farabi's political theory and epistemology is concerned, and so may well depart from Averroes. This is because it seems that for al-Farabi the epistemic elite, in so far as it constitutes those in a condition of absolute certainty, comprises only one member: the prophet. It is true that al-Farabi saw in Plato (and Aristotle) the idea regarding the necessity of rhetorical virtue in politics, but in his hands that is a corollary of the fact that proper *theoretical* certainty involves practical ability. It is not necessary for him as a means for a non-prophetic epistemic elite to keep the masses in check.

In al-Farabi's Fallibilism, when it comes to all but prophets' knowledge, we find the checks required for Islamic moderate Evidentialism not to spiral into a kind of extremism. Dialectics and allegory may well be required, even in a democratic state, for the diverse parts of the human community to work together in harmony—for the theoreticians to communicate and have their ideas enacted properly. But the theoreticians should not see themselves as part of an elite. In al-Farabi's system, as per the diagram earlier in the chapter, theoretical virtue is not at the head, as it is in the Platonic system—"in truth

there is no ruler among them, and no ruled", as he puts it. So while conceal-
ment of the fact that an allegory is an allegory may nonetheless be necessary
for the theoreticians to be effective, they cannot do so to *coerce* and *dominate*
since they will not be in a position of power. One may of course wonder
whether being knowledgeable of the theoretical de facto puts one in a position
of power. But one is supposed equally in a position of power by virtue of one's
practical and rhetorical virtues. And the theoreticians cannot *alone* do the
rhetorical work necessary for their noble lies to be effective.

Extremist Belief

To recapitulate, the idea I find in al-Farabi is a radically Fallibilist one, whose
dominant insight, it seems to me, is that this does not mean that we must be
sceptics and suspend judgement on any proposition—our beliefs can be justified even if they fall short of being justifiably certain. Put in the language of
modern "formal epistemology", we should never, or very, very rarely, have full
confidence, credence 1.0 with respect to any proposition, but rather the most
we can ordinarily have is something like a 0.8 credence: we do not need to
split the difference each time and suspend judgement (a 0.5 credence). As I
mentioned in the previous chapter, this has certain theoretical attractions with
respect to scepticism, and circumvents any criticism as regards whether this
one could "live" this Fallibilism, since we can justifiably have more than 0.5
credences and so easily act on them. It also, intriguingly, begins to tell us
something about what it is to have extremist belief, and what is uniquely
wrong with having extremist belief. Let me explain.

Consider two possible models for conceptualising extremist belief: what I
like to call "'the defective belief model" and the "over-belief model". I want to
present the latter as the model favoured by al-Farabi and the former the tacit
consensus view of the contemporary West. According to the "defective belief
model", someone has extremist beliefs when they believe propositions that are
morally bad to believe, such as that racism is permissible, perhaps, or that it is
permissible to torture non-combatants. The problem with this account is that
it does not seem—as we have already mentioned several times in this book—
that we have voluntary control over our beliefs. And if, as we discussed, "moral
ought implies can", then it looks as if we cannot be held to *moral* account over
what we believe. For example, it seems crazy for me to blame you, the individual reader, for the last monsoon rains in India, given that their happening
was something you could not control. But if our beliefs are outside our control, then they too should escape moral blame.

We might then make the following modification (staying within the model): what is defective about extremist beliefs has nothing to do with whether they are rightly subject to moral blame, but rather to do with their being grossly at odds with our evidence. We might then think that someone who does not believe in climate change, or who believes that the earth is flat, is as much of an "extremist" as someone who believes that non-combatants are legitimate targets during war. But the problem is that if extremist beliefs are just beliefs that are badly out of kilter with the evidence, then what's precisely *extremist* about them? Earlier today, I completely believed I had fed the cat this morning, against the evidence provided by a full tin of Whiskas and a hungry-looking animal. Does that make me an extremist? I think it doesn't.

Perhaps there are solutions to these problems for the "defective belief model"; but I think raising them does enough to motivate us to at least look at an alternative picture. Here, then, is the "over belief model", which I think one can derive from al-Farabi. Suppose, as I am interpreting al-Farabi, ordinary belief (for non-prophets) is more like a 0.8 credence than a full-on 1.0 credence. (We don't need to worry about the precise value so long as it is above 0.5 and under 1.0). Anything above a 0.8 credence is, then, other than in very unusual circumstances, to have too much credence in one's belief; it is to *over believe*. Put differently, we should nearly always allow for at least some small possibility that we might be mistaken: absolute certainty is almost always problematic relative to our evidence. To believe with absolute certainty, such that nothing could persuade us otherwise—to *over believe*—is to have extremist belief. The model circumvents the problem regarding ascribing moral responsibility to our beliefs when the latter are out of our control, since extremist beliefs are held to be problematic relative to the evidence (and not some moral standard). And the model identifies something unique that all extremist beliefs possess, and so differentiates them from non-extremist beliefs badly in tension with our evidence.

What I think this means politically is that one must be extremely careful—from a liberal point of view—about legislating on the limitations (or the conditions of the possibility) of a liberal state. As mentioned, that al-Farabi's radical fallibilism seems to recommend something like the latter may make us consider his view to be more germane to a kind of anarcho-socialism than an endorsement of modern liberalism as we know it. But perhaps this need not commit al-Farabi to anarcho-socialism as such, especially given that his fallibilism is meant to be consistent with the failure of scepticism. Perhaps, for instance, he could have accepted something like the claim that we can make legislation to ensure the continence of the liberal state, but that in making judgements about how to legislate, the best we can hope for is the judgement of something like a deliberative democracy—where that judgement is to be considered perforce revisable and never absolute.

Concluding Remarks

Islamic moderate Evidentialism began in the medieval Islamic world as a doctrine in response to an issue that arose specifically for doing philosophy in, as Nasr put it, the "land of Prophecy"—though as I mentioned in Chap. 4, the issue can generalise such that it is a secular one about expertise. It looked at first blush a very theoretical position, primarily about epistemology and metaphilosophy. But I hope this last chapter has shown how it underpinned the political philosophy of the day too; not only that, it has proved important to comprehending the political philosophies of more contemporary Muslim thinkers such as Sayyid Qutb and Edward Said. As Peter Adamson strongly emphasises throughout his monumental (2016) *Philosophy in the Islamic World*, Islamic philosophy has always been, and continues to be, very much in touch with its history. But the doctrine has proven crucial with respect to understanding influential figures in Western political thought such as Leo Strauss; and properly understood it could provide us with some of the tools for understanding deep-seated problems facing our modern world.

Study Questions

- Is it ever permissible for the state to *manipulate* the media as a means of getting its message across?
- Is there any sense that the narrative of modernism within the Islamic world is a kind of "Orientalism" as Said conceived of it?
- Could modern liberalism in theory have a place for a political philosophy that accepts the role of religion?

What to Read Next

- Al-Farabi: *The Political Regime—Al-Siyāsah al-Madanīyyah* Translated by Najjar, F.M. in R. Lerner and M. Mahdi (eds.) *Medieval Political Philosophy: A Sourcebook* (New York: Free Press).
- Qutb, S. 2006/1964: *Milestones* (Islamic Book Service).
- Mahdi, M.S. 2001: *Alfarabi and the Foundation of Islamic Political Philosophy* (Chicago: Chicago University Press).

Notes

1. Also in particular Malana Maududi (1903–1979). Unfortunately we won't have the space to discuss his views here.
2. For a survey of contemporary work, see Seth (2014).
3. For a lucid discussion, see Morris (2006).
4. For more on this parallelism, see Williams (1999).
5. Machiavelli, for Strauss, is the paradigm of a liberal thinker who rightly engaged in rhetorical and dialectical methods to get his message across. See his (1958) *Thoughts on Machiavelli*.
6. Strauss's criticisms of liberalism then, it must be emphasised, are "friendly-fire" criticisms. His aim is to protect liberalism from its otherwise inevitable decay. This is not of a piece with how some "Straussians" in the US Neoconservative movement have understood him.
7. Jason Stanley (2016) also describes ideology in a pejorative sense to be involved in propaganda.
8. This is often taken to be an idea taken from the German philosopher Friedrich Nietzsche in his famous *The Genealogy of Morals*.
9. Hence al-Farabi writes in *The Political Regime* that the tyrannical city will be governed by "the one most excellent at using stratagems, and the one most perfect in opinion about what they ought to do as always to be seen as dominators and to prevent others from dominating them … All of their traditional laws are traditional laws and prescriptions such that, when adhered to, they are fit to dominating others" (sec. 106).
10. This, even among so called epistemic "deontologists", since the latter merely defend the view that there are such things as epistemic *obligations*—that belief can be deontologically evaluated.
11. What is most original in Berker's article, however, is his demonstrating how making the epistemic end a synchronic end (as recommended by, for instance, Feldman 2000 and Foley 1993) does not help: the epistemic teleologists will nonetheless have to accept these unacceptable trade-offs, even if the epistemic aim is a synchronic one.
12. Though see Booth (2014, 2012) for a dissenting view.
13. Thus the ruler deserves his place in virtue of certain *natural* properties; as al-Farabi puts it: "Therefore the prince occupies his place by nature and not merely by will … This being the case, the theoretical virtue, the highest deliberative virtue, the highest moral virtue, and the highest practical art are realized in those equipped for them by nature: that is, in those who possess superior natures with very great potentialities" (al-Farabi *The Attainment of Happiness*, p. 34).
14. Note, however, that he never uses the word "prophet" in this context. This is presumably to avoid the possibility of being charged with blasphemy.

15. This of course in reference to Plato's *Republic*.
16. This echoes Aristotle's famous claim that "Man is a Political Animal".
17. I say anarcho-socialism, since, as I have mentioned, human happiness and freedom is, for al-Farabi, dependent of how the group functions as a whole—the virtues in humanity lie fragmented and can only come together (as in the state of the prophet) when the group is operating in harmony.
18. After the famous Harvard political philosopher John Rawls (1921–2002) who reanimates political philosophy in contemporary "analytic" philosophy (where it had become rather moribund) in his work *A Theory of Justice*.
19. For discussion (and reasonably sympathetic views of Qutb's work) see Thorpe forthcoming and Khatab 2006. The phrase "the Philosopher of Terror" is from the *New York Times*, cited in Thorpe forthcoming. As I mentioned earlier, we should be careful to distinguish Qutb's views from the views of those who sought to enact his theory, since their conception of Qutb is an odd mixture of what Qutb actually said with a Hanbalite world view that is actually anathema to the former.
20. For further discussion on this point see Shavit (2017).
21. There are some Muslim scholars, however, who question whether Sharia law ought to dictate the idea that apostasy is a capital punishment. For instance, Talbi (2006) argues that though the death penalty for apostasy has its authority based on a Hadith, "we have good reason to consider it a forgery" since it is mixed in the books of Hadith with rebellion and highway robbery, and there is no mention in the Koran of the death penalty for apostates.
22. For a much more detailed defence see Booth and Peels (2010, 2012) and Peels and Booth (2014).

References

Secondary Sources

Adamson, P. 2016. *Philosophy in the Islamic World. A History of Philosophy Without Any Gaps*. Vol. 3. Oxford University Press.

Berker, S. 2013. Epistemic Teleology and the Unity of Propositions. *Philosophical Review* 122: 337–393.

Booth, A.R., and R. Peels. 2012. Why Responsible Belief Is Blameless Belief. *Journal of Philosophy* 107 (5): 257–265.

Booth, A.R. 2012. All Things Considered Duties to Believe. *Synthese* 187 (2): 509–517.

———. 2014. Epistemic Ought Is a Commensurable Ought. *European Journal of Philosophy* 22 (4): 529–539.

Booth, A.R., and Rik Peels. 2010. Why Responsible Belief Is Blameless Belief. *Journal of Philosophy* 107 (5): 257–265.

Feldman, R. 2000. The Ethics of Belief. *Philosophy and Phenomenological Research* 60: 667–695.

Foley, R. 1993. *Working Without a Net: A Study in Egocentric Epistemology.* Oxford University Press.

Geuss, R. 1981. *The Idea of a Critical Theory.* Cambridge University Press.

Kahlidi, A.M. 2003. Al-Fārābi on the Democratic City. *British Journal for the History of Philosophy* 11 (3): 379–394.

Kelly, T. 2003. Epistemic Rationality as Instrumental Rationality: A Critique. *Philosophy and Phenomenological Research* 66: 612–640.

Khatab, S. 2006. *The Power of Sovereignty: The Political and Ideological Philosophy of Sayyid Qutb.* Routledge.

Morris, M. 2006. Akrasia in the Protagoras and the Republic. *Phronesis* 51 (3): 195–229.

Peels, R., and A.R. Booth. 2014. Why Responsible Belief Is Permissible Belief. *Analytic Philosophy* 55 (1): 75–88.

Said, E. 1978. *Orientalism.* Penguin.

Seth, S. 2014. The Politics of Knowledge: Or, How to Stop Being Eurocentric. *History Compass* 12 (4): 311–320.

Shavit, U. 2017. *Scientific and Political Freedom in Islam.* Routledge

Smart, J.C.C., and B. Williams. 1973. *Utilitarianism: For and Against.* Cambridge University Press.

Strauss, L. 1958. *Thoughts on Machiavelli.* Chicago University Press.

———. 1959. How Fārābī Read Plato's *Laws.* In *What Is Political Philosophy? And Other Studies.* Free Press.

Stanley, J. 2016. *How Propaganda Works.* Princeton University Press.

Talbi, M. 2006. Religious Liberty: A Muslim Perspective. In *New Voices of Islam: Rethinking Politics and Modernity: A Reader,* ed. M. Kamrava. I.B. Tauris.

Thorpe, L. forthcoming. Sayyid Qutb and Aquinas: Liberalism, Natural Law, and the Philosophy of Jihad. *Heythrop Journal.*

Williams, B. 1999. The Analogy of City and Soul in Plato's Republic. In *Plato,* ed. Gail Fine. Oxford University Press.

Appendix 1: Raphael's *The School of Athens* (Source: Alamy.com)

© The Author(s) 2017
A.R. Booth, *Analytic Islamic Philosophy*, Palgrave Philosophy Today,
https://doi.org/10.1057/978-1-137-54157-4

References

Greek Works Cited

Aristotle

Categories – translated by J.L. Ackrill (1975) *Aristotle: Categories and De Interpretatione* (Clarendon Press).

De Anima – translated by Hugh Lawson-Tancred (1987) *De Anima (On the Soul)* (Penguin Classics).

Metaphysics – translated by Hugh Lawson-Tancred (1998) *Aristotle: The Metaphysics* (Penguin Classics).

Nicomachean Ethics – translated by Hugh Tredennick (2004) *Aristotle: The Nicomachean Ethics* (Penguin Classics).

On the Heavens – translated by W.K.C. Guthrie (1960) *Aristotle on the Heavens* (William Heinemann Medical Books).

Physics – translated by P.H. Wicksteed & F.M. Cornford (1989) *Aristotle: Physics Books 1- IV* (Loeb Classical Library).

Posterior Analytics – translated by Hugh Tredennick & E.S. Forster (1989) (Loeb Classical Library).

Plato

Meno – translated by Adam Berensford (2005) *Plato: Protagoras and Meno* (Penguin Classics).

Phaedo – translated by David Gallop (2009) *Plato: Phaedo* (Oxford World's Classics).

Republic – translated by Desmond Lee (1974) *Plato: The Republic* (Penguin Classics).

© The Author(s) 2017
A.R. Booth, *Analytic Islamic Philosophy*, Palgrave Philosophy Today,
https://doi.org/10.1057/978-1-137-54157-4

Plotinus

Enneads – translated by Stephen Mackenna (1991) *Plotinus: The Enneads* (Penguin Classics).

Porphyry

Life – translated by Thomas Taylor (2016) *Select Works of Plotinus: Translated from the Greek with an Introduction Containing the Substance of Porphyry's Life of Plotinus* (Classic Reprint).

Alexander de Aphrodisias

De Anima – translated by Victor Caston (2014) *Alexander of Aphrodisias: On the Soul* (Bloosmbury's Ancient Commentators of Aristotle).
De Intellectu – translated by Robert B. Todd (1990) *Two Greek Aristotelian Commentators on the Intellect: The De Intellectu Attributed to Alexander de Aphrodisias and Themistus' Paraphrase* (Pontifical Institute: Medieval Sources in Translation).

Arabic Works Cited (Not in Translation)

Al-Farabi

Kitāb al-burhān: Al-ʿAjam, R. & Fakhry, M. (eds.) *Al-Mantiq ʿinda al-Fārābī* vol. 4 (Dar el-Machreq 1986).
Risālah fī al-ʿAql: Bouyges, M.S.J. (ed.) *Alfarabi Risālah fī al-ʿAql* (1938).
Sarāʿiṭ al-yaqīn: Al-ʿAjam, R. & Fakhry, M. (eds.) *Al-Mantiq ʿinda al-Fārābī* vol. 4 (Dar el-Machreq 1986).

Al-Ghazali

Fayṣal al-Tafriqa: Dunyā, S. (ed.) (Cairo: 1961).

Arabic Works Cited in English Translation

Al-Kindi

A Concise and Brief Statement About the Soul – translated by Peter Adamson & Peter E. Pormann (2012) *The Philosophical Works of al-Kindi* (Oxford University Press).

Discourse on the Soul – translated by Peter Adamson & Peter E. Pormann (2012) *The Philosophical Works of al-Kindi* (Oxford University Press).

Letter on the Method of How to Dispel Sorrows – translated by Peter Adamson & Peter E. Pormann (2012) *The Philosophical Works of al-Kindi* (Oxford University Press).

On First Philosophy – fi al-Falsafa al-Ūlā – Translated by Ivry, A.L. 1974: *Al-Kindi's Metaphysics* (SUNY Press).

On the Intellect – translated by Peter Adamson & Peter E. Pormann (2012) *The Philosophical Works of al-Kindi* (Oxford University Press).

That There Are Incorporeal Substances – translated by Peter Adamson & Peter E. Pormann (2012) *The Philosophical Works of al-Kindi* (Oxford University Press).

Al-Farabi

The Attainment of Happiness – Taḥṣīl al-saʿādah (Translated by M. Mahdi 2001 *Alfarabi: Philosophy of Plato and Aristotle* (Cornell University Press).

The Perfect State – Mabādi' ārā ahl al madīnat al-fāḍilah (Translated by Walzer, R. 1985: *On the Perfect State* (Oxford University Press).

The Philosophy of Aristotle – Falsafat Arisṭūṭālīs (Translated by M. Mahdi 2001 *Alfarabi: Philosophy of Plato and Aristotle* (Cornell University Press).

The Political Regime – Al-Siyāsah al-Madaniyyah (Translated by Najjar, F.M. in R. Lerner and M. Mahdi (eds.) *Medieval Political Philosophy: A Sourcebook* (Free Press).

Avicenna

Autobiography – (Translated by D. Gutas 2014: *Avicenna and the Aristotelian Traditon* (Brill)).

The Healing (Metaphysics) – Al-Shifā (al-Ilāhiyyāt) (Translated by Marmura, M.E. 2008: *The Metaphysics of the Healing* (Brigham Young University Press).

The Healing (Psychology) – Al-Shifā (al-Nafs) (Translated by Rahman, F. 1959: *Being the Psychological Part of Kitab al-Shifā* (Oxford University Press).

Averroes

Epitome of the Parvia Naturalia – Talḫīṣ al-ḥiss wa-l-maḥsūs (Translated by Blumberg, H. 1961: *Averroes' Epitome of the Parvia Naturalia* (Medieval Academy of America)).

Middle Commentary on Aristotle's Categories – Talkḥīs kitāb al-maqulāt (Translated by Butterworth, C.E. 1998: *Averroes' Middle Commentaries on Aristotle's Categories and De Interpretatione* (St Augustine's Press)).

The Decisive Treatise – Kiqtab Fasl al-Maqal (Translated by Hourani, G. F. 1961: *Averroes: On the Harmony of Religion and Philosophy* (Gibb Memorial Trust)).

The Incoherence of the Incoherence – Tahafut al-tahāfut (Translated by Van Den Bergh, S. 1954: *Averroes' Tahafut al-Tahafut* (Gibb Memorial Trust)).

Al-Ghazali

Deliverance from Error – al-Munqidh min al-Dalāl (Translated by McCarthy, R. 1980: *Freedom & Fulfillment* (Twayne Publishers)).

Moderation in Belief – Al-iqtiṣād fī al- iʿtiqād (Translated by Yaqub, A.M. 2013: *Al-Ghazali's Moderation in Belief* (Chicago University Press))

The Incoherence of the Philosophers – Tahāfut al-Falāsifa (Translated by Marmura, M.E. 1997: *Al-Ghazālī: Tahāfut al-Falāsifa* (Brigham Young University Press)).

Ibn Taymiyya

Against the Greek Logicians – Dar al-Taʿārud al-ʿAql wa-l-Naql (translated by W. Hallaq) (1993) (Oxford University Press) 1993.

Ibn Tufayl

Hayy Ibn Yaqzan – Ḥayy ibn Yaqzān translated by Lenn Goodman (2009) *Ibn Tufayl's Hayy Ibn Yaqzan: A Philosophical Tale* (Chicago University Press).

Suhrawardi

Philosophy of Illumination – Ḥikmat al-Ishrāq (translated by John Walbridge & Hossein Ziai) (2000) *Suhrawardi: The Philosophy of Illumination* (Brigham Young).

Other Primary Sources

Descartes

Discourse on Method – translated by Donald A. Cress (1998) *Descartes: Discourse on Method & Meditations on First Philosophy* (Hackett).

Brentano

Psychology from an Empirical Standpoint – translated by A.C. Rancurello & D.B. Terrell in Linda McAllister (ed.) (2014) *Brentano: Psychology from an Empircial Standpoint* (Routledge).

Clifford

The Ethics of Belief – edited by T.J. Madigan (1999) *The Ethics of Belief and Other Essays* (Prometheus).

Hume

Dialogues Concerning Natural Religion – edited by Dorothy Coleman (2007) *Hume: Dialogues Concerning Natural Religion* (Cambridge University Press).
Enquiry Concerning the Principles of Morals – edited by L.A. Selby-Bigge & P.H. Nidditch (1975) *David Hume: Enquiries: Concerning Human Understanding and Concerning the Principles of Morals* (Open University Press).

James

Pragmatism – (2017) *William James: Pragmatism* (Jovian Press).
The Will to Believe – (2017) *The Will to Believe: William James* (Jovian Press).

Kierkegaard

Concluding Unscientific Postscript – edited by A. Hannay (2009) *Kierkegaard: Concluding Unscientific Postscript* (Cambridge University Press).

Moore

Principia Ethica – (2017) *G.E. Moore: Principia Ethica* (Dover Books).

Nietzsche

On the Genealogy of Morals – translated by Michael A. Scarpitti (2013) *Nietzsche: On the Genealogy of Morals* (Penguin Classics).

Pascal

Penseés – translated by A.Krailsheimer (1995) *Blaise Pascal: Penseés* (Penguin Classics).

Russell

History of Western Philosophy – (2008) (Routledge).

Wittgenstein

On Certainty – translated by Denis Paul, edited by G.E.M. Anscombe & G.H. von Wright (1978) *Ludwig Wittgenstein: On Certainty* (Blackwell).

Secondary Sources

Adamson, P. 2005. On Knowledge of Particulars. *Proceedings of the Aristotelian Society* 105 (3): 273–294.
———. 2007a. *Al-Kindī.* Oxford University Press.
———. 2007b. Knowledge of Universals and Particulars in the Baghdad School. *Documenti e Studi Sulla Tradizione Filosofica Medievele* 18: 141–161.
———. 2016. *Philosophy in the Islamic World. A History of Philosophy Without Any Gaps.* Vol. 3. Oxford University Press.
Adamson, P. 2015. *Philosophy in the Islamic World: A Very Short Introduction.* Oxford University Press.
Aikin, S. 2014a. *Evidentialism and the Will to Believe.* Bloomsbury.
———. 2014b. Knowing Better, Cognitive Command, and Epistemic Infinitism. In *Ad Infinitum: New Essays on Epistemological Infinitism,* eds. John Turri and Peter Klein. Oxford University Press.
Al-Afgani. 1955. *The Refutation of the Materialists.* Cairo.
Al-Jabri, M. 1996. *Arab-Islamic Philosophy: A Contemporary Critique,* Middle East Monography Series. CMES.
Al-Jabri, M. 1999. *Arab-Islamic Philosophy: A Contemporary Critique.* Centre for Middle Eastern Studies, University of Texas at Austin.
Albertini, T. 2011. Ibn Rushd or Averroes? Of Double Names and Double Truth. In *After Appropriation: Explorations in Intercultural Philosophy and Religion,* ed. M. Joy. Calgary University Press.
Ali, Z. 2013. *Faith, Philosophy, and the Reflective Muslim.* Palgrave Macmillan.
Alston, W. 1989. The Deontological Conception of Epistemic Justification. In *Epistemic Justification: Essays in the Theory of Knowledge.* Cornell University Press.
Anscombe, G.E.M. 1957. *Intention.* Blackwell.

Antognazza, M.R. 2015. The Benefit to Philosophy of the Study of Its History. *British Journal for the History of Philosophy* 23 (1): 161–184.

Bakar, O. 1998. *Classification of Knowledge in Islam: A Study in Islamic Philosophies of Science*. Islamic Texts Society.

Bealer, G. 1996. A Priori Knowledge and the Scope of Philosophy. *Philosophical Studies* 81: 121–142.

Berker, S. 2013. Epistemic Teleology and the Unity of Propositions. *Philosophical Review* 122: 337–393.

Berman, L.V. 1961. The Political Interpretation of the Maxim: The Purpose of Philosophy Is the Imitation of God. *Studia Islamica* 15: 53–61.

Bishop, J. 2007. *Believing by Faith*. Oxford University Press.

Black, D. 1996. Practical Wisdom, Moral Virtue, and Theoretical Knowledge: The Problem of the Autonomy of the Practical Realm in Arabic Philosophy. In *Moral and Political Philosophies in the Middle Ages*, ed. B.C. Bazan, E. Andujar, and L.G. Sbrocchi. Legas.

———. 2006. Knowledge (ʿilm) and Certitude (yaqīn) in al-Fārābī's Epistemology. *Arabic Sciences and Philosophy* 16 (1): 11–46.

Bonjour, L. 1985. *The Structure of Empirical Knowledge*. Harvard University Press.

Bonjour, L. 1986. *Empirical Knowledge*. Rowman and Littlefield.

Booth, A.R. 2008a. A New Argument for Pragmatism? *Philosophia: Philosophical Quarterly of Israel* 36 (2): 227–231.

———. 2008b. Deontology in Ethics and Epistemology. *Metaphilosophy* 39: 530–545.

———. 2012. All Things Considered Duties to Believe. *Synthese* 187 (2): 509–517.

Booth, A.R., and Rik Peels. 2010. Why Responsible Belief Is Blameless Belief. *Journal of Philosophy* 107 (5): 257–265.

Booth, A.R., and R. Peels. 2012. Why Responsible Belief Is Blameless Belief. *Journal of Philosophy* 107 (5): 257–265.

———. 2014. Epistemic Ought Is a Commensurable Ought. *European Journal of Philosophy* 22 (4): 529–539.

———. forthcoming-a. Belief Is Contingently Involuntary. *Ratio*.

———. forthcoming-b. Advice for Infallibilists: DIVORCE & RETREAT! *Synthese*.

Booth, A.R., and D.P. Rowbottom. 2014. *Intuitions*. Oxford University Press.

———. 2014. Why Responsible Belief Is Permissible Belief. *Analytic Philosophy* 55 (1): 75–88.

Brentano, F. 1874 [1995]. *Psychology from an Empirical Standpoint*. Routledge.

Bronstein, D. 2016. *Aristotle on Knowledge and Learning: The Posterior Analytics*. Oxford University Press.

Chisholm, R. 1957. *Perceiving: A Philosophical Study*. Cornell University Press.

Clifford, W.K. 1877[1999]. The Ethics of Belief. In *The Ethics of Beleif and Other Essays*, ed. T. Madigan. Prometheus.

Clifford, W.K. 1887. The Ethics of Belief. *Contemporary Review*.

Conway, D. 1984. 'It Would Have Happened Already': On One Argument for a First Cause. *Analysis* 44: 159–166.

Davidson, H. 1992. *Alfarabi, Avicenna, and Averroes, on Intellect.* Oxford University Press.

De Boer, T.J. 1967. *The History of Philosophy in Islam.* Trans. E.R. Jones. Islamic Philosophy Online.

Deutsch, H. 1990. Real Possibility. *Noûs* 24 (5): 751–755.

Dougherty, T., and Chris Tweedt. 2015. Religious Epistemology. *Philosophy Compass* 10 (8): 547–559.

Douglas, A.X. 2015. *Spinoza & Dutch Cartesianism: Philosophy and Theology.* Oxford University Press.

Edmonds, D., and J. Eidinow. 2001. *Wittgenstein's Poker.* Faber & Faber.

Emilsson, E.K. 2017. *Plotinus.* Routledge.

Endress, G. 1980. Review of *L'Intellect selon Kindî* by J. Jolivet (1971). *Zeitschrift der Deutschen Morgenlandischen Gesellschaft* 130: 422–435.

Evans, C.S. 1998. *Faith Beyond Reason: A Kierkegaardian Account.* Edinburgh University Press.

Fakhry, M. 2002. *Al-Fārābī: Founder of Islamic Neoplatonism.* Oneworld.

———. 2004. *A History of Islamic Philosophy.* Columbia University Press.

Fantl, J., and M. McGrath. 2009. Advice for Fallibilists: Put Knowledge to Work. *Philosophical Studies* 142: 55–66.

Feldman, R. 2000. The Ethics of Belief. *Philosophy and Phenomenological Research* 60: 667–695.

Foley, R. 1993. *Working Without a Net: A Study in Egocentric Epistemology.* Oxford University Press.

Frank, R. 1983. Moral Obligations in Classical Muslim Theology. *Journal of Religious Ethics* 11: 205–223.

Frankfurt, H. 1971. Freedom of the Will and the Concept of a Person. *The Journal of Philosophy* 68 (1): 5–20.

Galston, M. 1990. *Politics and Excellence: The Political Philosophy of Alfarabi.* Princeton University Press.

———. 1992. The Theoretical and Practical Dimensions of Happiness as Portrayed in the Political Treatises of Al-Farabi. In *The Political Aspects of Islamic Philosophy*, ed. C.E. Butterworth. Harvard University Press.

Gettier, E. 1963. Is Knowledge Justified True Belief. *Analysis* 23 (6): 121–123.

Geuss, R. 1981. *The Idea of a Critical Theory.* Cambridge University Press.

Goldman, A. 2001. Experts: Which Ones Should You Trust? *Philosophy and Phenomenological Research* 63 (1): 85–110.

Goldziher, I. 1889. *Muhammedanische Studien I.* Niemeyer.

Griffel, F. 2004. Al-Ghazālī's Concept of Prophecy: The Introduction of Avicennan Psychology into Ashʿarite Theology. *Arabic Sciences and Philosophy* 14: 101–144.

———. 2009. *Al-Ghazālī's Philosophical Theology.* Oxford University Press.

———. 2012. *Al-Ghazali's Philosophical Theology.* Oxford University Press.

————. 2015. Al-Ghazālī at His Most Rationalist: The Universal Rule for Allegorically Interpreting Revelation. In *The Impact of al-Ghazālī: Papers on His 900th Anniversary*, ed. Georges Tamer. Brill.

Gutas, D. 1998. *Greek Thought, Arabic Culture: The Graeco-Arabic Translation Movement in Baghdad and Early Society.* Routledge.

Haack, S. 2001. The Ethics of Belief reconsidered. In *Knowledge, Truth, and Duty: Essays on Epistemic Justification, Responsibility and Virtue*, ed. M. Steup. Oxford University Press.

Harris, S. 2004. *The End of Faith: Religion, Terror, and the Future of Reason.* Norton.

Hasse, D.N. 2001. Avicenna on Abstraction. In *Aspects of Avicenna*, ed. Wisnovsky. Princeton University Press.

Hawthorne, J., and J. Stanley. 2008. Knowledge and Action. *Journal of Philosophy* 105 (10): 571–590.

Hawthorne, J., D. Rothschild, and L. Spectre. forthcoming. Belief Is Weak. *Philosophical Studies.*

Hetherington, S. 2011. *How to Know: A Practicalist Conception of Knowledge.* Wiley.

Hintikka, J. 1973. *Time and Necessity: Studies in Aristotle's Theory of Modality.* Oxford University Press.

Hoerber, R.G. 1960. Plato's *Meno. Phronesis* 5: 78–102.

Hume, D. 1779. Dialogues Concerning Natural Religion Original e-copy. http://www.davidhume.org/texts/dnr.html

Hunter, D. 2011. Alienated Belief. *Dialectica* 65 (2): 221–240.

Iqbal, M. 1974. *The Reconstruction of Religious Thought in Islam.* Kitab Bhavan.

Irwin, T. 1977. *Plato's Moral Theory.* Oxford University Press.

Jackson, F. 1986. What Mary Didn't Know. *Journal of Philosophy* 83: 291–295.

Jonas, S. 2016. *Ineffability and Its Metaphysics.* Palgrave Macmillan.

Jordan, J. 2006. *Pascal's Wager: Pragmatic Arguments and Belief in God.* Oxford University Press.

Kahlidi, A.M. 2003. Al-Fārābi on the Democratic City. *British Journal for the History of Philosophy* 11 (3): 379–394.

————. 2006. Orientalisms in the Interpretation of Islamic Philosophy. *Radical Philosophy* 135: 25–33.

Kallfelz, W. 2009. *Clifford Allgebra.* VDM Verslag.

Kant, I. 1785 [2005]. *Groundwork for the Metaphysics of Morals.* Routledge.

Kelly, T. 2003. Epistemic Rationality as Instrumental Rationality: A Critique. *Philosophy and Phenomenological Research* 66: 612–640.

Khatab, S. 2006. *The Power of Sovereignty: The Political and Ideological Philosophy of Sayyid Qutb.* Routledge.

Kripke, S. 1980. *Naming & Necessity.* Blackwell.

Kuhn, S. 1972. Objectivity, Value Judgement, and Theory Choice. In *The Essential Tension.* Chicago University Press.

Lameer, J. 2013. Avicenna's Concupiscence. *Arabic Sciences and Philosophy* 23: 277–289.

Laudan, L. 1984. *Science and Values: The Aims of Science and Their Role in Scientific Debate.* University of California Press.

Leaman, O. 1980. Ibn Rushd on Happiness and Philosophy. *Studia Islamica* 52: 167–181.

———. 1988. *Averroes and His Philosophy.* Curzon Press.

———. 2009. *Islamic Philosophy: An Introduction.* Polity Press.

———. 2016. *The Qur'an: A Philosophical Guide.* Bloomsbury.

Lerner, B. 1974. Introduction. Trans. *Averroes on Plato's Republic.* Cornell University Press.

Lewis, D. 1973. *Counterfactuals.* Blackwell.

Lewis, D. 1996. Elusive Knowledge. *Australasian Journal of Philosophy* 74 (4): 549–567.

Littlejohn, C. 2013. The Russellian Retreat. *Proceedings of the Aristotelian Society 3* (3): 293–320.

López-Farjeat, L.X. 2015. Al-Ghazālī on Knowledge (ʿilm) and Certainty (yaqīn) in al-Munqidh min aḍ-Ḍalāl and inal-Qisṭās al-Mustaqīm. In *Islam and Rationality: The Impact of al-Ghazālī – Papers Collected on His 900th Anniversary,* ed. Georges Tamer. Brill.

Lowe, J. 2014. Grasp of Essences vs. Intuitions: An Uneven Contest. In *Intuitions,* ed. Booth and Rowbottom. Oxford University Press.

Marebon, J. 2007. Latin Averroism. In *Islamic Crosspollinations. Interactions in the Medieval Middle East,* ed. Anna Akasoy, James Montgomery, and Peter Porman. Gibbs Memorial Trust.

Marmura, M.E. 1963. Avicenna's Psychological Proof of Prophecy. *Journal of Near Eastern Studies* 22 (1): 49–56.

Marnissi, F. 2011. *Beyond the Veil.* Saqi Books.

Matheson, D. 2005. Conflicting Experts and Dialectical Performance: Adjudication Heuristics for the Layperson. *Argumentation* 19: 145–158.

Maurusic, B. 2013. Promising Against the Evidence. *Ethics* 123 (2): 292–317.

McGinnis, J. 2010. *Avicenna.* Oxford University Press.

Moore, G.E. 1903. *Principia Ethica.* Cambridge University Press.

Morris, M. 2006. Akrasia in the Protagoras and the Republic. *Phronesis* 51 (3): 195–229.

Najjar, F. 1958. Al-Fārābī on Political Science. *Muslim World* 48: 94–103.

Nasr, S.H. 1998. Foreward. In *Classification of Knowledge in Islam,* ed. Osman Bakar. Islamic Texts Society.

———. 2006. *Islamic Philosophy from Its Origin to the Present: Philosophy in the Land of Prophecy.* SUNY.

Netton, I. 1992. *Al-Fārābī and His School.* Curzon.

O'Brien, M. 2015. *Heidegger, History & the Holocaust.* Bloomsbury.

Peels, R. forthcoming. Believing at Will is Possible. *Australasian Journal of Philosophy.*

Peels, R., and A.R. Booth. 2012. Epistemic Justification, Rights, and Permissibility. *Logos & Episteme* 3: 405–411.

Peels, R., and A.R. Booth. 2014. Why Responsible Belief Is Permissible Belief. *Analytic Philosophy* 55 (1): 75–88.

Philipse, H. 2012. *God in the Age of Science: A Critique of Religious Reason.* Oxford University Press.

Pines, S. 1970. Philosophy. In *The Cambridge History of Islam,* ed. P.M. Holt, A.K.S. Lambton, and B. Lewis. Cambridge University Press.

Plantinga, A. 2000. *Warranted Christian Belief.* Oxford University Press.

Prichard, D. 2005. *Epistemic Luck.* Oxford University Press.

Putnam, H. 1973. Meaning and Reference. *Journal of Philosophy* 70: 699–711.

Qutb, S. 2006 [1964]. *Milestones.* Islamic Book Service.

Rahman, F. 1958. *Prophecy in Islam: Philosophy and Orthodoxy.* Allen & Unwin.

Rawls, J. 1971. *A Theory of Justice.* Harvard University Press.

Reed, B. 2002. How to Think About Fallibilism. *Philosophical Studies* 107: 143–157.

———. 2007. The Long Road to Scepticism. *The Journal of Philosophy* 104: 236–262.

———. 2010. A Defence of Stable Invariantism. *Noûs* 44: 224–244.

Reinach, A. 1911. On the Theory of Normative Judgement. Trans. Barry Smith 1982. *Parts and Moments: Studies in Logic and Formal Ontology.* Philosophia.

Reisman, D.C. 2013. The Life and Times of Avicenna: Patronage and Learning in Medieval Islam. In *Interpreting Avicenna: Critical Essays,* ed. Adamson. Cambridge University Press.

Reisner, A. 2009. The Possibility of Pragmatic Reasons for Belief and the Wrong Kind of Reasons Problem. *Philosophical Studies* 145 (2): 257–272.

Rinard, S. forthcoming. No Exception for Belief. *Philosophy and Phenomenological Research.*

Rosenthal, E.I.J. 1958. *Political Thought in Medieval Islam.* Cambridge University Press.

Rosenthal, F. 2007. *Knowledge Triumphant: The Concept of Knowledge in Medieval Islam.* Brill.

Rowett, C. forthcoming. Why the Philosopher Kings Will Believe the Noble Lie. *Oxford Studies in Ancient Philosophy.*

Russell, B. 1912. In *The Problems of Philosophy,* ed. Skorupski. 2001 edn. Oxford University Press.

Said, E. 1978. *Orientalism.* Penguin.

Schaffer, J. 2010. The Least Discerning and Most Promiscuous Truthmaker. *Philosophical Quarterly* 60: 307–324.

Schwitzgebel, E. 2002. A Phenomenal, Dispositionalist Account of Belief. *Noûs* 36: 249–275.

Scott, D. 2006. *Plato's Meno.* Cambridge University Press.

Seth, S. 2014. The Politics of Knowledge: Or, How to Stop Being Eurocentric. *History Compass* 12 (4): 311–320.

Shah, N., and J.D. Velleman. 2005. Doxastic Deliberation. *Philosophical Review* 114: 497–534.

Shah, N. 2006. A New Argument for Evidentialism. *Philosophical Quarterly* 56: 481–498.

Shavit, U. 2017. *Scientific and Political Freedom in Islam.* Routledge

Shehaan, T. 2014. *Making Sense of Heidgger: A Paradigm Shift.* Rowman and Littlefield.

Sheehan, T. 2015. *Making Sense of Heidegger: A Paradigm Shift.* Rowman and Littlefield.

Shields, C. 1999. *Order in Multiplicity: Homonymy in the Philosophy of Aristotle.* Oxford University Press.

———. 2013. *Aristotle.* 2nd edn. Routledge.

Shoemaker, S. 2009. Self-Imitation and Higher-Order Belief. *Erkenntnis* 71: 35–51.

Shukri, A. 1991. *Aristotelian Logic and the Arabic Language in Al Fārābī.* CUNY Press.

Sinnott-Armstrong, W. 1999. Begging the Question. *Australasian Journal of Philosophy* 77 (2): 174–191.

Smart, J.C.C., and B. Williams. 1973. *Utilitarianism: For and Against.* Cambridge University Press.

Stalnaker, R. 1984. *Inquiry.* MIT Press.

Stanley, J. 2016. *How Propaganda Works.* Princeton University Press.

Strauss, L. 1958. *Thoughts on Machiavelli.* Chicago University Press.

———. 1959. How Fārābī Read Plato's *Laws.* In *What Is Political Philosophy? And Other Studies.* Free Press.

Strohminger, M., and Yli-Vakkuri. forthcoming. The Epistemology of Modality. *Philosophy Compass.*

Swinburne, R. 1981. *Faith and Reason.* Oxford University Press.

Talbi, M. 2006. Religious Liberty: A Muslim Perspective. In *New Voices of Islam: Rethinking Politics and Modernity: A Reader,* ed. M. Kamrava. I.B. Tauris.

Taylor, R.C. 2000. 'Truth Does Not Contradict Truth': Averroes on the Unity of Truth. *Topoi* 19: 3–16.

Thorpe, L. forthcoming. Sayyid Qutb and Aquinas: Liberalism, Natural Law, and the Philosophy of Jihad. *Heythrop Journal.*

Turri, J. 2011. Believing for a Reason. *Erkenntnis* 74 (3): 383–397.

Unger, P. 1975. *Ignorance: A Case for Scepticism.* Clarendon Press.

Van den Bergh, S. 2008. Introduction. In *Averroes: Tahafut al Tahafut.* Gibb Memorial Trust.

Walbridge, J. 2004. Suhrawardī and Illuminationism. In *The Cambridge Companion to Arabic Philosophy,* ed. Adamson and Taylor. Cambridge University Press.

Walzer, R. 1962. *Greek into Arabic: Essays on Islamic Philosophy.* Oxford University Press.

Watt, M. 1985. *Islamic Philosophy and Theology.* Edinburgh University Press.

Watt, M. 1987. *Islamic Philosophy and Theology.* Edinburgh University Press.

Weatherson, B. 2008. Deontology and Descartes' Demon. *Journal of Philosophy* 105: 540–569.

Williams, B. 1999. The Analogy of City and Soul in Plato's Republic. In *Plato,* ed. Gail Fine. Oxford University Press.

Williamson, T. 2007. *The Philosophy of Philosophy.* Blackwell.

Williamson, T. 2011. *The Philosophy of Philosophy.* Wiley Blackwell.

———. 2013. *Modal Logic as Metaphysics.* Oxford University Press.

Williamson, T. 2015. *Modal Logic as Metaphysics.* Oxford University Press.

Wolterstorf, N. 1996. *John Locke and the Ethics of Belief.* Cambridge University Press.

Wright, C. 1991. Scepticism and Dreaming: Imploding the Demon. *Mind* 100: 87–116.

Zagzebski, L. 2001. Recovering Understanding. In *Knowledge, Truth and Duty,* ed. M. Steup. Oxford University Press.

———. 2003. The Search for the Source of Epistemic Good. *Metaphilosophy* 34: 12–28.

Zimmerman, M. 1996. *The Concept of Moral Obligation.* Cambridge University Press.

Index[1]

---

[1] Note: Page number followed by 'n' denotes end note

© The Author(s) 2017
A.R. Booth, *Analytic Islamic Philosophy*, Palgrave Philosophy Today,
https://doi.org/10.1057/978-1-137-54157-4

Lightning Source UK Ltd.
Milton Keynes UK
UKHW021846270922
409538UK00004B/379